MIGRATION AND RACIALIZATION IN TIMES OF "CRISIS"

MIGRATION AND RACIALIZATION IN TIMES OF "CRISIS"

The Making of Crises and their Effects

Edited by Leila Benhadjoudja,
Christina Clark-Kazak, and Stéphanie Garneau
In collaboration with Magalie Civil,
Yacout El Abboubi, and Gina Vukojević

University of Ottawa Press
2025

Les Presses de l'Université d'Ottawa
University of Ottawa **Press**

Les Presses de l'Université d'Ottawa/University of Ottawa Press (PUO-UOP) is North America's flagship bilingual university press, affiliated to one of Canada's top research universities. PUO-UOP enriches the intellectual and cultural discourse of our increasingly knowledge-based and globalized world with peer-reviewed, award-winning books.

www.Press.uOttawa.ca

Library and Archives Canada Cataloguing in Publication
Title: Migration and racialization in times of crisis : the making of crises and their effects / edited
    by Leila Benhadjoudja, Christina Clark-Kazak, and Stéphanie Garneau ; in collaboration with
    Magalie Civil, Yacout El Abboubi, and Gina Vukojević.
Names: Benhadjoudja, Leila, 1982- editor. | Clark-Kazak, Christina R., 1975- editor | Garneau,
    Stéphanie, 1975- editor
Series: Studies in international development and globalization.
Description: Series statement: Studies in international development and globalization | Includes
    bibliographical references and index.
Identifiers: Canadiana (print) 20240490711 | Canadiana (ebook) 2024049072X |
    ISBN 9780776641713 (softcover) | ISBN 9780776641706 (hardcover) |
    ISBN 9780776641720 (PDF) | ISBN 9780776641737 (EPUB)
Subjects: LCSH: Crises—Social aspects. | LCSH: Crises—History. | LCSH: Social history.
Classification: LCC HN18.3 .M54 2025 | DDC 306—dc23

Legal Deposit: Second Quarter 2025
Library and Archives Canada

Production Team

Copy editing	Valentina D'Aliesio
Proofreading	Robbie McCaw
Typesetting	Édiscript enr.
Cover design	Benoit Deneault
Cover image	Tess Jenkins

---

uOttawa

PUO-UOP gratefully acknowledges the funding support of the University of Ottawa, the Government of Canada, the Canada Council for the Arts, the Ontario Arts Council and the Government of Ontario.

Canada

Canada Council Conseil des arts
for the Arts du Canada

ONTARIO ARTS COUNCIL
CONSEIL DES ARTS DE L'ONTARIO
an Ontario government agency
un organisme du gouvernement de l'Ontario

Ontario

Table of Contents

CHAPTER 5

COVID-19 in Montreal: Systemic Impact on Precarious
Im/migrant Workers and their Organizing Responses

CHAPTER 6

International Students and the "Crisis" of Higher Education
in Canada

List of Figures and Tables

Introduction

Leila Benhadjoudja, Christina Clark-Kazak, and Stéphanie Garneau

This book was conceived as a way to bring to a close several years of collaboration between professors and students working on racism or migration, within the framework of the *Collectif de recherche sur les migrations et le racisme* (COMIR) at the University of Ottawa. COMIR was an opportunity for researchers to come together around various academic activities and reflect on subjects as varied as the effects of neoliberalism and capitalism on migration and racism, issues of positionality in research, and state violence against racialized populations, among others. After four years of collective work, we wanted this volume—and its French-language companion—to be our record in bringing together students, emerging researchers, and professors. The chapters in these two books are the result of a call we launched in the midst of the COVID-19 pandemic, to mark the closing of the COMIR. It was at this juncture, often referred to as a "health crisis," that we felt it necessary to reflect on the issues the crisis raised for our research projects, for the meaning of our academic work, and for ourselves.

The pandemic, which represents "an organic crisis of capitalism" (McKay, 2023), underscored the need to question the notion of crisis, and more specifically its effects on marginalized, migrant, and racialized populations. Indeed, while the world was living through the rhythm of this crisis, other "crises" of different magnitudes were increasing or recurring in the four corners of the globe: political, social, and economic crisis in Venezuela; "security" crisis (Grinand, 2021) in Haiti; "mental health" crisis (Colly, 2021) in Lebanon; never-ending migration crises (Carastathis et al., 2018; Crawley, 2016; Jeandesboz & Pallister-Wilkins, 2016), whether in Greece, on the Polish border, in the Mediterranean, in Calais and the English Channel, in Venezuela, or on the roads of Central and South America; an anti-gas pipeline blockade crisis in Canada; economic and humanitarian crises in Afghanistan and Yemen; climate crises; "academic freedom crisis" in the United States, Canada, and France.

The haphazard listing of all these crises, which are not necessarily related to each other or to COVID-19, shows the extent to which the crisis approach has become a norm, with its own pathologizing and stigmatizing effects. Added to many other crises in recent history—the Oka crisis, student crises, agricultural crises, subprime crises, oil crises, the Darfur crisis—in such a way as to make crisis a perpetual state, as if the contemporary world were in itself "crisogenic" (Aguiton et al., 2019, p. 12). But if crisis is enduring, are we still permitted to talk about crisis? Is the normalization of crisis "a paradox that invalidates the very idea of crisis" (Aguiton et al., 2019, p. 10)? How, then, are we to think about such moments in history and their consequences?

As members of COMIR, the editors of this book (and the parallel volume in French) could not ignore the data and other facts reported daily in the newspapers since the COVID-19 crisis was declared: over-representation of infections in areas and neighbourhoods predominantly inhabited by migrant and racialized populations (Lindeman, May 13, 2020); undocumented workers sent to the front lines in essential sectors, without recognition or regulation of their status (TCRI, 2020); outbreaks in Indigenous communities in Canada; increased racial and social profiling during states of emergency (quarantines, confinements, curfews); the spread of infections in refugee and migrant camps; outbreaks in the working and living environments of temporary migrant workers, in factories as well as in greenhouses and fields; delays in the processing of asylum-seeker and refugee files; an increase in gender-based violence, in households as well as among displaced and refugee women and girls (UNHCR Canada, 2022). As Nancy Fraser reminds us, this was strong evidence that COVID-19 was "a perfect storm of capitalist irrationality and injustice" (cited in McKay, 2023, p. 21).

Contrary to the popular idea that the coronavirus did not discriminate and could affect anyone, it seems clear that racial, classist, and colonial logics were structuring the health crisis into which we were all thrown, albeit very unevenly. Indeed, despite the call for solidarity and care from several public decision-makers, the pandemic exacerbated the prison-like character and racial violence—particularly anti-Black—of our white capitalist societies. From the outset, this pandemic crisis has been marked by the over-representation of deaths and murders in Black communities as a result of structural violence, as in the case of the murder of George Floyd. As Black Canadian feminist Robyn Maynard reminds us:

> Even as economies and nations have been "closed down," the violence of police killings has been unceasing in North America and well beyond. The deaths of Ahmaud Arbery, Breonna Taylor and Tony McDade in the US, and D'Andre Campbell and Regis Korchinski-Paquet north of the colonial border, demonstrate that while labouring on the front lines of the pandemic, Black peoples are continuously outside the register of the "public" within common framings of public safety and health. (Maynard, 2020, p. 71)

Nor could we ignore the relentless anti-Chinese and anti-Asian violence, strongly fuelled and encouraged by right-wing and far-right groups.

Taken together, these elements showed that the health crisis had to be understood as a symptom requiring deep analysis. The effects of the coronavirus and its political management in many countries had only served to reveal racial and sexual inequalities, and recurrent dehumanization that we had been documenting and denouncing for years in our respective work. It therefore became productive to place this crisis, which we were told began in March 2020, in a long-term perspective, and to relate it to other crises that precede it and are still ongoing. In this book, we look at crises of all kinds, with the specific aim of shedding light on their colonial and racial roots, and their concrete effects on migrants, Black, racialized, and Indigenous people.

This two-volume collection brings together previously unpublished contributions from COMIR faculty members and students, as well a number of researchers from outside the University of Ottawa who responded to our call for papers. Putting these contributions together reveals how these crises are fundamentally racial and symptomatic of a crisis in the white supremacist system (De Genova, 2016; Rohland, 2020). Moreover, the very conditions of the production of this work are inscribed in the racial, gendered, and capitalist logics of this system we critique. Although we, as editors, do not all share the same racial positions, nor do we face the same oppressions or privileges, we are critically engaged through our profession in the neoliberal university. As much as the university constitutes a propitious space for the critique of racial capitalism, patriarchy, heteronormativity, and other systemic violence, we are aware that it also participates in such violence (Chatterjee & Maira, 2014) and mobilizes the notion of crisis specific to neoliberal logic (see Pasipanodya & Chowdhury, this volume) and academic capitalism (Boggs & Mitchell, 2018). In this context, we sought to work collectively during the writing process and its interruptions, the latter of which were numerous due to the pandemic and its effects on our own working conditions. Moreover, though we sought to support one another during the preparation of these volumes (these forms of support constituting for us concrete practices that are part of the critique of knowledge production in the neoliberal university), we had to deal with constraints that meant that the crises analyzed in this collection are ultimately not represented in all their diversity, at least not in the diversity we had wished for at the start of the project. The fact that many of the chapters published here are based largely on discourse-analysis methodologies betrays, in part, the difficult conditions under which a number of research projects were carried out in times of confinement. That said, discourse analysis remains powerful in the context of reflection on the processes by which crises are made; i.e., the ways in which they are circumscribed, defined, and debated by public authorities and other groups in society (Triandafyllidou, 2018).

This collection is therefore an opportunity to reflect on crises through the prism of migration and racialization, from multiple points of view: national (Ecuador, Spain, Canada, etc.), disciplinary (sociology, political science, criminology, etc.), and linguistic (French and English).

How to Define a Crisis? Looking Back at a Concept

As both a commonsense and political category, "crisis" is not easily understood in the social sciences, as it involves so many different epistemological dimensions. First borrowed from ancient Greek, and from its earliest polysemous usages ranging from "to choose" to "to decide" to "to judge," the word *crisis* had a medical and theological meaning in Latin languages such as French and English, before entering the political sphere (Koselleck, 2006). According to historian Reinhart Koselleck (2006), crisis is a socio-historical concept, and though it appears to be key in the modern social sciences, it has undergone such an expansion of meaning that it has lost its precision. This imprecision reveals an ambivalence, as the term can at once be understood as a conceptual and imaginative opening, as well as a "symptom of a historical crisis that cannot yet be fully measured" (Koselleck, 2006, p. 399).

In its political sense, the notion of crisis is historically associated with Marxist critique, and the act of studying crisis in this case means unveiling it, bringing it out into the open, and doing so in such a way as to denounce capitalism as a crisis-generating system (Roitman et al., 2019; Hage, 2015). In the Marxist perspective—which has long dominated the social sciences—crisis is indeed inherent to capitalism, the result of capital accumulation, exploitation, and alienation, and inevitably leads to class confrontation. The work of researchers in such a perspective, then, consists in identifying the sites of crisis generated by capitalism and is undoubtedly accompanied by a hope for social change and emancipation; the crisis can only produce a revolutionary political subject who will be able to take advantage of the structural flaw self-produced by the capitalist system so as to precipitate its implosion (Hage, 2015). In this case, the crisis appears as a brutal moment of rupture with the course of history, an opportunity for social critique, a possibility for redefining the world we live in—in short, a hope for the exit from capitalism. Over time, however, the Marxist analysis of crises seems to have faded—though not disappeared—giving way to a "crisis of critique" (Hage, 2015, p. 200) and the assumption that crises are not so much what social transformation will come about, but as what capitalist societies and economies manage to reproduce. In this analysis, however, racism as a fundamental structure of modernity remains a major afterthought. We shall see below how Black radical critique enables us to grasp capitalism differently, to renew our critique of it, and thus to rethink the very idea of crisis.

Other researchers, in the wake of the *Sociologie des crises politiques*, first published in 1986 by political scientist Michel Dobry, have moved away from the classic Marxist approach of rupture to the "hypothesis of continuity" (Dobry, 2009, p. 9). These works, particularly present in French-speaking political science, borrow from a sociology of action and point out that the "logic of disorder" and the call for innovation that appear in times of crisis do not completely escape the logic of order, notably the weight of habitus and social dispositions. Dobry and the work he inspired invite us to join order and disorder, structure and action, in order to turn our attention to an intermediate plane, that of "situational logics": moments of crisis, made up of routine logics as much as upheavals, produce singular constraints and opportunities that need to be elucidated. The idea here is to escape the double trap of seeking causal interpretations of the crisis (since situational dynamics can develop to the point of freeing themselves from the sources of their initial triggering) and teleological analysis (made *a posteriori*, oriented by knowledge of the end) in order to invest the crisis as a present, autonomous moment, and study "the crisis in the *making*" (Roger & Aït-Aoudia, 2015). Since then, researchers have adopted this constructivist approach to examine how the crisis constitutes a political arena. There is no shortage of empirical cases, since crisis management has become a preferred approach of states and organizations since the 1990s and the idea that "zero risk" does not exist (Lagadec & Guilhou, 2002). Research is therefore less interested in exploring the universe of possibilities opened up by crisis than in taking it head-on, that is, observing it: sometimes as an issue contested by actors with differentiated interests; sometimes as a situation appropriated by institutions to legitimize their existence and actions; sometimes as an object contested in its political and social consequences (Ambrosetti & Buchet de Neuilly, 2009; Aguiton et al., 2019).

It is undoubtedly Janet Roitman's book, *Anti-Crisis*, published in 2013, that offers a more radical line of analysis for thinking about crises. The author invites researchers to first take a step back: what if, before even pretending to study the ways in which the crisis is appropriated or denied by a plurality of institutions and actors with differentiated powers, we cast doubt on its existence? What if we did not take it for granted, as something that goes without saying, but rather tried to "suspend judgment" (Roitman et al., 2019, p. 116) about it? The very title of the book, *Anti-Crisis*, is Roitman's way of saying that the crisis does not exist *a priori*: "judging the crisis is necessarily a *post hoc* interrogation: what went wrong? [...] The foundations of knowledge about the crisis are neither questioned nor made explicit. This is why contemporary narratives of crisis evade two questions: How can we *know* the crisis in history and how can we know the crisis itself?" (Roitman, 2013, p. 10).

For the author, one of the blind spots in the scientific literature on crises, whether seen as moments of rupture or as the continuation of pre-existing logics, is that crises never seem to be called into question. Events obviously have objective effects on the people who are their victims — for example, dying from the consequences of a contagious virus in times of pandemic, or losing one's home in times of financial crisis — but is the concept of crisis essential to making these observations? Would it not be more relevant to take a closer look at what the political diagnosis of a crisis (the belief in it) and the measures subsequently put in place generate as collateral effects, producing other victims? Does taking the crisis for granted not sometimes prevent us from thinking outside the box, from finding alternatives to the only solutions that the crisis paradigm makes possible? This is what Roitman suggests when she notes that the *subprime* crisis in the United States led to certain actions (devaluation and foreclosure), yet the very possibility of foreclosure was never questioned, even by those on the left. Questioning, therefore, does not mean denying the consequences of the crisis, but rather invites us to take an interest in how the crisis is constructed, how the diagnosis of crisis is made, and what the acceptance of this diagnosis produces, particularly in terms of knowledge.

Thinking about "Crises" through the Prism of Racial Capitalism

The intention of this book, then, strongly inspired by Roitman's approach, is not to confirm or deny crises, but to analyze the ways in which they are proclaimed and put into practice, and to identify the various narratives to which they give rise and, conversely, those which they keep silent. In short, the guiding question is to look at the crisis rather than to look from the crisis, in order to reveal its blind spots, particularly in terms of the knowledge produced and the power stakes that maintain it.

This is where the concept of "racial capitalism" proposed by Cedric J. Robinson (2023 [1983]), which lies at the heart of Black radical perspectives, can help us take the step back that Roitman calls for, and thus accompany us as we reflect on the blind spots of the crises. First, Robinson helps us to decentre Marxism, which he describes as a "Western construction", in order to better see how this construction is also a European point of view (Robinson, 2023 [1983], p. 2). Robinson's major contribution, in fact, is to show that the development of the capitalist system was linked to slavery, genocide, and the colonization of the Americas (Issar, 2021, p. 59), and that the labour produced by slavery, contrary to what Marx proposed, is not an anomaly, but central to the development of racial capitalism (Issar, 2021, p. 59). Indeed, Robinson writes:

> The development, organization and expansion of capitalist society followed essentially racial directions, as did its social ideology. As a material force, therefore, it was to be expected that racialism would inevitably infiltrate the emerging social structures of capitalism. I have used the term 'racial capitalism' to refer to this development and the resulting structure as historical agentivity. (Robinson, 2023 [1983], p. 89)

Robinson shows that racialization is a process that began in Europe, primarily among Europeans, and that capitalism grew out of feudalism. In other words, capitalism developed around, with, and through racism. This approach invites us to think of modern labour and its division in terms of its racial character and how it engenders violence and the dehumanization of racialized bodies for the benefit of racialized capital. The richness and analytical force of Robinson's theoretical and conceptual proposal is such that it not only enables us to revisit European history, but also offers a break with Eurocentric historical interpretations that have erased African civilizations from "European consciousness and knowledge" in favor of a dehumanization of Africa and Africans (Robinson, 2023 [1983], p. 90). For Robinson, and this constitutes a major contribution of his work, Marx and Engels were mistaken in thinking of the proletarian as the revolutionary (and universal) subject, thus ignoring non-Western revolutionary movements, including African resistances, which are at the source of the Black radical tradition.

Black radical perspectives, unfortunately often marginalized in critical thinking in the social sciences, provide a way out of the racial ignorance of Marxism and its analytical and political effects. By recalling the racial order of capitalism, they help us to think that ways of defining "crises", their effects, and the devices put in place to overcome them, can neglect the angle of the reproduction of race.

Thinking in terms of racial capitalism thus invites us to constantly interrogate the terms of crisis insofar as they make possible a racial biopolitics and political economy. Following Black feminist and race-critical perspectives, the idea of being in crisis is necessary to maintain the necessary conditions for white supremacy sustained by racial capitalism. Whether a migratory, climate, or COVID-19 crisis, racial capitalism generates and regenerates itself through different grammars of crisis (Edwards, 2021; Pulido, 2016; Rohland, 2020). For example, in the case of the COVID-19 health crisis, Zophia Edwards (2021), sociology professor in Black studies, shows how responses to this crisis and the measures adopted follow the neoliberal ideology that promotes racial violence and the accumulation of white capital. In this sense, Black and racialized workers sent to the "front" by the states primarily enable the accumulation of capital. She points out that, at the same time, "neoliberal racial states further marginalize these same workers by excluding them from the social protections they so desperately need to cope with the impacts of Covid-19 on their health, incomes and general well-being" (Edwards, 2021, p. 23).

In this vein, seeking to secure a consensus on "crisis" becomes paramount, since it enables the paradox that Lauren Berlant (2011) describes in her seminal work *Cruel Optimism*. Berlant explains this paradox through the idea of "crisis ordinariness", i.e., an everyday moment as crisis "is not exceptional to history or consciousness but a process embedded in the ordinary that unfolds in stories about navigating what's overwhelming" (Berlant, 2011, cited in Boggs & Mitchell, 2018, p. 434). The trap, then, is that the dominant ways in which crises are enunciated plunge us into a constant dynamic of wanting to "fix" what we should, on the contrary, from an anti-racist feminist point of view, abolish. Consequently, the "crisis ordinariness" described by Berlant, or the migratory or pandemic crises declared by states or experts, can be understood as distractions from the abolition of white supremacy and its violence.

This assumption—that discourses of crisis are sources of the maintenance of racial capitalism and white supremacy—allies itself to a certain extent with the methodological posture Roitman adopts when she invites us to refuse to question what went wrong to bring about the crisis in the first place. This question "What went wrong?" (Roitman, 2013, p. 9) sometimes presupposes that the pre-crisis state was the normal state of affairs to which we must quickly return, sometimes that the crisis is the symptom of a system necessarily condemned to failure and therefore to transformation towards something "better":

> Yet, if [the crisis] did indeed take place, it would not simply gen-erate a critique of existing relationships and practices; it would

also be the occasion for a reorganization and transformation of these relationships and practices. If this transformation does not take place, then we need to extricate ourselves from the politics of crisis in order to consider, more clearly and explicitly, the effects and consequences of our adherence to this diagnosis. This is a different kind of political demand. (Roitman et al., 2019, p. 116; our translation)

As a result, most of the contributions to this book are not motivated by a desire to take the crisis as true, nor by a desire to understand what might have failed in order to bring it about. Rather, the aim is to understand, in the context of racial capitalism, what the crisis as a site of enunciation makes possible in terms of the fabrication of order and disorder, the normal and the pathological, the safe and the dangerous. "Not to take the crisis for granted" does not mean denying that a serious event took place, still less not taking seriously the effects of the event on individuals and communities. It means casting doubt on the exact location of the crisis, on the way it is defined, on the consequences it is supposed to have; in short, on the way in which the crisis is sociologically fabricated, and in so doing is likely—this is our thesis—to omit the racial order. Instead of asking what happened, it is more appropriate to ask what past, in relation to what normality (often exempt from the racial order in its dominant representation), the enunciation of a crisis intervenes. The chapters in this book present case studies from different national spaces—Ecuador, Haiti, Guatemala, Mexico, the United States, Canada, and Spain—and different sites of enunciation. They show how processes of racialization are at work in the making of crises, despite the particularities taken on by the racial order according to local and national contexts.

Ways of Thinking About Crises and Migrant, Black, Indigenous, and Racialized Populations

What is designated as a "crisis" is often no more than a revelation (cf. Escalante Rengifo and Pantaleón, volume in French) of a pre-existing situation of "crisis" that has been normalized: Indigenous peoples under colonial regimes of trusteeship for centuries; refugees locked up in camps for decades; health systems whose organization of work has been gendered, racially stratified, and underfunded for 40 years; migration policies that have made agricultural workers vulnerable for decades. The posture of defiance towards diagnoses of crisis taken by each of the contributors to this book, in their own way, gives rise to several methodological and epistemological avenues. These avenues provide useful reference points for studying the making of crises and their effects on marginalized populations who, like migrants, Black, racialized, and Indigenous people, can be directly singled out as scapegoats for a declared crisis (cf. Roy, volume in French). We have identified three main issues.

The first path taken by the contributions to this book is an epistemological one. Adopting a questioning stance towards the official declaration of a crisis undoubtedly implies, first, distancing oneself from the available corpus of literature on crises in the social sciences and from the usual theorizations of crises (cf. Civil and Couton, volume in French). Historically associated with the capitalist production system, as we have seen above, social crises have traditionally had an economic dimension. However, as explained above, capitalism developed *along with* racism, as a continuation of European feudalism rather than a rupture from it (Kelley, 2017). Serious consideration of the possible effects of colonialism and racism in a number of crises, including economic ones, not only makes visible the specific realities experienced by certain population groups generally left in the shadows, but is likely to reveal other crises not declared as such by the dominant powers, or other causes than those usually endorsed. In this way, Felices-Luna, Llaguno and Gomá, and Pasipanodya and Chowdhury, each in their own way, show how the dominant discourse on the "migration crisis" prevents us from thinking about both the capitalist and colonial roots of contemporary migratory flows. Illuminating the colonial blind spot of crises—from their causes to their solutions, via their interpretation—is a necessary first step towards the decolonization of imaginaries (cf. Sondarjee and Rugira, volume in French).

The second approach is more methodological and consists—as already put into practice by many of the authors mentioned above and others—in understanding the "belief in crisis" as a field of political action. The diagnosis of a crisis is often contested (think of the far-right conspiracy theories of QAnon, which claim that the COVID-19 pandemic was invented out of thin air), as are probably even more contested the measures put in place to respond to the crisis (still in relation to COVID-19, think of the various anti-mask, anti-vax, and other movements). A "crisis" thus brings into play groups of actors situated—in terms of race, gender, social class—with differentiated interests, and whose interests may moreover evolve over time to reveal negotiations, alliances, and rallies, as well as various strategies of opposition and struggle (Ambrosetti & Buchet de Neuilly, 2009). How are crises declared, when, and by whom? What terminologies do they bring into play, or even conflict with—a crisis of "academic freedom" or a crisis of "academic whiteness"? (cf. Romani, volume in French)—and what does this reveal? What do the declaration and vocabulary of crisis—for example, the use of the term "guardian angel" during the COVID-19 pandemic (Salamanca Cardona, volume in English; Leroy and Garneau, volume in French)—commit as visibility effects and, at the same time, from what realities do they divert attention? What populations do they overshadow, or what solutions do they prevent? Vargas-Aguirre's chapter (volume in English) shows, for example, how the Ecuadorian government's construction of Venezuelan migrants as both "risks" and "victims" authorizes the implementation of restrictive policies that lead to their irregularization and, ultimately, legitimize their exclusion from the territory. What modes of management and governance are thus set in motion, and what effects do they have, in turn, on the populations we are concerned with? What legitimate ways of living through the crisis do they impose? Crisis diagnosis remains the privilege of politicians and experts, but questioning the different narratives involved and documenting the technologies of government and their effects is a first way of taking a critical distance from the crisis and putting back at the heart of the analysis the power relationships, including those potentially exercised by researchers (cf. Glockner and colleagues, volume in English), that run through it and participate in shaping it.

Finally, a third and equally methodological line of analysis aims to think about "crisis" in terms of its potentially multiple spatial and temporal scales. Is the crisis in question shocking and brutal, or does it tend to settle stealthily into the long timeframe of social life and governmentality? Is the crisis international, national, communitarian, or individual, and how does it play out on these different scales?

Crises are both produced and "producing," so there can be crises within crises, like a domino effect. Different crises can be superimposed or chained together, and this process of stacking crises unfolds all the more as the state of crisis tends to become permanent and normalized. In their article, based on their observations of the economic crisis in Cameroon, Mbembe and Roitman (1995) report that when a crisis becomes long-lasting and marks intimate experience, particularly in its most dramatic aspects, the inexplicable tends to prevail. The effort to understand the crisis can then deviate from the socio-political and historical framework to become normality. These authors show how the economic crisis in Cameroon has settled into the routine actions of daily life, giving rise to the bricolages and improvisations that have become the new reality. In this routine experience of crisis, tactics of resourcefulness are deployed, but also frustration and violence when there is no longer any concordance between everyday practical and material life, and the corpus of meanings available to understand the world.

Analyzing crises from scale to scale shows how a crisis at the global level can lead to a national crisis, then to a community crisis, then how everyday inter-individual arrangements can generate, over time, other forms of crisis—dispersal of authority, petty corruption, everyday violence—until they give rise to new regimes of subjectivity (Mbembe & Roitman, 1995) as well as various tactics of survival and self-reconstruction. What does this level tell us about the subjectivities and routine actions woven by people to cope with incoherence, instability, and uncertainty in their everyday existence? Conversely, looking at crises "from the bottom up", using these scales of context (Revel, 1996), i.e. moving up the ladder, can help us depart from a psychologizing or naturalizing analysis, and re-inscribe what, at first glance, appear to be individual crises at the heart of relations of domination. It is through the lens of colonial relations, for example, that the seemingly intimate crises that punctuate the individual trajectories of Innu mothers marked by youth protection services can be read (cf. Croteau, volume in French).

While reading the chapters in English and French gives rise to these three cross-cutting avenues of reflection, their respective richness is far from exhausted. Each of the collective's 13 original chapters (six in the English volume and seven in the French volume) stands on its own, documenting the realities of specific crises.

Overview of the Volume in French

The French-language volume includes seven previously unpublished chapters. In the first chapter, **Vincent Romani** immerses us in the "N-word crisis" that rocked the University of Ottawa campus and French-speaking Quebec academic circles in the fall of 2020. Based on a quantitative and qualitative analysis of over a hundred articles written by university actors in the Quebec print media, Romani goes beyond this seemingly isolated incident to analyze it within the broader framework of a sociology of racism in academic circles. To this end, he invites us to reflect on the crises of "racial panic" that have shaken various national higher education spaces in the Global North in recent years. Using the theoretical and methodological tools of social sciences, the author convincingly demonstrates the racial and masculine subjectivity at the heart of the Quebec (and Western) academic institution and invites members of the white academic community to make the same detachment and distancing from themselves that they demand of racialized people.

The next two chapters also focus on media discourse, but this time specifically on epidemic or pandemic crises. Drawing on 2,437 articles from six Canadian media sources on the spread of four diseases (tuberculosis, H1N1, Ebola, and Zika), followed by a brief incursion into the COVID-19 pandemic at the end of the chapter, **Mélissa Roy** examines the distortions and transformations undergone by "epidemic narratives" throughout the "crises" generated by their outbreak and management. She has identified three periods—three "chronotopes"—during which specific figures of otherness appear and are blamed. While the forms of otherness tend to evolve and are therefore plural, the figure of migrant, racialized, and Indigenous people appears in all the cases analyzed as guilty and/or inferiorized.

Jeanne Marie Rugira and **Maïka Sondarjee** show, based on an analysis of 40 press articles published in online newspapers in France, the United Kingdom, Canada, and the United States, the extent to which part of the Western media discourse on Africa was alarmist and Afropessimistic from the very first months of the COVID-19 pandemic. The comparison between the media's treatment of the African "exception" and that of New Zealand is striking, echoing the inferiorization of Africa (and the valorization of the West/whiteness) observed by Mélissa Roy. Whereas for Africa, the low number of contaminations is attributed, at best, to the weakness of the statistical system on the continent, and, at worst to a miracle, for the island country of Oceania, it is credited to the success of the state's management of the pandemic. After showing the shortcuts and interpretation biases of Western journalists and experts, the authors invite us to reflect on epistemic injustices and call for the decolonization of thought and imaginations.

As in the case of Africa, **Magalie Civil** and **Philippe Couton** share the view that we need to move away from the pitying and defeatist discourse on Haiti. According to the authors, in the case of Haiti, the notion of crisis is overexploited, so much so that "it is overused to signify almost all societal issues" (our translation). After explaining their posture of doubt and mistrust of the notion of crisis, Civil and Couton analyze the ways in which certain Haitian intellectuals tend to mobilize this analytical grid to interpret the upheavals running through the country's history, making Haiti a country in "perpetual crisis". At the same time, the two researchers point to a blind spot in the dominant analysis, slavery and colonialism, and thus the Haitian revolution, which has not yet succeeded but continues to be led by the popular masses.

Karine Croteau's chapter, too, invites us to suspend our judgement as to the proven nature of the crises declared by political, journalistic, and intellectual elites in order to reinscribe the analysis of crises in the long timeframe of colonialism. The author invites us into the lives of nine Innu mothers whose children have been taken away from them by the Quebec Youth Protection Branch. By illuminating this ordeal in the context of the many other losses and sufferings that punctuate the biographical trajectory of these women, this non-Indigenous Canadian researcher reminds us of the colonial, racist, and sexist sources, and therefore the historical and collective character, of the recurring and seemingly individual or family "crises" experienced by these women. The angle taken by the author rightly emphasizes the strengths mobilized by Innu women to overcome "crises" and reclaim their role as mothers, despite the obstacles. Against the backdrop of the COVID-19 pandemic and the crisis paradigm that accompanies it, the reflections by Croteau, Civil, and Couton put the crisis paradigm into perspective—what crisis, and for whom?—and question the appropriate temporal scale for thinking about the source of the challenges and upheavals encountered. By returning to colonialism, the focus is on the coloniality of power, highlighting a number of other dimensions that are usually invisible in the analysis of today's "crises", thereby opening the door to new political alternatives.

Finally, chapters by Leroy and Garneau and Escalante Rengifo and Pantaleón attempt to shed light on the effects of the COVID-19 "crisis" and its management on migrant and racialized workers. **Handy Leroy** and **Stéphanie Garneau** offer an analysis of the policies and discourses of the Coalition Avenir Québec (CAQ) government towards healthcare workers who were sent "to the front" during the first months of the "health crisis"—a few thousand of whom turned out to be asylum seekers or undocumented migrants. The authors first present the contradictions between a political discourse that, on the one hand, speaks of frontline workers as "guardian angels,' and practices that, on the other, aim to delegitimize and exclude undocumented migrants or those awaiting status from this category. The chapter goes on to explain how this apparent paradox is to be understood in the light of the CAQ's ideology of identity-based nationalism and its ultimate aim of reducing immigration to Quebec.

Guadalupe Escalante Rengifo and **Jorge Pantaleón**'s chapter looks at the social representations conveyed in certain media about Guatemalan and Mexican temporary farm workers in Quebec and Ontario. Based on their analysis of 347 articles published in Canada's French-language print media, the text shows the extent to which discourses of "crisis" (labour shortages, the H1N1 epidemic, COVID-19) play a part, to a certain extent, through various processes of legitimization or denunciation, in the structuring of Quebec and Ontario agribusiness. By comparing the periods 2010–2011 (H1N1) and 2020–2021 (COVID-19), the authors show how the representations conveyed in the newspapers by various actors (agricultural employers, Foundation for Foreign Agricultural Worker Recruitment (FERME) agents, workers, migrant rights collectives, journalists), while remaining utilitarian during the two periods studied, leave more room for the vulnerability of workers in the second. This finding suggests that poor working conditions intensified during the COVID-19 pandemic to such an extent that the work of migrant workers' rights collectives and the discourse on human rights succeeded in establishing themselves in the media narrative.

Overview of the Volume in English

The English-language volume contains six original chapters. We, as editors, decided to start with chapters that set the methodological (Chapter 1) and discursive contexts (Chapter 2) of "crisis" before presenting a series of case studies in Ecuador (Chapter 3), Spain (Chapter 4), Quebec (Chapter 5), and Canada (Chapter 6) where these "crises" are made manifest. While representing diverse geopolitical contexts and themes ranging from the COVID-19 pandemic to migrant labour to higher education, each chapter demonstrates how governments have framed disparate issues as "crisis" to justify policies that perpetuate racialized inequalities. The chapters can be read alone but, taken together, they paint a picture of broader structural processes that produce and reproduce "crises" as a mode of governance at local, national, and transnational levels.

In the first chapter, **Valentina Glockner** and colleagues explore the praxis of *acompañamiento* as an epistemological, methodological, and ethical approach to research action with people in precarious migration contexts. Drawing on examples of work carried out with unaccompanied young people attempting to cross the border between Mexico and the United States, and with Indigenous communities in Guatemala, the authors show how the effects of intersecting "crises"—manifested through migration—can be mitigated by researchers' acts of resistance. However, *acompañamiento* is not a quick fix. Literally and figuratively, "walking alongside others in solidarity and resistance in the face of oppression" requires a long-term commitment and deep reflexivity to refocus voices and experiences that have been marginalized by "crises". As this chapter shows, this approach encourages researchers to reflect carefully on their position—in relation to those they "accompany", as well as to the power relations that (re)produce crises—and to adjust the timing, objectives, and methodologies of research projects.

Maritza Felices-Luna analyzes the construction of "crises" in Calais through media discourses, which serve to validate government policies to create and then dismantle camps for migrants waiting to cross the Channel between France and England. Her chapter demonstrates how "crises" are made visible and invisible by popular discourses and government policies that "transform migrants into a (racial) spectacle". Through a textual analysis of media coverage of Calais by three regional newspapers, Felices-Luna focuses on the figurative worlds underlying the news stories. Her analysis reveals two dominant and contrasting narratives of French nationalism: solidarity with migrants, evoking France as the birthplace of human rights; or, a sovereign France under threat. However, while they are contrasting, these two imaginary worlds are connected by humanitarian securitization. Through this lens, discourses of "crisis" are used to construct migrants as both victims and threats, which require management.

Similarly, in Chapter 3, **Martha Alexandra Vargas Aguirre** uses Foucault's notion of problematization to demonstrate how the Ecuadorian government has constructed the mass migration of Venezuelans as both a "risk" and "victims". Indeed, Ecuador has used tactical humanitarianism through erratic changes in its migration policy that often undermine its progressive, pro-migration constitutional framework. In particular, Vargas Aguirre explores how the migration of Venezuelans to Ecuador was first facilitated, then problematized as a "humanitarian crisis" that needed to be managed. The government of Ecuador used both the manufactured urgency of "crisis", as well as the humanitarian-securitization nexus to introduce policies that contradicted the legal right to freedom of movement by aiming to first facilitate the temporary transit of, and then exclude and expel, Venezuelans. In particular, the imposition of a visa requirement, with monetary and documentation costs, caused an increase in the number of Venezuelans with irregular status in Ecuador.

In their chapter, **Tatiana Llaguno** and **Marina Gomá** focus on the case study of Barcelona's unionized street vendors to interrogate Europe's alleged immigration "crisis". In the context of the criminalization of both migration and street vending, the creation of a union and the clothing cooperative "Top Manta" is a form of anti-racist praxis. The authors analyze the messaging and images inscribed on Top Manta clothing to demonstrate how both the branding itself and the processes of collective self-organization serve to challenge dominant discourses of national citizenship, waged labour, and racial capitalism. Their analysis shifts our focus to the ways in which those at the centre of intersecting "crises" navigate and resist racist laws that criminalize survival.

Similarly, in Chapter 5, **Manuel Salamanca Cardona** analyzes the effects of the COVID-19 "crisis" on racialized, precarious im/migrant workers in Quebec. Based on ethnographic research with the Immigrant Workers Centre (IWC) and surveys and semi-structured interviews with refugee claimants, he situates this "crisis" within the context of historical, systemic discrimination in neoliberal labour market structures. The chapter not only shows how racialized im/migrant workers, especially those who are undocumented, were disproportionately affected by the pandemic, but also how their unjust working conditions radicalized class awareness and galvanized collective action. Salamanca provides nuanced insights into the disconnect between "essential workers" and "guardian angel" discourses on the one hand, and the realities of precarious conditions that undermined the health and rights of im/migrant labourers on the other hand. Similarly, the chapter describes the tensions within the IWC and other advocacy organizations which worked more closely with governments to provide services, while at the same time challenging the fundamental exclusionary logics within these same state structures.

Continuing with the theme of racialized and precarious immigrants, **Chiedza Pasipanodya** and **Tahseen Chowdhury**, in Chapter 6, analyze the commodification of higher education in Canada and how international students are exploited within this system, and also constructed as "the other" within the perceived crisis of immigration. Using critical race theory, the authors interrogate interlocking systems of oppression within the discourses of the Government of Canada's International Education Strategy and press coverage of its release, as well as the internationalization strategies of four universities and one college. This textual analysis reveals systemic racism, "manufactured crises" of scarcity, competition, and fraud, and contradictory policies of temporary status with promised, but elusive, long-term residency. While international students are fundamental to the economic functioning of the neoliberal higher education system in Canada, they are also constructed as undermining the immigration system and/or the Canadian economy—what Pasipanodya and Chowdhury refer to as "crisis by design."

References

Aguiton, S. A., L. Cabane, & L. Cornilleau (2019). Politiques de la "mise en crise". *Critique internationale, 85*(4), 9–21.

Ambrosetti, D., & Y. Buchet De Neuilly (2009). Les organisations internationales au cœur des crises : configurations empiriques et jeux d'acteurs. *Cultures & conflits, 75*, 7–14.

Berlant, L. G. (2011). *Cruel optimism.* Duke University Press.

Boggs, A., & N. Mitchell (2018). Critical university studies and the crisis consensus. *Feminist Studies, 44*(2), 432–463.

Carastathis, A., N. Kouri-Towe, G. Mahrouse & L. Whitley (2018). Introduction: Feminist approaches to the refugee "crisis." *Refuge, 34*(1), 3–15.

Colly, A. (2021, 16 December). "J'étais chez moi, je voulais boire de l'eau de javel" : le Liban, un pays à bout de nerfs, Le reportage de la rédaction, *France Culture.*

Crawley, H. (2016). Managing the unmanageable? Understanding Europe's response to the migration "crisis." *Human Geography, 9*(2), 13–23.

De Genova, N. (2018). The "migrant crisis" as racial crisis: Do black lives matter in Europe? *Ethnic and Racial Studies, 41*(10), 1765–1782.

Dobry, M. (2009). *Sociologie des crises politiques. La dynamique des mobilisations multisectorielles.* Presses de Sciences Po.

Edwards, Z. (2021). Racial capitalism and COVID-19. *Monthly Review, 72*(10), 21–32.

Grinand, A. (25 October 2021). La crise sécuritaire, nouvelle menace haï-
tienne ? *Le Nouvelliste Numérique*.

Guilhou, X., & P. Lagadec (2002, 5 March). La fin du risque zéro, *Le Monde*.

Hage, G. (2015). La critique de la crise et la crise de la critique dans Tremblay,
André et Marie-Claude Haince (dir.), *Crise et mise en crise, actes du colloque de l'ACSALF 2012*, Éditions de l'ACSALF.

Issar, S. (2021). Listening to black lives matter: Racial capitalism and the critique of neoliberalism. *Contemporary Political Theory, 20*(1), 48–71.

Jeandesboz, J., & Pallister-Wilkins, P. (2016). Crisis, routine, consolidation: The
politics of the Mediterranean migration crisis. *Mediterranean Politics,
21*(2), 316–320.

Kelley, R. (2017). What did Cedric Robinson mean by racial capitalism?.
Boston Review. https://bostonreview.net/race/robin-d-g-kelley-what-
did-cedric-robinson-mean-racial-capitalism

Koselleck, R. (2006). Crisis. *Journal of the History of Ideas, 67*(2), 357–400.

Lindeman, T. (2020, May 13). "Why are so many people getting sick and dying
in Montreal from Covid-19?" *The Guardian*. https://www.theguardian.
com/world/2020/may/13/coronavirus-montreal-canada-hit-hard

Maynard, R. (2020). Police abolition/black revolt. *Topia, 41*(1), 70–78.

Mbembe, A., & Roitman, J. (1995). Figures of the subject in times of crisis,
Public Culture, 7(2), 323–352.

Pulido, L. (2016). Flint, environmental racism, and racial capitalism. *Capitalism,
Nature, Socialism, 27*(3), 1–16.

Revel, J. (Éd.). (1996). *Jeux d'échelles. La micro-analyse à l'expérience*. Gallimard/
Le Seuil.

Robinson, C. J. (2023[1983]). *Marxisme noir : la Genèse de la tradition radicale
noire*. Entremonde.

Roitman, J. (2013). *Anti-crisis*. Duke University Press.

Roitman, J., Aguiton, S.A., Cabane, L., & Cornilleau, L. (2019), Anti-Crisis :
penser avec et contre les crises. Entretien avec Janet Roitman, *Critique
internationale, 4*(85), 107–121.

Roger, A., & Aït-Aoudia, M. (ed.) (2015). *La logique du désordre. Relire la sociologie de Michel Dobry*. Presses de Sciences Po.

Rohland, E. (2020). COVID-19, Climate, and white supremacy: Multiple crises
or one? *Journal for the History of Environment and Society, 5*, 23–32.

Table de concertation des organismes au service des personnes réfugiées et
immigrantes (TCRI) (2020). *Demandeurs.se.s d'asile travaillant dans les services essentiels : près de 400 témoignages*. Montreal.

Triandafyllidou, A. (2018). A "Refugee crisis" unfolding: "Real" events and
their interpretation in media and political debates. *Journal of Immigrant
& Refugee Studies, 16*(1–2), 198–216.

UNHCR Canada (2022). La pandémie du COVID-19. https://www.unhcr.ca/
fr/notre-travail/situations-durgence/pandemie-covid-19/

The Theoretical and Practical Potential of *Acompañamiento* for Research with People Marginalized through Immigration Controls

Valentina Glockner, Walter Flores, Elaine Chase, Jennifer Allsopp,
Ian Warwick, Deborah Zion, Brad Blitz, Ricardo Muniz-Trejo,
Penelope Van Tuyl, and Theresa Cheng

This chapter is dedicated to the memory of Valentina Glockner Fagetti. Valentina was a dear colleague, friend, and exceptional academic. As an anthropologist, her work was dedicated to meaningful collaboration with migrant, refugee, and Indigenous women and children through practices of solidarity and advocacy. Valentina's commitment to social and environmental justice in Mexico and the Global South was and continues to be deeply inspirational.

Immigration control procedures have for many decades been generative of crisis, provoking devastating impacts on the lives of migrant communities and people on the move. While social science research can highlight these effects and suggest more humanitarian approaches, there remain multiple questions of how best to engage with migrant communities in ways which help formulate contextually meaningful, timely, and actionable responses to their situations. These questions are particularly pertinent in contexts of plural "crises" faced by Indigenous migrant peoples which emerge from the combined effects of the complex factors driving migration, deeply embedded racialized and class-based global politics, and punitive migration governance regimes creating daily crises of incoherence, instability, and uncertainty.

Drawing on illustrative examples from the work of two members of an interdisciplinary research team working with Indigenous migrant communities in Mexico, Guatemala, and the United States, this chapter explores the concept of *acompañamiento* and considers its theoretical and practical relevance in shaping modes of enquiry and action. We first outline how the concept has been operationalized across disciplines (from international development, critical education, feminist, legal, and anthropological perspectives) before disentangling how it is underpinned by ideas relating to participation, positionality, ethics, and research activism. We discuss the hitherto under explored application of the concept to migration studies alongside the ethical dilemmas it raises. We conclude with reflections on the potential and limitations of *acompañamiento* as a process of non-hierarchical, knowledge co-production, and action (praxis) which ultimately seeks to unsettle existing power structures and promote social justice in contexts of individual and collective intersecting crises. In doing so, we recognize how such crises, rather than only coming into existence via political declarations at particular moments in time, are experienced as the sustained products of persistent and long-term racialized and class-based immigration control procedures and other forms of political violence; and their co-incidence with other factors such as conflict, climate change, and global pandemics.

Vignette 1.1: *Acompañamiento* in Mexico (Valentina Glockner)

In November 2018, Norman and Edilson, two Honduran teenagers aged 17 and 15, respectively, were travelling through northern Mexico as part of the first massive migrant caravan crossing the country to reach the border with the United States.[1] They had been driven from their native countries by intersecting crises: environmental degradation and food insecurity but mainly due to the effects of armed violence and the presence of criminal groups in their neighbourhoods: the murder of Edilson's father by gang members, and an attempt of forced recruitment for Norman. Very close to achieving their objective, both were detained by Mexican authorities and transferred first to a detention center and then to a government shelter for unaccompanied migrant children. It was at the shelter where Norman and Edilson met and became friends. At first, their relationship was more of a necessity and a strategy to deal with the constant threats and intimidations meted out by the female child protection officer of the National Migration Institute (INM). Before being sent to the children's shelter, they reported that Mexican authorities had coerced them into signing their own deportation certificates, without having even listened to (in the case of Edilson) and without taking into account (in the case of Norman) the reasons why they had fled Honduras and wanted to request asylum in the United States.

After several tense days, Norman realized that although their ultimate goal was to request asylum in the United States, requesting asylum in Mexico could be a strategy to delay his deportation. Yet when he claimed his right to protection in Mexico, the officer's anger increased, as she was obliged to comply with the procedure and guarantee his right to international protection. Days later, she appeared at the shelter to announce INM had already purchased the plane tickets to send all the young people at the shelter back to their countries of origin. Norman and Edilson decided to rebel against this imposition and, that same night, they escaped from the government shelter.

I met Norman and Edilson the next day, while they were hiding in a church near the shelter where parishioners had promised to protect them from the police and immigration and child protection officers. We met the caravan, thanks to a network of scholars and activists accompanying and monitoring it, which by then had already reached the Tijuana/San Diego border and which the boys had contacted via a hidden cell phone. During the next two and a half months, I carried out an *acompañamiento* and documentation process designed to defend Norman and Edilson's right to migrate, as well as their right to seek asylum in the United States. This resulted in Norman and Edilson reaching the Nogales-Sonora border where they were admitted by Customs and Border Protection (CBP) authorities as unaccompanied children seeking refuge in early 2019. At the end of 2020 Norman won his case for asylum in an immigration court and in June 2021 he graduated from high school while working at a restaurant. Edilson is studying and working and will soon turn 18. His asylum case is being supported by pro bono lawyers from a non-profit child advocacy organization.

This process of *acompañamiento* was made possible thanks to the solidarity, advice, and support provided by a network of NGO activists, academics, advocates, lawyers, students, government officials, and family and friends on both sides of the Sonora and Arizona border, as well as other cities in Mexico. The network was formed in a spontaneous yet purposive way to respond to Edilson and Norman's needs for immediate help and defence. The *acompañamiento* of Norman and Edilson became, at the same time, an interpellation and an extension of my work as a researcher and an anthropologist. It arose from a conviction to produce forms of documentation that make possible the defence of the right to migrate, as well as collectively constructing both a critical account of the border regime and its effects on children and youth, and a *memoria del presente* (memory of the present) focusing on the ways in which the current migratory regime—through migration and child protection authorities in this case—violates the human rights of migrants and asylum seekers.

Acompañamiento emerges as a way of building strategies to record the knowledge, experiences, and participation of children and young people to recognize them as protagonists and fundamental actors of contemporary migration. In that sense, I agree with Alicia Re Cruz (2018) that in an era in which migration policies put the lives and security of migrants and refugees at risk, anthropology and research should serve as an instrument for the construction of social justice.

Vignette 1.2: CEGSS—Guatemala (Walter Flores)

Over ten years ago, CEGSS (Centre for the Study of Equity and Governance in Health Systems) started its first action-research project with rural Indigenous communities of Guatemala.[2] The United States Congress had recently passed a new law promoting citizen participation in the planning and monitoring of public services. Our project aimed to develop and field-test a participatory model for training communities to engage in planning and monitoring of the local healthcare services.

While working with the communities, we realized there was a distrust between communities and local health authorities. In addition, some community leaders that tried to implement an active citizen role, as stated in the new law, found themselves facing threats from local authorities for asking questions about use of public resources. In one of our dialogues with communities, they said they trusted us and wanted to continue learning about the law. Because of the threat from authorities, they wanted legal advice and that we do not "leave them alone."

Our project grant was about to finish and we were a team of public health professionals—not experienced in conflict resolution and legal aid. We understood these communities needed *acompaña-miento* and that if we were to continue working with them, we had to expand our team to include a lawyer and team members that spoke local Indigenous languages. CEGSS then started a new model of work where in addition to capacity-building and technical assistance, we provide *acompañamiento* to communities in their struggles for equitable access to public services and confronting the historic social exclusion they suffer. As part of our *acompañamiento* strategy, community leaders have a major role in discussing and deciding, together with CEGSS, what research we needed to do and the strategies for advocacy. As the *acompañamiento* evolved, CEGSS expanded its team skills to include anthropology, political sciences, informatics, and journalism.

Our relationship and trust with communities also deepened. We got to know more about their lives and they also learned more about ours. All of us working at CEGSS are acutely aware of how we enjoy social privileges that rural Indigenous communities do not have, yet we share a commitment to do whatever is within our reach to support communities' struggles and demands for well-being. But our relationship is not based on paternalism. Communities decide their own actions, and there are multiple disagreements about strategies which are resolved through dialogue. Rather, we understand our relationship as one of inter-class solidarity. In the past few years, communities have approached CEGSS to help them address the effects in their communities resulting from the increasing migration from rural Indigenous areas to Mexico and the United States. Families risk the very little they have in order to make the trip and many are deported in the process, returning in an even more vulnerable condition than they left. In our more recent consultations with communities, we have identified other factors which exacerbate vulnerability among rural Indigenous families. The storms and hurricanes in late 2020 destroyed their crops and access roads, and COVID-19 travel restrictions did not allow them to seek temporary work elsewhere. Despite the efforts by Indigenous communities to oppose such actions, extractive industries continue expanding in their territories, often using violence and sometimes with the support of public security forces. Intersecting vulnerabilities are displacing entire families and others are migrating abroad. Currently, our *acompañamiento* involves being responsive to these changing dynamics, documenting together with communities the intersecting crises, and implementing tailored rights literacy campaigns through virtual programs adapted to the COVID-19 reality.

Aims and Scope

The accounts of Edilson and Norman, and the efforts to support members of Indigenous communities in Guatemala, capture the violent and dehumanizing aspects of racialized immigration regimes and how they combine with other crises such as climate change, armed conflict, extreme poverty, and the recent COVID-19 pandemic. The vignettes illustrate how the effects of these plural crises can be somewhat tempered or suspended (momentarily or long term) through the actions of others who help operationalize resistance to regimes of oppression through the practice of *acompañamiento*. In this chapter, we write collectively as a group of academics, based in Mexico, Guatemala, the United Kingdom, the United States, and Australia seeking to better understand the impacts of migration governance on people's lives. From the reflections offered by Valentina and Walter, we consider the broader relevance of the concept of *acompañamiento* for research in contexts of migration and (im)mobility, typically spaces of intersecting crises generating ethical and methodological dilemmas.

The paper draws on emerging findings from the UKRI-funded Life Facing Deportation[3] study on the impacts of migration governance in the United States, Mexico, and Guatemala on people's lives, with a view to informing advocacy and strategic litigation to promote the rights of migrant communities. After providing some context, the paper introduces *acompañamiento* as a concept, with examples of how it is understood and applied across disciplines and connecting it to ideas of positionality, ethics, participation, and research activism. We illustrate how studies of (im)mobility can be generative of *acompañamiento*, since migration is often at once a response to and a means of exposing oneself to intersecting crises. Migration scholars are often required to accompany research participants—in person or through narrative—across borders of place and time. The practice of "journeying with" someone is thus well established in the field. We conclude with reflections on the potential of *acompañamiento* as a process of non-hierarchical, knowledge co-production, and action (praxis) which ultimately seeks to unsettle existing power structures and promote social justice in contexts of immigration control and other intersecting crises.

Migration, Deportations, and Marginalization in Central America

Despite international global compacts claiming to enable the "safe, orderly and regular" movement of people (IOM 2018) and promote cooperation and sharing of resources to support refugees (UN 2018), in reality national and regional policies across the globe have long been generative of crises of humanity and care (Rosen et al., 2023) through the production of increasingly securitized borders, limitations to free movement, and the imposition of punitive regimes of control and violence on those who move (Álvarez Velasco, 2017; Varela Huerta, 2018). These produce extended periods of immobility, liminality, induced poverty, marginalization, and forms of politically induced precariousness (Butler, 2006) which prevent people from living the lives they aspire to or exercising their continuously obscured, elusive, and contested rights.

The context of the United States and Central America, where our research is situated, generates particular risks and challenges for people on the move. Recent years have seen an increase in the migration of families and unaccompanied minors from Central America crossing in large numbers (CBP, 2018) and an increase in applications for asylum (Camargo, 2014). Restrictions on people's movement (Cantalapiedra & Quintero, 2018), including children and youth (Glockner, 2019) along the so-called vertical border (Varela Huerta, 2018) between the United States and Mexico include the increased use of charges for illegal entry and re-entry, detention, deportation, and tightened immigration controls in the interior of the USA. Some of the most controversial policies relate to the separation of children from families and their detention for indefinite periods of time (Human Rights Watch, 2019; Glockner & Sardao, 2020).

Bi-lateral arrangements between the United States and neighbouring governments, such as the Migrant Protection Protocol, also known as the "remain in Mexico" program (DHS, 2019), have made Mexico increasingly a forced destination country for hundreds of thousands of migrants who became trapped by a US immigration system denying them legitimate avenues for mobility and to asylum (Álvarez Velasco, 2017). As part of this arrangement, Mexico has been directly involved in the deportations of thousands of unaccompanied children and young people (Amnesty International, 2021; Glockner & Sardao, 2020). More recently the US government has exploited the COVID-19 pandemic through the application of Title 42 immigration restrictions to summarily remove thousands of migrants from the United States on the grounds of public health, without having to deploy the usual paraphernalia associated with deportations (Blue et al., 2021).

Guatemala is both a sending and receiving country in international migration between Central America, Mexico, and the United States. While large numbers of people have migrated since the 1980s due to civil wars, in the past decade migration has increased as a result of extreme poverty and violence, mainly related to drug trafficking and urban gangs. In 2019 alone, close to 55,000 Guatemalan citizens were deported by air back to Guatemala from the United States (Government of Guatemala, 2020). The largest number of deportees originate from municipalities with a majority of Indigenous populations and high levels of poverty. In July 2019, the US government designated Guatemala a "safe third country" and under the US-Guatemala agreement devolved the processing of asylum applications from Honduras and El Salvador to Guatemalan authorities. Guatemala has hence become a major receiving state, even though it is unsafe, has an "embryonic" asylum system (Adams, 2019), and thousands of its own citizens have sought sanctuary in the United States (Carasik, 2019).

Understanding Acompañamiento

Rooted in Indigenous thought and ethics (Carranza, 2021) and tied closely to ideas of liberation theology (Freire, 1970; Gozuieta, 2001), the essence of *acompañamiento* is captured by the idea of walking along-side others and to share their struggles in a show of solidarity and resistance in the face of oppression. It requires a deep sense of empathy and justice, implies a commitment to affirming people's humanity, dignity, and personhood, and is intrinsically political. While often read as a religious ethic, for example in the mission of the Jesuit Refugee Service (to "accompany, serve, and advocate"), the concept resonates with several bodies of work and disciplines. Among others, it is aligned with a feminist ethos of care (Edwards & Mauthner, 2012), an ethics of social and spatial justice (Askins, 2018), and providing a basis of a social contract (or Acción Social) in the pursuit of justice—whether, for example, to alleviate poverty, resist, and advocate against forms of displacement (Guerra, 2006), or to support families of the "disappeared" in Colombia to discover what has happened to their loved ones (Garcia et al., 2018). Whatever practice engaged in, *acompañamiento* requires working as "converts" in Freirean terms or as "privileged allies" in the words of Sepúlveda (2011) to re-centre the voices, demands, and needs of those on the margins (Spivak, 1988) and to back them up and help sustain their struggle once they have spoken or acted. In contexts of migration, *acompañamiento* has emerged as a practice of care, solidarity, and political activism among migrants, which transforms illegality into humanity (Nuñez-Janes & Ovalle, 2016), and as a discursive strategy by humanitarian organizations to assert control over the social encounter between locals and refugees in the face of hostile border regimes (Carpi & Şenoguz, 2019).

    Acompañamiento is implicit within disciplinary practices relevant to our own areas of work. For example, the practice of human rights law based on feminist legal collaboration (Jacobson, 2020) promotes the building of alliances with people whose rights are contested, thus revealing the political possibilities in socio-legal spaces of attending to situated needs and injustices and generating a process of co-production of legal responses (Castro Neira, 2019). In the field of education, *acompañamiento*-as-pedagogy has considered how marginalized and migrant young people can be enabled to speak back to society and the educational institutions—or "liminal spaces of schooling"—around them through a process of what Sepúlveda (2011) refers to as a "pedagogy of the borderlands" (p. 550). This seeks to redress the disconnect between the lived experiences of migrant students and the curricula and pedagogies they are presented with, and avoid the spatial, academic, and social separations (or "socialization into marginality") through education. In development practice, *acompañamiento* has been associated with progressive feminism (Wilson & Whitmore, 1995) and bound to the core principles of empowerment and participation (Freire, 1970).

Inherent in the concept is *movement*, and it is thus not surprising that the genesis for our thinking about *acompañamiento* is migration research. Beyond established feminist research ethics, which centre on establishing "where we stand" and speaking from that bordered space of power in order to mitigate its harmful effects (Cockburn, 2005), the practice of *acompañamiento* is driven by the needs and desires of those whose lives we seek to document, and in ways which are most meaningful to them in any given place and time. The movement associated with *acompañamiento* does not necessarily have a specific or predetermined point of arrival or end point. It might not even have a single or clearly defined goal but involves action which is sustained and vigilant to what is happening in real time. In practical terms, if a participant is deported or detained, it suggests not only documenting what happens but recognizing a responsibility to mobilize opposition against the immigration system depriving them of their freedom and right to migrate. It is our belief that *acompañamiento* offers a possibility to take seriously questions of power and to establish a research approach that can accommodate a meeting of bodies and minds on the move.

Bringing Acompañamiento *to Research*

In practical terms, *acompañamiento* has implications for every stage of research from how we enter the "field", what we search for, and how we position ourselves as researchers whose interests go far beyond documentation and interpretation of reality. Our initial objective in the Life Facing Deportation project was to generate a better understanding of the impact of deportation threats, processes, and procedures on people's lives and consider the legality of these actions and how we might support advocacy and strategic litigation to contest policies and practices of violence. As captured in the vignettes, however, the feasibility of this broader project is complicated by the immediacy and complex intertwining of the multiple crises migrant people are facing, along with the criminalization and dehumanization tactics coming from the borderization regimes. Thus, an asynchronicity emerges between the strategies and timing of a research plan and what people need in the here and now to pursue their own goals and improve their lives. Such dilemmas bring us to fundamental questions of our positionality and commitment as "researchers" — why we are there; what values we bring; what must be prioritized; what we do and how we do it.

Positionality and Motivation

The vignettes suggest several motivations for why researchers might adopt the mantel of *acompañamiento* and become involved in such intimate ways in people's lives. Glockner describes a commitment to documenting what is happening to young people as a form of defence of their right to migrate, while at the same time producing concrete strategies that will allow them to claim their right to asylum, and creating collective memory of the violence of the border regime and its impact on young people. She situates anthropology as an instrument for social justice in the face of violence and the failures of national states and the international community to fulfill their responsibility towards unaccompanied migrant children and asylum seekers. Flores speaks of the importance of recognizing privilege vis-à-vis those we hope to accompany and entering a form of social contract of inter-class solidarity to redress the various forms of violence encountered by Indigenous communities. In both scenarios the researcher has an explicit intention beyond finding out and documenting what is happening. Research and the production of knowledge become a secondary purpose and a direct result of the process of *acompañamiento* and defence of people's interests and rights. Glockner is defending children's right to migrate and claim asylum in the United States, while Flores and colleagues are getting behind a community's struggle for equitable access to public services and challenging historic exclusions of Indigenous communities that result in extreme poverty and marginalization. In both situations, the agenda is determined by those defined in orthodox terms as "research subjects", but who in the process of *acompañamiento* become actors and protagonists, drivers of the research and action process.

Having understood the goals and intentions of Edilson and Norman, Glockner rallies to the support of others who have encountered them on the route, to come up with a collective strategy to protect the boys from deportation. Her role as ethnographer is explicit in that documentation of state-produced violence within migratory regimes is the result of a process of *acompañamiento* whose most important aim is to collectively guarantee Norman's and Edilson's well-being, freedom, and right to seek asylum. Therefore, academic research and documentation emerge through the process of producing personal accounts that will help them strengthen their respective asylum cases, advocacy strategies, and legal defence against deportation, as through negotiating and confronting government officials and immigration institutions. While *acompañamiento* helps Edilson and Norman achieve what they most value (that is, requesting asylum in the United States), it also connects their personal experiences to the wider impacts of immigration regimes which transcend the individual and create spaces of violence and oppression for migrants across the globe. Hence beyond responding to the idiosyncrasies of situated experience, *acompañamiento* is concerned with documenting and amplifying commonalities in experiences across people, context, and time.

Flores and colleagues within CEGSS in Guatemala describe a well-intended motivation to facilitate a government policy allegedly designed to allow people a greater say in access and quality to health services. Their interactions with communities based on *acompañamiento* reveal the chasm between policy rhetoric and what is happening on the ground. This situated and contextualized understanding informs a positionality adopted by Flores and his team who commit to supporting the struggles of the community and respond to the explicit plea that "they not be left alone". In both situations we can recognize interpellation through which researchers actively question and reorientate what they do given the contextualized realities of the situations they find themselves in and the aspirations and requests of others.

The researcher within this dialogic, relational space is no longer the neutral bystander but aligns themselves in solidarity with the "oppressed", building bridges between the (often privileged) "scientific" world of academia and people's lived experiences across the "humanitarian border" (Walters, 2011). Given the acuteness of the violence and harm facing migrant communities, the practice of *acompañamiento* becomes at once a methodological, ethical, and moral necessity and form of commitment and *implicación* (implication). It suggests a shift from sporadic data collection at pre-set intervals to a dynamic and extended interaction with people (Askins, 2018) which is moulded to the rhythms and patterns of their lived realities.

Relationship of Acompañamiento *to Particular Research Approaches*

While difficult to situate the practice of *acompañamiento* within a single research paradigm, we recognize synergy with several research approaches. Alderson's (2019) application of critical realism to contexts of conflict and disruption is a cogent example. This is because critical realism foregrounds the importance of values as central to all social relations and prioritizes the engagement with unseen "causal mechanisms" of people's lived realities (understanding how these may be occurring within multiple micro, meso, and macro systems) alongside other social structures such as power, inequality, and dependency (Alderson, 2019). Hence it is an approach that connects what is happening in space and time to these broader influences. Alderson details four planes of critical realism which are relevant to our current work.

The first refers to human bodies in nature and involves understanding how wider factors such as climate change, violence, and poverty incite migration; the second, interpersonal relations, explores how human agents work with each other within a given context; the third considers the social structures, in this case the immigration and border regimes that generate forms of violence; and the fourth is about the values and emotions that drive our actions. In this case, it is a combination of commitment to redress the inequalities and marginalization generated by systems of immigration control and deportation, combined with feelings that vary from anger, sadness, and empathy, in relation to the observed impact on people's lives. Hence in the context of migration and (im)mobility, research becomes a process of understanding how injustices and oppression come about (including the multi-level and often hidden factors shaping migratory outcomes); incorporating a historical and geopolitical analysis of how power imbalances are generated; and minimizing power differentials in the research process through unsettling the epistemic power typically held by those with privilege. In their accounts of *acompañamiento*, both Glockner and Flores point to these processes of broader analysis, the emphasis on relationships—especially relations of care, reciprocity, and solidarity—attention to structural violence, and the role of values and emotions.

Such ideas also suggest a methodological orientation informed by critical pragmatism (Lewis-Beck et al., 2004), an approach which is experimental and adaptable to situation and context, but which purposefully sets out to illuminate ideological domination, hegemonic practices, and social injustices. At the same time, fixed labels and categories of "vulnerability" such as "vulnerable children" and "vulnerable women" are problematized and, instead, there is engagement with the intersectional and multi-layered factors and sources of vulnerability, which are intrinsically related to context (Lunar, 2019), recognizing that precarity—or politically induced precariousness (Butler 2006)—is produced by the systems, policies, institutions, and structures that people in migratory contexts have to endure (De Vries & Guild, 2019).

The Ethics of *Acompañamiento*

Acompañamiento also raises fundamental ethical questions about how researchers are to conduct themselves and what they can do and cannot do in the field. The ethical stance in both scenarios rests on a process of not only "walking" with, learning from, and documenting people's lived realities, but learning how to "de-centre" oneself from the process of knowledge production and decision-making. This "de-centring" implies the practice and commitment of *escucha activa* (active listening), a process which involves not only listening, learning from, and recognizing people's voices, experiences, needs, and desires, but actively acknowledging your role in their struggle, and identifying and mobilizing the resources and opportunities your positionality, privilege(s), and class could contribute. Therefore, *acompañamiento* rests on the ethical premise of what narrative practice (White, 2007) calls to remain "de-centered but influential"—that is, to become politically and ethically de-centred but deeply engaged and active.

This approach rejects any notion that research is value-free and instead accepts it as a political project, concerned with unsettling

exploitative power dynamics and building intimate research relationships (Maynard, 1994; Leyva Solano & Speed, 2015). In the context of Indigenous people's migration, it is purposefully revelatory of
the historical, political, economic, racialized, and class-based factors
producing the lived realities of daily crisis, and seeks to disrupt what
are understood as the normal and acceptable modes of migration
governance.

Acompañamiento aligns itself with a feminist ethics of care
(Edwards & Mathener, 2012) which situates care, rather than research
outcomes, justice, and rights at the core of interactions—though these
may be by-products of the process. It emphasizes deontology or duty,
a deep concern with issues of power, the centrality of personal experience and emotions, and the building of relationships which are affec-
tionate and nurturing (Porter, 1999). From a feminist care perspective,
there is an acknowledgement that daily dilemmas are shaped by
social divisions of race, class, ethnicity, citizenship, and legal status;
and that such dilemmas are embedded in particular relationships that
involve emotions as well as a deep commitment with auto-reflexivity
and self-criticism. Hence the ethics of research practiced in such contexts involves a constant process of dialogue and negotiation within
research teams and with communities and people, in order to establish consensus about what is morally and ethically the right course of
action. Denzin (1997) talks about the role of ethnography as a process
of being "with and for the other" and bringing about transformations
to the public and private spheres of life. Glockner starts from understanding what are the immediate needs and most valued desires and
aspirations, and then works in collaboration with others to understand how they can be supported. Flores speaks of building consensus
for action through a constant process of dialogue with communities.
In both situations, *acompañamiento* involved intensive and long-term
commitment. Glockner worked with the boys for more than eight
months to help them escape deportation, get to the border, request
asylum, and find suitable sponsors; while Flores and colleagues have
worked with communities over many years to respond to the intersecting crises generated by climate change, political violence, poverty,
and migration governance.

Supporting what others want to achieve involves working
beyond who and what we know. Glockner aligned herself with others (the church, community activists, advocacy organizations, family
networks, and other academics on both sides of the border), who were

able to provide direct forms of shelter and support to Edilson and Norman. Flores and colleagues identified others who could support what Indigenous communities were trying to achieve and then built other alliances and expanded their team so that they could provide appropriate support and continue to work alongside the community. Hence *acompañamiento* speaks to generating and sustaining communities of solidarity and leveraging the relevant expertise of others to support what they want to achieve, such as, in the case of Flores and colleagues, legal aid, journalism, and political science. Such an approach aligns with Carranza's (2021) idea of being invited into spaces and at the same time working with people's own values and objectives whilst enabling them to retain possession of their knowledge and stories and use them for their own ends (see also Pittaway et al., 2010).

Acompañamiento suggests a research ethic which transcends ideas of "doing no harm" and instead engages in *investigación comprometida* (committed research) (Glockner, 2022), and forms of reciprocity, what Pittaway et al. (2010) define as giving back something of value to the community which is determined by them. As such, research, advocacy, mediation, and enablement are intrinsically intertwined—all research has the purpose of unsettling structures and systems which generate and perpetuate crises of oppression and marginalization. This requires a criticality with regard to power dynamics and a commitment to research which unsettles rather than reproduces existing power structures (Dietz & Cortés, 2007).

Implications for Co-creating Knowledge

For the purposes of research as practice, *acompañamiento* closely links to participatory methods of engagement, conscientization, and praxis (Freire, 2000). However, a key difference is that *acompañamiento* does not assume the need for "conscientization," the idea embedded within critical pedagogy, but instead engages with the ideologies, philosophies, principles, and values of different, individual, and collective participants; and recognizes the plurality, situatedness, and intersectionality of knowledges (Gordon, 2014). At the same time, it promotes horizontal and de-centred forms of dialogue which recognize the multiple "invested positionalities" involved (Carranza, 2021) whilst holding at heart a fundamental concern for social justice and enabling people to achieve what they most value. Embedding ideas of *acompañamiento* in research means dismissing ideas about the neutrality of research (Lather, 1986). At the same time, researchers must reject dominant Western constructions of "modernity" which associate progress and advancement with positivism and objectivity as defined by hegemonic institutions of "knowledge-power" residing in the Global North. This dominant approach too often relegates the rest of the world to backwardness, ignorance, and disadvantage, a viewpoint that migration studies has far from elided (Mayblin & Turner, 2021). Hence *acompañamiento* engages also with ideas of colonialism and coloniality, or how the legacies of colonialism transcend the postcolonial world (Quijano, 2007), and accepts that academic approaches based on colonialism have caused violence to Indigenous methods of knowledge production.

Instead, *acompañamiento* captures the relational nature (Biesta, 2007) of knowledge production; that is, its emergence through relationships and interactions between different actors. Aligning with new materialist approaches, knowledges are recognized in their plurality, as more than "systems of thought" and as socially produced in relation to multiple forms of materiality (including human bodies, nonhuman animals, material objects, artistic representations, and artefacts) and incorporating meanings associated with space, place, the natural and built environment, and material forces such as gravity and time (Fox & Alldred, 2019).

In terms of practice, knowledge generated through *acompañamiento* is put to a practical purpose, determined by the communities we work with as necessary for both their own and collective well-being and the pursuit of sustainable lives, and lives that are worth living (Butler 2006). It suggests a degree of immediate action and personal and collective engagement, rather than procrastinated change, often typical of orthodox research. Flores speaks of having to respond simultaneously to communities' concerns with the impacts of migration from rural Indigenous areas, the hurricanes which have destroyed crops and livelihoods, and the limitations imposed by COVID-19 on people's movement to find work. Such crises require immediate advocacy for political change while promoting critical rights literacy to strengthen community action in the long term. Similarly, Glockner and colleagues recognize their duty not just to document Edilson and Norman's situation but to facilitate the boys' immediate access to (immigration) justice and asylum.

Conclusion

The Life Facing Deportation project set out to document the experiences of people facing deportation and the impacts on their lives. It had a designated objective of supporting advocacy and strategic litigation through building a body of evidence which could be channelled through relevant systems, structures, and institutions dedicated to defending human rights and redressing social injustices. Bringing *acompañamiento* into the frame suggests something different, and it has implications for how we generate knowledge and what stance and action we take in the process. It raises fundamental questions about why we are in the space in question; what our role is, what values, resources, connections, and commitments we bring, what knowledge is generated, who lays claim to such knowledge, and how it is used.

In contexts of intersecting crises encountered through our work and generated by migration governance systems, political repression, industrial and commercial violence, climate change, and global pandemics such as COVID-19, *acompañamiento* exerts a duty on researchers not just to witness and document people's suffering but to take action to alleviate it. Hence it challenges the neutrality of research and transforms it into a political project underpinned by an ethics of care and commitment. At the same time, given the fluidity of the contexts within which people live out their struggles, *acompañamiento* suggests that research objectives might best be conceived of as floating anchors, requiring ongoing processes of engagement and dialogue to keep them fit for purpose and meaningful to people's lived realities.

We would argue that *acompañamiento*, whilst aligned with participatory action research based on ideas of critical pedagogy, goes further since it starts from a recognition of the knowledge and expertise of communities (not assuming a required awakening), is essentially driven by those seeking justice and change, is based on forging relationships that recognize the protracted effects of inequality and oppression, and is founded on the principle of contingencies (ability to respond and take action in relation to shifting crises). It requires a profound shift in the epistemological and methodological relevance of the academic endeavour (Glockner, 2019) and an openness and reciprocity which sits at odds with traditional academy.

Acompañamiento can keep research grounded and meaningful in a constantly changing world, guide us away from its often-extractive dynamics, and strengthen the centrality of relationships of knowledge co-production and the dialogic nature of action. In the context of migration, it offers a methodological approach for researchers, if they so choose, to work in solidarity with others to collectively resist and disrupt the norms which perpetuate ontological crises for people on the move through systematic forms of racialized and class-based oppressions, which have long typified migratory governance and other political actions or inactions.

Notes

1. Names have been changed for reasons of privacy and security.
2. Centre for the Study of Equity and Governance in Health Systems, https://cegss.org.gt/en/.
3. Life Facing Deportation, https://www.deporting-lives.co.uk.

References

Adams, D. C. (2019, August 5). Guatemala's "embryonic" asylum system lacks capacity to serve as safe U.S. partner, experts say. UnivisionNews. https://www.univision.com/univision-news/immigration/guatemalas-embryonic-asylum-system-lacks-capacity-to-serve-as-safe-u-s-partner-experts-say

Alderson, P. (2019). Education, conflict, peace-building and critical realism. *Education and Conflict Review, 2*, 54–58.

Álvarez Velasco, S. (2017). Movimientos migratorios contemporáneos: entre el control fronterizo y la producción de su ilegalidad. Un diálogo con Nicholas De Genova. *Iconos. Revista de Ciencias Sociales*, 153–164.

Amnesty International (2021, June 11). USA and Mexico deporting thousands of unaccompanied migrant children into harm's way. https://www.amnesty.org/en/latest/press-release/2021/06/estados-unidos-mexico-deportan-miles-ninos-migrantes-situaciones-peligro/

Askins, K. (2018). Feminist geographies and participatory action research: co-producing narratives with people and place. *Gender, Place & Culture, 25*(9), 1277–1294.

Biesta, G. (2007). Towards the knowledge democracy? Knowledge production and the civic role of the university. *Studies in Philosophy and Education, 26*(5), 467–479.

Blue, S., Devine, J., Ruiz, M., McDaniel, K., Hartsell, A., Pierce, C., Johnson, M., Tinglov, A., Yang, M., Wu, X., Moya, S., Cross, E., & Starnes, C. (2021). Im/Mobility at the US–Mexico Border during the COVID-19 Pandemic. *Social Sciences, 10*(2), 47.

Butler, J. (2006). *Precarious life: The powers of mourning and violence.* Verso.

Camargo, A. (2014). Arrancados de Raíz: causas que originan el desplazamiento transfronterizo de niñas, niños y adolescentes no acompañados y/o separados de Centroamérica y su necesidad de protección interna-cional. Ciudad de México: ACNUR.

Cantalapiedra, T., & Quintero, J. C. (2018). Mexico, a vertical border? Policies for the control of irregular migratory transit and their results, 2007–2016. *Social and Humanistic Studies, 16*(2), 87–104.

Carasick, L (2020, July 30). *Trump's Safe Third Country Agreement with Guatemala Is a Lie.* Foreign Policy. https://foreignpolicy.com/2019/07/30/trumps-safe-third-country-agreement-with-guatemala-is-a-lie/

Carpi, E., & Şenoguz, P. H., (2019). Refugee hospitality in Lebanon and Turkey. On making "the other." *International migration, 57*(2), 126–142.

Carranza, M. E. (2021). "From our own selves": Acompañamiento with indigenous women in Perú. *International Social Work.* https://doi.10.1177/0020872820970261

Castro Neira, Y. (2019). Las caravanas de migrantes. Racismo y ley en los éxo-dos masivos de población. *Iberoforum. Revista de Ciencias Sociales de la Universidad Iberoamericana, 14*(27), 8–48.

Cockburn, T. (2005). Children and the feminist ethic of care. *Childhood, 12*(1), 71–89.

Customs and Border Protection (CBP). (2018). *Border patrol southwest border apprehensions by sector FY 2018.* https://www.cbp.gov/newsroom/stats/usbp-sw-border-apprehensions: U.S. CBP.

De Vries, L.A., & Guild, E. (2019). Seeking refuge in Europe: spaces of tran-sit and the violence of migration management. *Journal of Ethnic and Migration Studies, 45*(12), 2156–2166.

Denzin, N.K. (1997). *Interpretive ethnography: Ethnographic practices for the 21st century.* London: Sage.

Dietz, G., & Cortés, L. M. (2011). Indigenising or interculturalizing universi-ties in Mexico? Towards an ethnography of diversity discourses and practices inside the Universidad Veracruzana Intercultural. *Learning and Teaching, 4*(1), 4–21.

Edwards, R., & Mauthner, M. (2012). Ethics and feminist research: Theory and practice. In Miller, T., M. Birch, M. Mauthner, & J., Jessop (Eds.). *Ethics in qualitative research* (2nd ed.). SAGE Publications Ltd.

Fox, N. J., & Alldred, P. (2019). New materialism. In P. Atkinson, S. Delamont, A. Cernat, J. W. Sakshaug, & R. A. Williams (Eds.), SAGE Research Methods Foundations. https://www.doi.org/10.4135/9781526421036768465

Freire, P. (2000). *Pedagogy of the oppressed.* Bloomsbury.

Garcia, S., Pérez-Sales, P., & Fernandez-Lina, A. (2018). Exhumation pro-cesses in fourteen countries in Latin America. *Journal for Social Action in Counseling & Psychology, 2*(2), 48–83.

Glockner, V. (2019). Las caravanas migrantes como estrategia de movilidad y espacio de protección, autonomía y solidaridad para los adolescentes Centroamericanos. *Iberoforum*, XIV (27), 145–174.

Glockner, F., V. (2022). Restitution and the anthropology of childhood: An ethical and political practice. In Razy, E., de Sureiman, C. & Alvarado, N. (Eds.), *Children in ethnographic restitution*. Presses Universitaires de Liège.

Glockner F., V. & Sardao C., E. (2020, December 4). *Euphemisms of violence: Child migrants and the Mexican state*. North American Council on Latin America.

Goizueta, R.S. (2001). *Caminando con Jesus: Towards a Hispanic/Latino theology of accompaniment*. Orbis Books.

Gordon, L.R. (2014). Disciplinary decadence and the decolonisation of knowledge. *Africa Development*, 39(1), 81–92.

Government of Guatemala. (2020). *Guatemalans deported from the USA by air*. guatemaltecos-deportados-vía-aérea-de-usa-al-3-diciembre-2019.pdf (igm.gob.gt)

Guerra, C. T. (2006). Desplazamiento Forzado Y Acompanamiento Psicosocial : A propósito de la emergencia de nuevos actors politícos. *Univ. Psychol. Bogotá*, 5(1), 147–162.

Human Rights Watch. (2019). *US: Family separation harming children, families*. https://www.hrw.org/news/2019/07/11/us-family-separation-harming-children-families

IOM. (2018). *Global compact for safe, orderly and regular migration*. IOM.

Jacobsen, M.H. (2020). Practical engagements in legal geography: Collaborative feminist approaches to immigration advocacy in Denmark. *Area*, 53(4), 1–8.

Lather, P. (1986). Issues of validity in openly ideological research: Between a rock and a soft place. *Interchange*, 17(4), 63–84.

Lewis-Beck, M. S., Bryman, A., & Futing Liao, T. (2004). *The SAGE encyclopedia of social science research methods*. (Vols. 1-0). Sage Publications, Inc. https://www.doi.org/10.4135/9781412950589

Leyva Solano, X., & Speed, S. (2015). Hacia la investigación descolonizada: nuestra experiencia de co-labor. In X. Leyva Solano, C. Pascal, A. Köhler, H. Olguín Reza, & M. d. R. Velasco Contreras (Eds.), *Prácticas otras de conocimientos: entre crisis, entre guerras* I, (pp. 451–480). Taller Editorial La Casa del Mago.

Luna, F. (2019). Identifying and evaluating layers of vulnerability: A way forward. *Developing World Bioethics*, 19(2), 86–95.

Mayblin, L., & Turner, J. (2021). *Migration studies and colonialism*. Polity Press.

Maynard, M. (1994). Methods, practice and epistemology: The debate about feminism and research, in M. Maynard and J. Purvis (Eds.), *Researching women's lives from a feminist perspective* (pp. 10–26). Taylor & Francis.

Nuñez-Janes, M., & Ovalle, M., (2016). Organic activists: Undocumented youth creating spaces of *acompañamiento*. *Diaspora, Indigenous, and Minority Education, 10*(4), 189–200.

Pittaway, E., Bartolomei, L., & Hugman, R. (2010). "Stop stealing our stories": The ethics of research with vulnerable groups. *Journal of Human Rights Practice, 2*(2), 229–251.

Porter, E. (1999). *Feminist perspectives on ethics*. Pearson Education.

Quijano, A. (2007). Coloniality and modernity/rationality. *Cultural Studies, 21*(2–3), 168–178.

Re Cruz, A. (2018). Cuando Fronteras y testimonios se confabulan para el surgimiento de una Antrapología de Emergencia. En A, Cortés y J. Manjarrez (Eds). *Género, migraciones y derechos humanos*. 205–226.

Rosen, R., Chase, E., Crafter, S., Glockner, V., & Mitra, S. (2023). *Crisis for whom? Critical global perspectives on childhood, care and migration*. UCL Press.

Sepulveda, E. (2011). Toward a pedagogy of *acompañamiento*: Mexican migrant youth writing from the underside of modernity. *Harvard Educational Review, 81*(3), 550–572.

Spivak, G. (1988). Can the subaltern speak? In C. Nelson & L. Grossberg (Eds.) *Marxism and the interpretation of culture* (pp. 271–313). University of Illinois Press.

United Nations. (2018). *Global compact on refugees*. UN. https://www.unhcr.org/5c658aed4.pdf

Varela Huerta, A. (2018). Migrants trapped in the Mexican vertical border. *Oxford Law Faculty*. https://www.law.ox.ac.uk/research-subject-groups/centre-criminology/centreborder-criminologies/blog/2018/06/migrants-trapped

Walters, W. (2011). Foucault and frontiers: Notes on the birth of the humanitarian border. In U. Bröckling, S., Krassman, & T., Lemke (Eds.), *Governmentality: Current issues and future challenges* (pp. 138–164). Routledge.

White, M. (2007). *Maps of narrative practice*. W. W. Norton.

Wilson, M. G., & Whitmore, E. (1995). Accompanying the process: Principles for international development practice. *Revue Canadienne d'études du Développement, 16*(4), 61–77.

CHAPTER 2

Vive la France! Exalting French Nationalism through News Media Narratives of the "Migrant Crisis" in Calais

Maritza Felices-Luna

In this chapter I argue that figured worlds (Gee, 2011), found in news media reporting of the "migrant crisis"[1] in the region of Calais during the past decade, exalt a French nationalism that reproduces white supremacy and conceals the role of neoliberal capitalism and colonial logics in generating population movement inequalities.[2] The first section situates the chapter within two distinct literatures: scientific knowledge produced on the case of Calais and scientific knowledge produced on media discussions of migrants. In the second section I discuss the conceptual approach and methodological tools used in this chapter. I then explore in detail the particularities of and similarities between the two figured worlds evoked through news media narratives. I conclude by suggesting that through alternating accounts, appealing on one hand to values of solidarity and humane treatment of migrants, and advocating for the securatization of migrants in the name of protecting the homeland on the other, news media coverage contribute to an unequal distribution of social goods where the French national is reclaimed and reconstituted as a moral subject and the legitimate inhabitant of the territory, while the migrant is condemned and consigned to humanitarian securitization.[3]

Foregrounding and Erasing Migrants: Towards a News Media Analysis of the "Migrant Crisis" in Calais

Since the 1990s, the region of Nord-Pas de Calais et Picardie in France has been a nodal point for migrants seeking to reach the United Kingdom because of its geographical proximity and multiple human-made points of entry (train, tunnel, and ports) (Jouve, 2018). Because crossing the Channel is an arduous feat, Calais and its surroundings have become a waiting area for thousands of people looking for an opening to embark on the last leg of a perilous journey (Sanyal, 2017). The presence of migrants has been dealt with in a multiplicity of ways, depending on a variety of factors, and has garnered attention from regional, national, and international news media (Van Isacker, 2019). In order for politicians, humanitarian organizations, and/or different levels of government to call for imminent intervention, they construe a particular situation as a "crisis" by pointing to a real or purported increase in the number of migrants in the area, and signalling a surge in a variety of problematic situations resulting from the presence of migrants, as well as denouncing migrants' inhumane living conditions. Once the situation is successfully construed as a "crisis," a camp is either created or formalized, aid is provided, and officials attempt to persuade migrants to desist from attempting to cross the Channel. When the situation within the camp is said to be untenable, another "crisis" is said to be occurring, which leads to the camp being dismantled and migrants constrained to either disperse or be forcefully relocated somewhere else (Aris Escarcena, 2019; Queirolo Palmas, 2021). When this happens, all traces of the camp are erased and police intervention and other violent means are used to render migrants invisible until the next crisis is publicly constituted once again. The "migrant crisis" is thus dependant on the politics of (in)visibility.

Having read about Calais for many years, I knew the existent scientific literature tended to focus on the phenomenon of migration and its mechanisms (Reinisch, 2015; Guenebeaud, 2019); the experiences of migrants (Agier et al., 2019; Djigo, 2016; Djigo, 2019); the camps (Rygiel, 2011; Davies et al., 2017; Sanyal, 2017; Agier et al., 2018; Ibrahim & Howarth, 2018); policies and other forms of intervention and governance (Guiraudon 2002; Millner, 2011; Aris Escarcena, 2019; Van Isacker, 2019; Atoui, 2020; Nahaboo & Kerrigan, 2021); humanitarian aid and solidarity (Rygiel, 2011; Abbas, 2018; Bouagga,

2018; Sandri 2018; Anghel & Grierson, 2020); as well as vigilantism (Gardenier, 2018; Guenebeaud, 2021).

I wanted to contribute to this literature but did not want to do it by asking migrants to retell tales that have been told so many times by so many different people for the sole purpose of being consumed by researchers, journalists, politicians, and the public. I was initially interested in the mechanisms through which the migrant crisis was made (in)visible and the (in)visible ways in which migrants were used and disposed of for political purposes, but the more I read, the more I became interested in unveiling what else was being achieved through publicly circulated statements about the migrant crisis besides attempts to influence policy and practice. In other words, I wanted to explore how, as a public discourse, the migrant crisis contributed to constituting the collective self that was confronted to the "crisis." I opted to focus on news media narratives of the migrant crisis given that these discourses are the ones most widely circulated, but also because it is through news media that those not engaging directly with migrants or the "crisis" access the discourses produced by public figures speaking on the "migrant crisis."

The scientific literature on news media reporting on "migrant crises" in Europe has mostly focused on the frames[4] the news media uses in their narratives. They have found that despite deploying a diversity of frames at the beginning of the "crisis," these frames will eventually crystallize into a narrower and simplistic set (Greussing & Boomgaarden, 2017) regardless of political leanings and type of newspaper (KhosraviNik, 2010; Greussing & Boomgaarden, 2017; Cooper et al., 2020).[5] The five main narratives entail negative depictions of migrants: the administrative challenges and costs of dealing with migrants; migrants as security threats (terrorism, crime, deviance, health); migrants as economic harm; migrants as a threat to national identity and culture; and migrants as scapegoats for all sorts of social problems (Innes, 2010; KhosraviNik, 2010; Schemer, 2012; Greussing & Boomgaarden, 2017; Bhatia, 2018; Cooper et al., 2020; Shan-Jan, 2021). Although news media narratives do deploy humanitarian frames and provide readers with some background information on the refugees' situation, this is done much less frequently (Steimel, 2010; Greussing & Boomgaarden, 2017; Ibrahim & Howarth, 2018). Furthermore, despite departing from negative framings of migrants, they contribute to the production of good/bad, deserving/undeserving, victim/threat, in need of help/profiting, honest/dishonest categorizations where one side of the dyad is dependent upon the existence of the other (Steimel, 2010; Chouliaraki & Stolic, 2017; Holzberg et al., 2018; Atoui, 2020). In either case, news media reporting transform migrants into a (racial) spectacle (Bhatia, 2018; Chouliaraki & Stolic, 2017; Ibrahim & Howarth, 2018).

I did not want to contribute to the use of migrants as a racial spectacle and therefore opted to precisely de-centre migrants from the "migrant crisis." I decided to contribute to this literature by analyzing what else is made visible and invisible through news media narratives on the "migrant crisis." I wanted to observe the question, what would come into focus once we blurred the migrant or the "migrant crisis" from the narrative? What would we be able to see more clearly? In other words, if we looked at the underlying plots made possible through the telling of the usual "migrant crisis" plot, what would we find? What is being protected, and what is implicitly or explicitly brought into existence through the telling of the "migrant crisis"? What does the discourse on the "migrant crisis" hide? What does it unnoticeably prop up?

News Media Narratives of the "Migrant Crisis" as Constructive Practices (Re)producing Figured Worlds

The scientific literature deploys crisis as a concept to describe and tackle a particular condition or to analyze the political effects and potentialities of naming a situation a crisis. In either instance, crisis is used as a source of intelligibility (of making sense) of a particular event, situation, or condition. In this chapter I conceive of discourse as a constitutive practice (Hammersely, 2013) and therefore explore how news media discourses on the "migrant crisis" contribute to the production of the social. Specifically, by unpacking the underlying figured worlds produced by news media narratives of the "migrant crisis," I analyze the (re)construction of the collective self as a product of the order/disorder produced by "crisis" discourses and the power relations they maintain.

A figured world is a "socially and culturally constructed realm of interpretation in which particular characters and actors are recognized, significance is assigned to certain acts, and particular outcomes are valued over others" (Holland et al., 1998, p. 52). Figured worlds work on the premise that we use words based on the stories, theories, or models that exist in our mind about what is normal or typical for a particular social or cultural group in order to understand and act in the real world (Gee, 2011). Regardless of whether specific figured worlds are partially or completely espoused (Hoffman et al., 2016) as simplified stories, they allow people to make sense of their collective past and construe current identities (Urrieta, 2007). Yet, figured worlds are not solely in our heads but out in the world, whether it is in books, media, other people's heads, and talk (Gee, 2011). Precisely because figured worlds imply ideologies, assumptions, and expectations that are mobilized to interpret discourse, actions, activities, and artefacts (Goble & Stafford, 2022), by analyzing them we can unveil social constructions and structure-in-practice (Günter et al., 2023), as well as the harm caused by the dismissive or derogatory assumptions about people embedded in them (Gee, 2011). For instance, though a story might be about solidarity, in the telling of it, the journalist might have been summoning a figured world that calls for the securatization of migrants. Contrary to discursive frames whose purpose is to uncover the lens provided to the reader to interpret a particular situation, figured worlds allow us to see how particular worldviews are strengthened and revitalized through a narrative process that evokes or alludes to certain ways of being in the world, as well as social values and cherished traits.

In order to identify the figured worlds evoked by news media, I sampled from three regional newspapers. I chose *La Voix du Nord*[6] and *Le Journal des Flandres*,[7] because they are the two most widely circulated newspapers in the region, and *La Gazette Nord-Pas de Calais*[8] because it is a specific newspaper focusing on the economy. I accessed all articles published through their website from 2012 until 2021.[9] I sampled from a data set of over 8,000 articles[10] looking for diversity in terms of time period and location but mostly looking for different types of stories and characters.[11] I was not looking for repetition in order to identify key trends in reporting; instead I was looking for diversity in the stories that might lead to a diversity of figured worlds.[12] I manually coded approximately 250 articles having as an overarching question "how are the relevant figured worlds here helping to reproduce, transform or create social, cultural, institutional and/or political relationships?" (Gee, 2011, p. 96)

Given that figured worlds do not take centre stage in any story precisely because their role is to evoke common understandings and worldviews that are already embedded in the reader, they remain in the background—they are the implicit backdrop of the story. When trying to unveil figured worlds, the actual story acts as a distraction by maintaining our attention focused on the explicit and discouraging us from wandering into the implicit. A very simple form of narrative analysis allowed me to tease out the figured worlds embedded in the news media stories of the "migrant crisis." I started by identifying the main plot of the story being told (what is this a story of?) as well as the main and secondary characters in the story (the attributes that were given to them as well as the role they played in the story and the purpose for which their words were used). Then, I focused on the secondary plots (what else is being told?), the absent characters (who does not appear?), and the missing components of the story (what is not being talked about?). I paid as much attention to what was there as to what was not there. The most flagrant absence was the voice of the migrants themselves and this strengthened my conviction that news reports on migrants and the "migrant crisis" were a means through which to tell other stories. In this chapter I analyze those other stories.

Through the analysis I sought to identify and describe the figured worlds the news media evoked and to explore their conse-quences on the social, specifically their contribution to the constitu-tion of a collective self. My focus being on the constitutive effects of the story, I had no interest in attempting to identify the *intent* of the journalist in narrating the story the way they did. Just as the intent of the journalist is not relevant to my analysis, neither is the story itself. Not wanting the reader distracted by the story, I do not contextualize quotes and instead use them selectively and abridged to allow the reader to remain focused on the figured world that is being evoked. Furthermore, given that the quotes are used to highlight the implicit and not the explicit, I have interpreted them instead of providing a literal translation of them. The purpose is to show how they bring about certain images in the readers' minds. For this same reason, I have included a series of quotations as a rhetorical strategy that uses repetition to provide the reader not only with an intellectual under-standing of different components of each figured world but also with the experience of it, with an impression, a sense, of that figured world.

Unpacking the Figured Worlds

Although the figure of the migrant is omnipresent and essential to the news media stories of the "migrant crisis," migrants are rarely a fully developed character of the story. Despite being central to the story, migrants rarely speak but are instead spoken about and spoken for. Part of the story, their histories, experiences, thoughts, feelings, ideas, values, motivations, and so on are presented through someone else's words and someone else's perspectives, values, interests, and aspirations. In some such instances, the migrant is an object that is spoken about, that is described, that is explained, that the main characters of the story have to deal with. In other stories, the migrant becomes a phantom-like entity that haunts the main characters of the story by creating obstacles and opportunities for them, by creating situations that move along the plot of the story. Finally, in some stories, the figure of the migrant and of the "migrant crisis" is that of a forever present spectre; that is, the backdrop, the context, in which the story takes place. Thus, the stories about migrants and the "migrant crisis" become the excuse for or the means through which other stories are told, where fully fleshed-out heroes and villains can come into existence to articulate what being French is all about. These stories have two distinct figured worlds embedded in them that evoke the essence of the French nation and in doing so contribute to the constitution of the collective self.

France as a Humanitarian Nation

The first figured world is that of France as the birthplace of human rights, where solidarity is thought to be the essence of what France is and therefore synonymous with being French. Put simply, being French means helping those in need regardless of whether they should or should not be in the territory. It is about caring for others and not being indifferent to people's suffering. Not doing this is almost an affront to the nation; it is going against what being French is all about.

> "Someone from Doctors without Borders confided in me saying that the camp of La Lande was the worst camp they had ever seen. And they travel around the globe [...] I am so ashamed!" (*Le Journal de Flandres*, December 12, 2015)[13]

> A volunteer with one of the community organisations stated in response to a speech by Macron about the need to control the irregular flux of migrants from Afghanistan: "It is horrible [...] We have a neighbour whose house is burning and we place a water curtain so that the fire doesn't come onto our property. It is horrible!" The mayor of a city also commented indignantly "This is France for God's sake." (*Le Journal de Flandres*, August 26, 2021)

Solidarity is about being human and recognizing the humanity of the other, acknowledging the other as a human being.

> "We'll bring tarpaulins, stakes, rope [...] whatever is needed to help migrants rebuild. I don't care if it is considered as aiding individuals in an irregular situation. We come here to help human beings! This exceeds any other logic or reason." (*La Voix du Nord*, April 6, 2012)

> "Would we see people across the street and not help them? That would be unthinkable. If I see someone who is hungry I give them a sandwich. [...] We cannot just stand there and do nothing." (*Le Journal de Flandres*, November 18, 2015)

> "The elections are setting the tone. Dismantling camps and other such policies show that we are turning into a country losing its humanitarian values; we are becoming a self-centred and selfish people worried about maintaining its privileges." (*La Voix du Nord*, June 15, 2021)

In rare instances migrants speak in the story to indicate a clash between what France is supposed to be and what the state or its representatives are actually doing.

> "If they destroy the camp I don't know what I will do. I will be at a loss. I thought France was a democratic country that would find solutions and would treat us as human beings. We should have something to eat, something to drink, somewhere to sleep, access to toilets. It is the minimum as human beings. I never thought France would receive us like that." (*Le Journal des Flandres*, September 28, 2016)

> Another migrant mentions that a policeman urinated on his belongings. "Why must they treat us like that? We are humiliated on top of being mistreated. We are human beings." (*Le Journal des Flandres*, June 19, 2019)

Yet, these quotes also contribute to painting migrants as representing a material cost to the state and as being demanding.

"They were really thankful and showed gratitude. We were really moved by their words because on a daily basis they just complain, we only hear criticisms from them." (*Le Journal des Flandres*, April 7, 2016)

Solidarity is not only directed to migrants but also applies to one's own community, between the communes and within the French nation.

"It was constant fear for everyone, Calaisians were under invasion" so on the day the camp was dismantled she came as a gesture of solidarity towards Calaisians. (*Le Journal de Flandres*, November 4, 2016)

"Out of solidarity Morbecque must help Calais, so it is important we participated to this collective effort." (*Le Journal de Flandres*, October 14, 2016)

A territory contract was signed between the state, the department, the region and the city of Calais worth 150 million Euros. The name of the contract was national solidarity and was signed to make up for the negative impact of migrants in the region. (*La Gazette*, October 4, 2016)

In this figured world the government is deemed responsible for acting in solidarity. However, the French citizen is equally if not more responsible than the French state.

"As long as there are elected officials and community organizations like you, France will remain loyal to its values." (*Le Journal de Flandres*, May 30, 2016)

"It is our individual duty of solidarity to ensure that those in need have shelter and food. However, it is the state's responsibility to prevent people's suffering in our territory. Each one has its own role." (*La Voix du Nord*, June 15, 2021)

"I was surprised to see how much France does for migrants. But nothing will replace the collective conscience and mobilisation of its citizens." (*Le Journal de Flandres*, November 3, 2016)

This figured world is summoned through three types of stories. First, we find stories where the main character is an ordinary French citizen who is more or less actively involved with a community organization.[14] The main character is presented in a way that evokes whiteness. They are described in positive terms and are said to be helping because it is the right thing to do, because it is unacceptable to let people live in inhumane conditions, because people who suffer must be helped. In these stories the main character's commitment to help migrants comes from their humanity and solidarity, not from espousing a particular political stance. This type of story is supported through the words of migrants who praise the generosity, the selflessness, and the humanity of the French citizen.

In the second type of story, the main character tends to be a locally elected official who is making resources available to migrants and the associations helping them; calling the citizens of the commune to help out and act in solidarity; challenging decisions by other government levels that hinder or limit the aid that is given to migrants. The emphasis is on the individual and not on their political party (which is rarely mentioned). Their motivation comes from being committed citizens, not elected officials.

The final type of story is one where the activities of community organizations are discussed. It is not an exposé on the organization (in fact, I was surprised not to find any); the story positions the community organization as the main character who feeds, clothes, heals, educates, supports, advocates for migrants.

> A collective of community organizations are demanding the city establishes a garbage collection point in the camps. Currently it is the community organizations that are organising trash pick up. "This is a matter of sanitation [...] it is about public health, particularly during a pandemic [...] it also impacts the environment." (*La Voix du Nord*, September 22, 2020)

These stories are about the actions of the community organizations responding to specific migrants needs and the challenges they face. These actions are a stop gap—a temporary solution due to the lack of state intervention or due to a heightened need, but they are not proposing or positioning themselves on what a permanent solution might be. In these stories it is frequently mentioned that the organizations offer help with filling documents to regularize their status, but it is never a condition to receiving the services they provide.

Although these types of stories might contain criticisms of government (in)action or might include specific demands made by community organizations, there is once again no explicit political positioning and no challenge to the authority of the state in deciding who can legally stay in the country. Within this figured world, opening up the borders or allowing everyone to stay is not an option.

Most of the organizations named in these stories have French names but many are staffed by non-French volunteers, yet the stories do not mention this. The overall impression given by these types of stories is that these are French citizens.[15] They evoke French solidarity as opposed to international solidarity.

Within these three types of stories, individuals and community organizations respect the rule of law. Despite the limitations or complications that municipal regulations, city ordinances, and state laws (e.g., *délit de solidarité*) have in their activities, they do not contravene the law.[16] Although they might occasionally engage in certain forms of civil disobedience (for example, dumping garbage in front of the mayor's office to demand trash collection in the camps sites), they mostly use advocacy and legal channels to challenge them. Consequently, the rule of law functions as the boundary of "acceptable" solidarity. It also implies that the rule of law allows for solidarity and for being humane, and therefore does not need to be challenged.

I was surprised by what I did not find within this figured world. I expected cosmopolitanism to be at the core of this figured world but there is no appeal to the right to free movement. This figured world upholds France's sovereignty over its national territory and the need for state borders.

> "The only thing we can do is give them a status within French territory. […] I am not encouraging for them to stay in France only to regularize their situation in France." (*La Voix du Nord*, October 5, 2013)

I was also surprised not to find the notion of fraternity. Aside from an article calling for fraternity between communes (*Le Journal de Flandres*, October 17, 2016) and a manifesto by the *Ligue des droits de l'homme*[17] claiming that "the xenophobic reactions migrants are victims of, tarnish the motto of our Republic: Liberté, Égalité, Fraternité[18]" (*Le Journal de Flandres*, November 25, 2016), there was no call for action in the name of brotherhood. It was solely about solidarity and humanity, which implies recognition of the other as human and of their plight as a human being, but not fraternity, which would imply a recognition of the other as part of the community or as belonging to the imagined national community.[19]

This figured world is a palatable French nationalism that "feels good" because of the values and image it fosters as a tolerant, benevolent, altruistic, and humane nation, but is non-threatening as it does not challenge social order, undermine rule of law, or challenge French sovereignty over the territory.

France as a Nation Under Attack

The second figured world embedded in news reporting of the "migrant crisis" is that of France as a republic whose territory is being constantly violated either by the (in)actions of other countries or by people who have no right to be there.

> "If other countries are letting migrants get into Europe, we should let them get into the UK. The UK should take care of its own borders, it should not be France's responsibility." (*La Gazette*, August 11, 2015)

> "I am calling on the government and the army to come to Calais." (*Le Journal de Flandres*, December 26, 2016)

> "I came to defend the territory but it is hard. It is hard to be anti-immigration, hard to argue against emotional points. There is a lot of sentimental arguments on migrants but the problems are real." (*Le Journal de Flandres*, January 13, 2016)

> "What I want is for the state to intervene and enforce the law. People who are in an irregular situation should not be in our territory [...] we should not be victims of crimes that also harm the environment. [...] Migrants undermine the image of a welcoming and clean city. The problem is that they drink, they are drunk and that creates public nuisance. They eat and then throw things on the ground [...] they walk through people's yards, they steal, they deface the city." (*La Voix du Nord*, September 5, 2020)

The feeling of being under attack is provoked through numerous stories focusing on individual or groups: charging the port or the tunnel, trying to get into trucks crossing into the United Kingdom, blocking the highway or avenues leading to the port and tunnel, engaging in violent confrontations with the police and with French citizens, taking over private land, squatting on abandoned buildings, and defacing the city. In these stories, specific objects and places are emblematic of the territory and breaches or damage to them are considered violations of the territory and, consequently, of French sovereignty.

> "The barriers to the tunnel have to be repaired every morning because every single night migrants damage them attempting to break through them." (*La Gazette*, August 18, 2015)

> "I was walking and saw that they had taken down the barriers and they had set up camp. The cops came right away to tell them they were violating private property. I understand they are fleeing war but I cannot endorse them living in unsanitary conditions. Don't think I don't care, I feel for them, I am a nurse but it is the government that must take necessary action. They set up camp in my property. They cut down trees to build shelter and they set up latrines in the fields." (*Le Journal de Flandres*, June 24, 2016)

> "To avoid another camp, we'll have to occupy the territory." (*La Gazette*, October 4, 2016)

> The bylaws in place since 2017 are geared towards stopping what the mayor called "abusive, prolonged and repetitive occupation of the industrial zone of the Dunes, the woods of Dubrulle and of the main square by migrants and community organisations distributing meals and other basic necessities." (*La Voix du Nord*, August 20, 2020)

Within this figured world, there is a sense of being constantly in danger or at risk. It is not only about crime but of being exposed to a variety of potential harms to the point where the normal life of French citizens feels perilous and therefore is in peril.

> "The camp is just there, people are afraid, they tell us. [...] It is not a matter of shoplifting, it is a matter of hygiene [...] it is the clients who are afraid when they come in." (*La Voix du Nord*, October 4, 2014)

"These are public health issues, these are unsanitary conditions and we must protect the environment, these woods are one of the last green lungs of the city and we are seeing rats around. It shouldn't be up to us to handle this but if no one does anything the problem won't be solved [...] In order to get the migrants to help we have to bribe them, we are offering bananas to those who help clean up." (*La Voix du Nord*, March 7, 2015)

"It has become a matter of civilization. How can we welcome refugees and ensure social cohesion at the same time?" (*La Gazette*, September 29, 2015)

Before it was only truck drivers that were assaulted now also tourists are afraid of taking the highway because migrants attack cars and trucks. (*La Gazette*, December 6, 2016)

A race was cancelled because the organizers couldn't ensure the security of the runners and volunteers [...] "the migrant camp nearby urges us to be careful." (*Le Journal de Flandres*, February 29, 2016)

Migrants were burning toxic materials in the backyard where a newborn baby lives. (*Le Journal de Flandres*, August 26, 2021)

Stories of the police's constant dismantling of camps is another way to conjure this figured world. It is not through the story itself, but its frequent repetition under different forms, that it is evoked. The same applies to the idea that migrants are draining resources. Whether it is about rescuing migrants at sea or trapped in trucks and containers; police intervention to stop them from attempting to cross over; opening up shelters during cold winter nights; providing a space to quarantine during COVID-19; vaccinating migrants; healing them when they are injured or curing them when ill; locking them up when they are caught; building barriers and installing barbed wire to protect infrastructure; clearing the roadblocks they set up; the constant recurrence of these stories summons this figured world on a daily basis.

Firefighters took over two hours to rescue a migrant in a composting truck. A lot of resources were needed. (*Le Journal de Flandres*, May 15, 2015)

> Eurotunnel invests 20 million euros in security every year. Aside
> from private security, there is a permanent police liaison and over
> 500 cameras in place. (*La Gazette*, January 31, 2017)

Within this figured world, migrants are also responsible for the economic woes of the region. They scare investors, scare tourists, affect
businesses who have fewer customers but must invest in security
while having their property defaced, redirect commercial traffic to
other ports, devalue property, damage agriculture, etc.

> Factories have chosen to leave and others won't come because of
> migrants. (*La Gazette*, November 24, 2015)

> "Us farmers, we have nothing against migrants we understand
> they suffer but we ask them to respect our farmed lands." It is
> not only that what they have sown won't grow but there is also
> the problem of the bottles, plastics, shoes, clothing, blankets.
> When the machines go to harvest the crops, they get damaged.
> (*Le Journal de Flandres*, April 1, 2016)

> Between 2015 and 2016 the port lost 3.4 million passengers
> because of the jungle. (*La Gazette*, January 29, 2019)

Migrants tarnish the image of Calais and it is a constant struggle to
protect it.

> "There are enough walls and barbed wire because of the migrant
> crisis. We cannot and are not going to spoil our coastline with
> barbed wire and a big wall." (*La Gazette*, September 20, 2015)

> Tourists aren't coming. The image of the territory has suffered
> tremendously. (*La Gazette*, November 24, 2015)

Within this figured world, the French citizen and the French territory
are therefore victims of migrants.

> A representative of the truckers' union asked the government for
> help regarding the fines the British hand them when they find
> migrants in the trucks. "We are not smugglers, we are victims."
> (*La Gazette*, July 5, 2016)

> After the dismantling of the camp the port is optimistic but watchful. The port now breathes, the ambience is less stressed. The highway leading to the port is relieved. During 2016 the traffic suffered a lot. [...] It was disrespectful to the port to have brought migrants 500m away from it. (*La Gazette*, December 6, 2016)

> "We have suffered for months on end despite the jungle having been dismantled for over a year." (*La Gazette*, January 23, 2018)

> "If someone has suffered, it is the port of Calais and it has yet to receive any compensation." (*La Gazette*, February 4, 2020)

This figured world feeds off a perceived rivalry between the needs of French citizens and migrants.

> "This is rubbish, what you are doing is rubbish. They are cutting the heating off from the French who have worked all their lives in this country you know?" (*La Voix du Nord*, April 6, 2012)

> "Migrants suffer but we also live in insecurity. It is no longer tenable for them or for us." (*Le Journal de Flandres*, October 6, 2016)

> There is a feeling of a battle of miseries where solidarity towards migrants means that there is less done for the homeless and other French in precarious situations. (*Le Journal de Flandres*, May 8, 2021)

At the essence of being French is the commitment to the republic and its territory.

> A representative of the state talks about the France that he loves to serve, the values, the honesty, truthfulness and loyalty owed to the territory he serves. [...] France cannot exist without its communes. (*La Gazette*, October 14, 2016)

> "The Republic is first of all union, cohesion, unity and fraternity." (*La Voix du Nord*, May 13, 2016)

Within this figured world, securitizing the territory does not preclude humanitarian intervention.

"We have been working hard and have been effective in not letting another camp spring up. However, in winter we tolerate a few tents here and there because it would be difficult to accept the life of these people being compromised by the harshness of winter." (*La Voix du Nord*, April 6, 2012)

The prefect of the region promises to be firm but humane in dealing with migration issues and the camps. The state presence will be uncompromising in terms of camp security but migrants will live in decent conditions. Aside from controlling migrant flux is about ensuring decent support. (*La Gazette*, May 13, 2016)

"It is not a migrant hunt. I don't know how they experience it because of the language barrier but we are saving their lives." (*Le Journal de Flandres*, September 24, 2021)

This figured world produces a French nationalism that is protective of its territory and identity, defensive of real or perceived attacks, that feels victimized and alone without succumbing to a fascist nationalism. It is a nationalism that claims to want to treat migrants humanely, as long as it does not put France and its way of life in peril.

The Points Where Both Figured Worlds Meet

Both figured worlds heighten France as a sovereign territory, a nation state. This implies a clear distinction between locals/nationals and migrants. Locals and nationals are good people while migrants do not contribute to the French nation, representing a drain or a danger to it. Furthermore, within the first figured world the contributions of international volunteers are hidden or ignored (only the French are humanitarian), while in the second figured world the belonging of second generation or third generation migrants to the nation is undermined (being born in France does not mean you are French).

When a bus diver attempts to explain Calaisians that they can't get in the bus because there is already too many people they tell him "anyway it is normal, you are the same colour as them." (*Le Journal de Flandres*, July 30 2021)

In both figured worlds the government is not doing enough, especially at the national level.

> "All the state does is let the communes come up with solutions of solidarity while limiting what the local elected officials can do. That is the state's policy!" (*La Voix du Nord*, April 6, 2012)

> "We will continue to help migrants wherever they are as long as the state refuses to be accountable and respect their fundamental rights." (*Le Journal de Flandres*, June 13, 2016)

> "The government and its management of the migrant crisis can be characterised as lethargic and disengaged." (*La Voix du Nord*, September 7, 2021)

However, in the first figured world, the local governments also hinder solidarity and humanitarian aid.

> Legal recourses have been put in place to limit the work of community organisations. "This can be understood as an attempt to block the work we do: blocking the installation of temporary showers, blocking food distribution and now blocking food preparation." (*La Voix du Nord*, March 13, 2017)

The European Union and other countries (particularly the United Kingdom) undermine France's sovereignty and harm migrants.

> "The migrants in Calais attempting to cross over to the UK have passed through Italy, Greece and other countries. France is only another transit country for them." (*La Voix du Nord*, August 2, 2015)

> L'auberge des migrants[20] is organising a demonstration in Brussels to "take hold of the European officials regarding the unacceptable living conditions of the communities in exile in the north of France and throughout Europe. [...] These conditions are the consequences of the failures of the Dublin system." (*La Voix du Nord*, November 28, 2018)

In both figured worlds the causes of migration are sometimes stated but never explored in depth. The first figured world names war and conflict as the main reason.

> Community organizations are attempting to parry the precarious situation of these exiles who are running away from war, from dictatorships and/or precarious living conditions in their own country. (*Le Journal de Flandres*, July 23, 2015)

> "People who are suffering daily barbaric situations [bullying, violence...] have seen through the internet how we live here. That has encouraged migration for sure." (*Le Journal de Flandres*, November 18, 2015)

The second figured world emphasizes the economy.

> "Any long-lasting response to migratory pressures necessitates a reduction in the number of people leaving Africa to come to Europe for economic reasons." (*La Voix du Nord*, August 2, 2015)

> "They are convinced that Europe is paradise. They believe it with a religious devotion." (*Le Journal de Flandres*, January 13, 2016)

The stories construe the French nationalism inherent to each figured world as reasonable. This is done by contrasting the acceptable actions and emotions of both figured worlds to the unacceptable actions and emotions of those deemed extremists.

> Announcing a far-right anti-migrant sit-in, the organiser states "all migrants are the same. They are harmful, three quarters of them are potential aggressors." Fear and insecurity is a constant feeling mixed with hate and rage towards migrants. (*La Voix du Nord*, November 6, 2013)

> Calais Migrant Solidarity (a branch of No Borders demanding the opening up of the borders) voiced slogans "No one is illegal" and "Reject expulsions". They also carried a banner that read "From conflict to cage, welcome to Europe"[21] [...] Various provocative messages against the police who were simply carrying their mission were posted on Twitter by Calais Migrant Solidarity. Pictures

of the police were followed by the caption "fascists." (*La Voix du Nord*, December 31, 2015)

Sauvons Calais[22] has links to volatile groups such as Génération identitaire[23] or L'oeuvre française,[24] they attract those on the right of the right, the identity block and those types of groups. (*Le Journal de Flandres*, January 13, 2016)

The police report identified them as three militants from no-border one Irish, one English and one German. [...] They incited migrants to attack the police. They were yelling (in English of course) "Fuck you, you losers, you Nazis," "Fuck you bullshit police" and one of them also threw rocks at the police. (*Le Journal de Flandres*, April 12, 2016)

In a public letter French army Generals decry the "disintegration of the motherland" and state they are "ready to support any policy that protects the nation. [...] if nothing is done, current laxity will continue to spread [...] provoking an explosion and forcing our active comrades to intervene in a perilous mission geared towards protecting our civilizational values." (*Le Journal de Flandres*, April 28, 2021)

The French National as Custodian of French Values and Guardian of French Sovereignty

By drawing on the concept of figured worlds, this chapter demonstrates how media stories regarding the "migrant crisis" generate the conditions of possibility for the continuation of white supremacy and racial capitalism. Both figured worlds are anchored on French citizens enacting French values, protecting French sovereignty, and defending the French national state, whose current situation is in part due to the (in)action of other countries and the inadequacy/incompetence of the European Union. By excluding the potential extremes of each figured world and by denouncing them, both figured worlds remain safe, palatable, and unchallenging to social structures and global forces. There are no attempts to explain how the population movement that results from a specific war or dictatorship, an environmental disaster, or the economic collapse of certain regions are the direct consequences of colonialism and capitalism. Furthermore, both figured worlds support neoliberal modes of governance. The apolitical French citizen in the first figured world is being responsible and charitable, compensating for the state's withdrawal from providing social assistance. Solidarity is therefore framed as a private decision made by its autonomous and responsible citizens who willingly deploy their resources (time, money, land, emotions, knowledge, even tolerance)[25] to support those who they deem deserving of it. The victimized French citizen of the second figured world is requesting from the state to defend the integrity of the territory, to regulate more through law and order, and to protect the economy and the French way of life in order to ensure the continuity of the (imagined) nation.

The coexistence and the effects of the two figured worlds evoked through news media stories of the "migrant crisis" in Calais renders possible humanitarian securitization.[26] The first figured world pushes for solidarity and humane treatment of migrants in the name of essential values of the homeland while the second figured world demands the securitization of migrants for their own well-being and in protection of the homeland. In return, humanitarian securitization invigorates French nationalism(s) by perpetuating the opposition between non-French entities and identities to French entities and identities. Through the telling of stories that emphasize the first and/or the second figured world, news media alternatingly evokes them both as the essence of what being French is. Through the telling of multiple stories, news media effectively attributes worth, value, legitimacy, and therefore continuity to both forms of French nationalisms.

The "migrant crisis" is not a "crisis" about migration and is not a "crisis" around unregulated population movement. The "migrant crisis" is the means through which two distinct nationalisms are reconciled. Although it would appear as two contradictory nationalisms, one focusing on France as solidarity and the other as France under attack, they are one and the same — it is a matter of degree and evaluation of the situation, not a difference in essence. In other words, the France as solidarity is a France that is not under attack and that can therefore be in solidarity with suffering non-nationals. However, the France under attack is the result of too much solidarity, which allows an increase in "undeserving non-nationals" whose actions threaten the viability of France as solidarity. The narrative analysis demonstrates that even though at first glance the news stories are about "migrants" as threat or as in need of aid, the real story, the story that is being told, is that of French nationalism. Through discourses on the "migrant crisis" news media reporting is actively contributing to the constitu-tion of white supremacy by using migrants as characters existing only to allow the hero (the French citizen) to protect and uphold the imag-ined French nation. This protection is the quest the hero embarks on. The telling of these stories serves also as means to maintain the distri-bution of social goods. On one hand, the French national is presumed to be white and born in France, whose natural goodness is evident through the care, solidarity, and generosity towards others, whose worth and value are intrinsic and unchallengeable and are therefore deserving of protection, safety, security, prosperity, and most impor-tantly feeling at home. On the other hand is the migrant who, whether presumed as deserving or undeserving, is attributed with vulnerabil-ity and need or dangerousness and deviousness. Migrants must there-fore be either monitored and controlled while receiving humanitarian assistance or provided with the bare necessities while awaiting being expelled because, in both instances, they are subjected to humanitar-ian securitization because they represent a threat to the continuity of the imagined nation and to the safety and well-being of its nationals.

Notes

1. I use the term "migrants" to avoid drawing on legal categories that produce legitimate/illegitimate, regular/irregular, deserving/undeserving distinctions. It is also the most common term used by news media coverage of the region.
2. I use scare quotes throughout the chapter to highlight the contentiousness of certain words.
3. "Social goods consist of anything people in a society want and value such as rights, protection, solidarity, care, humane treatment [...] and that lead to mate-rial and social benefits. Social goods are granted by being recognized as good, normal, proper, or deserving according to the expectations of a social group, they are also withheld when deemed bad, guilty, undeserving [...]" (Gee, 2011).
4. The way in which news media presents information encourages certain inter-pretations while discouraging others; it encourages the reader to understand the situation as a certain type of problem needing a particular solution.
5. Špadijer (2020) argues that the linguistic performance differs between left-wing and right-wing news media.
6. Daily newspaper, left-leaning.
7. Weekly newspaper, left-leaning.
8. Weekly newspaper, right-leaning.
9. I began by using *migrants* and *Calais* as search terms for the three newspaper sites. I was curious to see if other (combinations of) terms would yield different results, so I searched for *refugees* and *Calais*, as well as *immigration* and *Calais*, and those keywords produced fewer results but not a distinct set of articles. *Migrants* and *Calais* yielded the most comprehensive results and this was the combination I used as the basis of my data set.

10. I read all the articles to select my sample. It was a time-consuming effort but allowed me to be more thorough and get a clear sense of the different types of stories to ensure I included typical and atypical stories for the analysis. It also allowed me to get an overall feel for what was being reported and how.
11. I was looking for news articles on different cities, communes of the region, as well as articles reporting on other locations than just migrant camps.
12. Furthermore, the sampling I conducted would not have allowed me make any claims about any trends such as the frequency of figured worlds or correlations between figured worlds and newspapers.
13. Quotation marks are used to indicate speech.
14. This term refers to the *associations* which can be more or less organized, more or less formalized, implying paid work or volunteer work.
15. I am not stipulating the proportion of French versus non-French citizens volunteering/working within these organizations. I am signalling that despite there being a large number of non-French volunteers, these stories tend to invisibilize them.
16. French law considers it an offense to help migrants who are not authorized by the French government to transit or be in French territory.
17. Human Rights League.
18. Freedom, equality, and brotherhood.
19. I borrow from Hage (2000), who describes the imagined nation as necessitating a defined territory or national space, an ideal of what the nation used to be (look, smell, sound like) and an imagined mode of inhabiting the nation. It is also tied to the desire to be at home (therefore others should go back home), which is dependent upon familiarity (practical spatial and linguistic knowledge), which leads to a sense of community, and both lead to a sense of security, which requires the absence of what is considered a threatening other.
20. The migrants' inn.
21. The three slogans were in English, not in French.
22. Save Calais (where the subject is a collective "we," not requesting for someone else to save Calais).
23. An extreme-right political movement founded in 2012.
24. An extreme-right ultranationalist, anti-Semitic political organization founded in 1968.
25. According to Hage, the notion of tolerance presupposes a national subject entitled to decide on the fate of the nation who carries with them a national fantasy that guides what is deemed tolerable and what is not. The right to be intolerant is anchored in the exercise of tolerance. Discourses on tolerance do not empower the victims of exclusionary practices to resist. Those who are tolerated are reduced to objects that the national subject is encouraged to protect until they no longer fit the national fantasy.
26. This chapter contributes to the work of Ticktin (2011), Vaughan-Williams (2015), Chouliaraki & Georgiou (2017), Djebali (2019), and Sanyal (2020), who have pointed to the contradictory nature of government intervention, which on one hand claims to act under values of solidarity and human rights while implementing securitization policies that render migrants simultaneously as an object of care in need of protection and saving, and a threat to be controlled, contained, surveilled, and managed.

References

Abbas, M. (2018). Working as a medical doctor in the Calais migrant camp. *Medicine, Conflict, and Survival, 34*(2), 69–73.

Anghel, R., & Grierson, J. (2020). Addressing needs in a liminal space: the citizen volunteer experience and decision-making in the unofficial Calais migrant camp - insights for social work. *European Journal of Social Work, 23*(3), 486–499.

Ansems de Vries, L., & Guild, E. (2019). Seeking refuge in Europe: spaces of transit and the violence of migration management. *Journal of Ethnic and Migration Studies, 45*(12), 2156–2166.

Agier, M. et. al. (2018). *La Jungle de Calais : les migrants, la frontière et le camp.* Paris: PUF.

Agier, M. et. al. (2019). *The Jungle: Calais' Camps and Migrants.* Cambridge: Polity Press.

Aris Escarcena, J. P. (2019). Expulsions: The construction of a hostile environment in Calais. *European Journal of Migration and Law, 21*(2), 215–237.

Atoui, F. (2020). The Calais crisis: Real refugees welcome, migrants don't come. In K. Lynes, T.K. Morgenstern, & I.A. Paul. (Eds.), *Moving Images Mediating Migration as Crisis.* Transcrip Verlag.

Bhatia, M. (2018). Social death: The (white) racial framing of the Calais "jungle" and "illegal" migrants in the British tabloids and right-wing press. In M. Bhatia, S. Poynting, & W. Tufail (Eds.), *Media, Crime and Racism.* Palgrave Macmillan.

Bouagga, Y. (2018). Calais, carrefour des solidarités citoyennes. *Mouvements, 1*(93), 137–148.

Chouliaraki, L., & Stolic, T. (2017). Rethinking media responsibility in the refugee 'crisis': A visual typology of European news. *Media, Culture and Society, 39*(8), 1162–1177.

Chouliaraki, L., & Georgiou, M. (2017). Hospitability: The communicative architecture of humanitarian securitization at Europe's borders. *Journal of Communication, 67,* 159–180.

Cooper, G., Blumell, L., & Bunce, M. (2021). Beyond the "refugee crisis": How the UK news media represent asylum seekers across national boundaries. *The International Communication Gazette, 83*(3), 195–216.

Davies, T., et al. (2017). Violent inaction: The necropolitical experience of refugees in Europe: Violent inaction. *Antipode, 49*(5), 1263–1284.

Djebali, T. (2019). Africans in Calais: Migrants, rights, and French cosmopolitanism. In E.B Luczak, S. Dayal, & A. Pochmara (Eds.), *New Cosmopolitanisms, Race, and Ethnicity.* Walter De Gruyter Poland. 26–42.

Djigo, S. (2016). *Les migrants de Calais : enquête sur la vie en transit.* Marseilles: Agone.

Djigo, S. (2019). *Aux frontières de la démocratie : de Calais à Londres sur les traces des migrants*. Le Bord de l'eau.

Gardenier, M. (2018). Sauvons Calais, un groupe anti-migrants. Une perspective : « rétablir l'ordre » *Revue européenne des migrations internationales, 34*(1), 235–256.

Greussing, E., & Boomgaarden, H. (2017). Shifting the refugee narrative? An automated frame analysis of Europe's 2015 refugee crisis. *Journal of Ethnic and Migration Studies, 43*(11), 1749–1774.

Gee, J. P. (2011). *An Introduction to discourse analysis: Theory and method*. Routledge.

Goble, R. A. & Stafford, C. (2022). Mid-aged Latin@s in the U.S. Midwest narrating sustained bilingualism through figured worlds of bilingualism research, professionalization, and advocacy. *International Journal of Bilingual Education and Bilingualism, 25*(7): 2636–2652.

Guenebeaud, C. (2019). "Nous ne sommes pas des passeurs de migrants" : le rôle des transporteurs routiers et maritimes dans la mise en œuvre des contrôles à la frontière franco-britannique. *Lien social et Politiques, 83* : 103–122.

Guenebeaud, C. (2021). J'aime Calais: Mobilisations et luttes de pouvoir contre la présence de migrants à la frontière franco-britannique. *Champ pénal* (23).

Günter, K.P., Ahnesjö, I., & Gullberg, A. (2023). "I try to encourage my students to think, read, and talk science" intelligible identities in university teachers' figured worlds of higher education biology. *Journal of Research in Science Teaching*, 60: 1195–1222.

Guiraudon, V. (2002). Logiques et pratiques de l'Etat délégateur : les compagnies de transport dans le contrôle migratoire à distance. Partie 1. *Culture et Conflits*, 45 (printemps), 1–10.

Hage, G. (2000). *White nation: Fantasies of white supremacy in a multicultural society*. Routledge.

Hammersley, M. (2013). Divergent analytical strategies. In *What is Qualitative Research?* Bloomsbury, 47–65.

Hoffman, S. J., Tierney. J.D., & Robertson, C.L. (2017). Counter-narratives of coping and becoming: Karen refugee women's inside/outside figured worlds. *Gender, Place & Culture*. 24(9): 1346–1364.

Holland, D., Lachiotte, W., Skinner, D., & Cain, C. (1998). *Identity and agency in cultural worlds*. Harvard University Press.

Holzberg B, Kolbe, K., & Zaborowski, R. (2018). Figures of crisis: The delineation of (un)deserving refugees in the German media. *Sociology, 52*(3), 534–550.

Ibrahim, Y. & Howarth, A. (2018). *Calais and its border politics: From control to demolition*. Routledge.

Innes A. J. (2010). When the threatened become the threat: The construction of asylum seekers in British media narratives. *International Relations, 24*(4), 456–477.

Jackson, R. (2005). *Writing the war on terrorism: Language, politics and counter-terrorism.* Manchester University Press.

Jouve, J. (2018). *Rencontres à Calais: Sur la route des migrants.* Lille: Hikari Editions.

Khosravinik, M. (2010). The representation of refugees, asylum seekers and immigrants in British newspapers: A critical discourse analysis article. *Journal of Language and Politics, 9*(1), 1–28.

Millner, N. (2011). From "refugee" to "migrant" in Calais solidarity activism: Re-staging undocumented migration for a future politics of asylum. *Political geography, 30*(6), 320–328.

Nahboo, Z., & Kerrigan, N. (2021). Migrants, borders and the European question: the Calais jungle. Palgrave MacMillan.

Queirolo Palmas, L. (2021). "Now is the real jungle!" Institutional hunting and migrants' survival after the eviction of the Calais camp. *Society & Space, 39*(3), 496–513.

Reinisch, J. (2015). "Forever temporary": Migrants in Calais, then and now. *The Political Quarterly, 86*(4), 515–522.

Rygiel, K. (2011). Bordering solidarities: migrant activism and the politics of movement and camps at Calais. *Citizenship Studies, 15*(1), 1–19.

Sandri, E. (2018). "Volunteer humanitarianism": Volunteers and humanitarian aid in the jungle refugee camp of Calais. *Journal of Ethnic and Migration Studies, 44*(1), 65–80.

Sanyal, E. (2017). Calais's "Jungle": Refugees, biopolitics, and the arts of resistance. *Representations, 139*, 1–33.

Schemer, C. (2012). The influence of news media on stereotypic attitudes toward immigrants in a political campaign. *Journal of Communication, 62*(5), 739–757.

Shan-Jan, S.L. (2021). Framing immigration: A content analysis of newspapers in Hong Kong, Taiwan, the United Kingdom, and the United States. *Politics, groups and identities, 9*(4), 759–783.

Špadijer, S. (2020). L'analyse du discours des journaux de presse français à propos de la crise de migrants en France, en 2016. *French Cultural Studies, 31*(3), 230–245.

Steimel, S. (2010). Refugees as people: The portrayal of refugees in American human interest stories. *Journal of Refugee Studies, 23*(2), 219–237.

Ticktin, M. I. (2011). *Casualties of care: Immigration and the politics of humanitarianism in France.* University of California Press.

Urrieta' L. (2007). Identity production in figured worlds: How some Mexican Americans become Chicana/o activist educators. *The Urban Review, 39*(2), 117–144.

Van Den Hoonaard, D. K. (2012). *Qualitative research in action: A Canadian primer.* Oxford University Press.

Van Isacker, T. (2019). Bordering through domicide: Spatializing citizenship in Calais. *Citizenship Studies, 23*(6), 608–626.

Vaughan-Williams, N. (2015). *Europe's border crisis: Biopolitical security and beyond.* Oxford University Press.

CHAPTER 3

The Venezuelan "Migratory Crisis" in the Ecuadorian Context: Problematizing Immigrants as Victims and Threats

Martha Alexandra Vargas Aguirre

Important migratory processes have taken place in the Andean countries and Ecuador, the smallest territory in this region, has experienced important migratory exoduses. During the 1990s, the strong economic and political crisis that affected this country, Ecuador, caused massive migration of its citizens, mainly to the United States (Herrera & Torres, 2005). Similarly, the armed conflict that has affected Colombia for more than 25 years produced the massive movement of people seeking refuge in Ecuador (Barbieri et al., 2020). Finally, the political and humanitarian crisis affecting Venezuela, that resulted in one of the largest migratory outbursts in the region (Brito Siso, 2021), led to the migration of Venezuelan citizens to various South American countries. Among the main receiving countries of this population, Ecuador is in third place, after Colombia and Peru. As of 2021, it was determined that more than 400,000 Venezuelan citizens were in this small Andean country (UNHCR, 2021).

The Ecuadorian government has responded to this large movement of people with a series of erratic changes in migration policy that in most cases contradict the progressive and pro-migration constitutional framework of this country. In this context, in August 2018, the Ministry of Foreign Affairs and Human Mobility declared a "state of emergency," claiming the need of a "contingency plan" to implement "humanitarian assistance" for the thousands of Venezuelans arriving in the country (El Comercio, 2018a; El Universo, 2018a). The declaration initially encompassed Carchi, El Oro, and Pichincha, the three provinces hosting the largest number of Venezuelan citizens (Ministerio de Relaciones Exteriores y Movilidad Humana, 2018a), and it was subsequently extended to the rest of the country (Ministerio de Relaciones Exteriores y Movilidad Humana, 2019a).

To better understand this governmental response, this chapter analyzes the measures that were implemented by Ecuador in the framework of this declaration. Consequently, this chapter does not approach immigration as a pre-existing entity waiting to be discovered (and be subsequently addressed by public policy) but instead conceives it as a problematization in Foucauldian terms (Foucault, 1984). In other words, it analyzes this phenomenon as an object that has been produced as a particular problem with and through the various governmental practices that target it (Carson, 2018; Moffette, 2018).

Following this analytic framework and inspired by the scholarship that conceives humanitarianism and securitization as intertwined logic that governs migrant bodies (Agier, 2011; Harrell-Bond, 1999; Pereira, 2019; Ticktin, 2014; Watson, 2011; Župarić-Iljić & Valenta, 2019), I argue that through the declaration of a state of emergency the Ecuadorian government implemented a humanitarian crisis management approach. In this framework, between 2018 and 2019, Ecuador carried out a strategic deployment of measures that can be understood as tactical humanitarianism. Thus, Venezuelan migrants were produced as a "risk" that must be contained and at the same time as "victims" that must be rescued and safely channelled out of the Ecuadorian territory.

Analytical Framework and Methodology

Migration, in its diverse forms, is a complex and messy phenomenon. Its regulation—like the regulation of most social phenomenon—is not linear (Moffette, 2018); consequently, its study must be undertaken through analytical categories that will help us understand the intricacy of these governmental processes (resulting in the coexistence of various underpinning logics).

Following this line of thought, this chapter does not consider migration as a pre-existing and fixed entity awaiting to be discovered (Glynos & Howrot, 2007) and subsequently regulated through governmental intervention. It examines it as an issue that has been defined and constructed as a problematic and governable "truth" (Foucault, 1990; Foucault, et al., 2003) that has emerged through practices.

In a simultaneous process, the object of government (in this case, Venezuelan immigration) appears through an ensemble of practices that have been conceived as a means for its regulation (Bacchi, 2009; Foucault, 1984; Moffette, 2018). In other words, governmental problems only exist in the practices that create them. This does not mean that issues are not real; however, they do not become objects of thought until they are targeted by practices (Bacchi & Goodwin, 2016). Foucault (1984, p. 75) describes practices as "places" where "what is said and what is done, rules imposed and reasons given, the planned and the taken for granted meet and interconnect." In this sense, Foucault posits that problematizations are constituted by an ensemble of discursive (ways of thinking) and non-discursive practices (practical action) (Foucault, 1984).

Problematizations question how and why specific issues have been defined as problematic truths (Foucault, 1983) that must be governed. Hence, this perspective seeks to analyze the process of formation of these truths, or the process of how certain objects are produced as objects of thought that "pose problems to politics" (Foucault, 1984). Within this framework, it must be understood that public policies are considered the entry point for revealing the dynamics at play when it comes to governing subjects. In this sense, public policies are specific answers to determined "problems." Therefore, as Rose (2000) argues, problematizations focus on uncovering what type of questions do these answers—expressed in policy—respond to.

Understanding immigration policy as answers to specific questions implies interrogating what type of representation[1] of the "problem" is contained in these answers (Bacchi & Goodwin, 2016), and this is the intention in this chapter. In other words, to examine the problematization of an issue like immigration means to shed light on the "conceptual premises underpinning problem representations" (Bacchi & Goodwin, 2016, p. 17).

Hence, this analysis views migration as an object that has been produced as a particular problem with and through the various governmental practices that target it (Carson, 2018; Moffette, 2018). Consequently, my methodology allows me to observe the different power dynamics within immigration policy that enable immigration to emerge as an object that must be governed in a particular way. In this regard, policies are understood as answers to a specific set of questions. Therefore, my starting point of analysis is the answers (policy responses). As Bacchi and Goodwin (2016) contend, this exercise implies an analytic process that will develop from front to back; that is, from the proposal or solution to the problem. The objective of this inverted strategy of analysis is to reveal the "deep-seated assumptions" embodied in the political responses given to certain phenomena (Bacchi & Goodwin, 2016). The backward process that uncovers problematizations has been operationalized through the post-structural policy analysis of Bacchi and Goodwin (2016), which guides the methodology of this chapter.

In this vein, Foucault posits that access to problematizations is possible through "practical texts," which has a prescriptive nature since they are "written for the purpose of offering rules, opinions, and advice on how to behave" (Foucault, 1986, p. 12–13). Following Foucault's recommendation when studying problematizations, this chapter analyzes policy documents focused on the Venezuelan population issued from August 2018 to March 2020 (21 ministerial agreements, one executive decree), as well as the legal regulations underlying these documents. This research used a database called Fiel Web[2] to search for its targeted policy documents as well as the official websites of the Ecuadorian presidency (Presidencia del Ecuador), the Ecuadorian Ministry of Government (Ministerio de Gobierno), former Ministry of Interior (Ministerio del Interior), the Ecuadorian Ministry of Foreign Affairs and Human mobility (Ministerio de Relaciones Exteriores y Movilidad Humana) or chancellery (Cancillería), and the Secretariat Risk Management (Secretaría de Gestión de Riesgos).[3] The interpretation strategy adopted for these data was thematic content analysis (Robert & Bouillaguet, 1997/2007).

Context

International immigration and emigration were minor social and political issues in Ecuador until the first half of the twentieth century. Nevertheless, this South American country—and many other peripheral countries—was marked by significant flows of emigration to the United States and Europe, which gradually became a priority policy issue. Conversely, international immigration to Ecuador was a matter of little notoriety in state policy until the end of the twentieth century. However, since 2000, the trends in international immigrants arriving in Ecuador began to change gradually, and the governmental reaction transformed as well.

Migration is a complex phenomenon, and while the rise in immigration rates depends on a variety of factors and not only on the domestic policy and legislation of the receiving countries (Herrera, 2019), the promulgation of the twentieth and last constitution of Ecuador (known as the Constitution of Montecristi) marks a significant milestone for the transformations in immigration patterns in this country. This constitution, often considered to be one of the most progressive in the region (Minteguiaga & Ubasart-González, 2015), develops a series of guarantees and rights to protect and promote human mobility in its various forms. It addresses migratory issues in seven of its nine titles and devotes an entire section to the rights of migrants. For instance, it recognizes the right to migrate and promotes the gradual elimination of "foreigner" and "illegal" as legal statuses.

In this context, the Ecuadorian Ministry of Foreign Affairs and Human Mobility announced in June 2008 that, by presidential decree, all foreigners, without exception, would be able to freely enter the country and remain in national territory for 90 days (a visa exemption for tourists called the open-door policy by the Ecuadorian government) (El Universo, 2008; La Hora, 2008).[4] The president of Ecuador at that time, Rafael Correa, applying the principles contained in the constitution, took this measure to "dismantle that invention of the twentieth century that were passports and visas," (La Hora, 2008) and to facilitate the entry of all people wishing to visit Ecuador as tourists.

I argue that it is possible to identify two turning points in the patterns of immigration in Ecuador. Both led to an exponential increase in the number of foreigners entering this country, and to diversification beyond the patterns of intraregional immigration (characterized by Peruvian and Colombian immigration) (Quiloango Tipanluisa, 2011). The first turning point happened immediately after the implementation of the open-door policy for tourism in 2008. After its announcement, Ecuador started to record a significant number of entries from Chinese and Cuban nationals (INEC 2011: 23-32).[5] The number of Haitians arriving in this country also increased markedly (Burbano Alarcon, 2015, p. 207). Likewise, entries from other extra-continental nationalities were also occurring from Africa (mostly Nigeria and Eritrea) and Asia (mainly Bangladesh).

The second moment of rupture began with the arrival of hundreds of thousands of people from Venezuela fleeing the political and humanitarian crisis. During most of the twentieth century, Venezuela was one of the most stable economies in Latin America and was a migrant-receiving country in the region. However, during Chavez's presidency (1999–2013) it gradually became the country with the highest number of emigrants in the American continent. The financial, political, and social collapse that began during the government of this president, and worsened during Nicolas Maduro's term of office, drove the massive migration of Venezuelan citizens to various destinations, mainly in the South America region (Vargas Ribas, 2018). In this context, the smallest Andean country, Ecuador, became one of the main recipients of Venezuelans.

In 2013, Ecuador began to register an increase in the number of Venezuelan citizens entering Ecuador, and these figures started to exceed 100,000 entries as of 2016 (Ramirez, Linares, and Useche, 2019). The Ministry of Government registered 285,651 entries of Venezuelan citizens and a migratory balance of 60,752, and in 2018 it registered 509,285 entries and a migratory balance of 115,846 (Ministerio de Gobierno, n.d). However, starting in 2019, the implementation of new and more severe constraints to access the country caused a significant decrease in the number of entries (Ramirez, 2020).

Historically, the Venezuelan population did not face major restrictions or cumbersome processes to enter Ecuador and regularize their immigration status. It should be noted that citizens belonging to MERCOSUR (Southern Common Market) or UNASUR[6] (Union of South American Nations) may enter Ecuador simply by presenting an identity document. Therefore, as Venezuela forms part of UNASUR its citizens could easily enter this country. Regarding the regularization processes for temporary or permanent residency, in 2010 Ecuador and Venezuela signed a migratory statute whose objective was to facilitate the migratory processes between citizens of both countries.[7] Between 2010 and 2016, this agreement allowed the first Venezuelan immigrants to enter Ecuador without major inconveniences.

In 2017, following the enactment of the Ecuadorian Human Mobility Law (Ley de Movilidad Humana)—a legal instrument that replaces the former Migration Law (Ley de Migración) and Law on Foreigners (Ley de Extranjería)—a new visa modality known as the UNASUR visa was established as a mechanism to favour free mobility among South American citizens. This type of visa allowed thousands of Venezuelans to regularize their immigration status in Ecuador with relative ease (Herrera & Cabezas, 2019). However, since the number of Venezuelan migrants began to increase, the ability to enter Ecuador and eventually regularize their status began to be progressively limited. In

August 2018, Ecuador experienced its highest peak in the number of Venezuelan citizens trying to enter the country. During this month the Ministry of Government of Ecuador registered around 3,000 entries per day (quoted in Ministerio de Relaciones Exteriores y Movilidad Humana, 2018b, p. 3), and the United Nations High Commissioner for Refugees (UNHCR) estimated that more than 30,000 Venezuelans entered Ecuador during the first weeks of August (El Comercio, 2018). The large number of entries and presence of Venezuelan citizens at the Ecuador-Colombia border put the Ecuadorian government on "state of alert" (Ministerio de Relaciones Exteriores y Movilidad Humana, 2018a, p. 4) and it is from this moment on that the arrival of Venezuelans begins to be managed as an "unusual flow."

In this context, the first measure adopted by the Ecuadorian government is the declaration of a state of emergency in the three provinces with the largest Venezuelan influx: Carchi, El Oro, and Pichincha. This declaration was subsequently extended to the entire country and renewed consecutively until March 2020 (Ministerio de Relaciones Exteriores y Movilidad Humana, 2020). This moment marks an essential shift in the regulation of Venezuelan migration; consequently, this can be considered as what Foucault (1984) called a "problematizing moment", where relevant shifts in practices could be identified, and where "givens become questions." Therefore, this paper reflects upon what has been said and what has been done about Venezuelan migration in Ecuador since this moment of rupture.

Managing Venezuelan Immigration as a Crisis

The dialectic between security and humanitarian logic has been identified particularly in the European context, where intense migratory movements have been labelled as "humanitarian crises" (Lukić, 2016; Malkki, 1995; Šelo Šabić, 2017) in need of extraordinary intervention. With the aim of capturing this phenomenon, various theorizations have emerged. For instance, the humanitarian regime is a conceptual category that has been developed to understand the policies and practices put in place by state and non-governmental agencies to provide aid and relief to populations considered in a state of vulnerability (Harrell-Bond, 1999). These policies and practices are presented and conceived as neutral and beneficial for those represented as victims and subjects of this type of intervention. However, in the migratory context, this regime is not as neutral as it is made out to be (Hameršak

& Pleše, 2018); it also works in an intertwined manner within a securitized logic that, depending on the circumstances, aims to repress or expulse those it seeks to target.

In this line of thought, Watson (2011) presents how the logic of crisis management develops within a humanitarian-securitization nexus. For Watson, humanitarianism constitutes a sector of securitization. Security has been used as the logic that justifies the use of extraordinary measures. However, Watson (2011) considers that not only the discourse framed in security has made possible the implementation of measures that otherwise would be questioned, but that humanitarianism has also been implemented as a measure of legitimization of restrictive and exclusionary responses in times of "crisis." In this vein, Agamben (2013) argues that the concept of "crisis" has become the "motto of modern politics" and "an instrument of rule", which facilitates and legitimizes immediate authoritarian intervention. Hence, it does not require detailed analysis or prolonged parliamentary discussions. Therefore, counterproductive measures in the shape of "humanitarian response" can be introduced as a quick and effective mechanism to deal with what has been framed as an emergency or crisis.

Likewise, Chimni (2001) argues that the idea of humanitarianism does not have clear limits. Its conceptual boundaries are vague and can be easily manipulated. Consequently, it can be effortlessly used to justify practices that are not related to aid or charity responses. Following these theorizations, I posit that the Ecuadorian government tactically used the vagueness of humanitarianism to deploy a series of security-based measures with the aim of restricting Venezuelan migration.

Although the number of Venezuelan migrants began to increase progressively since 2013 (Ministerio de Gobierno, n.d), the Ecuadorian government did not take a clear position or action related to this phenomenon. However, in 2018, following exponential increase, Ecuador decided to establish measures to face these arrivals. In this framework, the Ministry of Government determined that Ecuador faced "an unusual flow" of Venezuelan migrants (Ministerio de Gobierno, 2018a). Thus, for the first time, these arrivals were constituted as an extraordinary situation that needed to be managed using extraordinary measures. Like most South American countries (Barbieri et al., 2020), Ecuador decided to represent the movement of Venezuelans as a "migratory crisis" (El Comercio, 2019a; Cancillería del Ecuador, n.d; Ministerio de Gobierno, 2019; Ministerio de Gobierno, 2020; Presidencia del Ecuador, 2018). Consequently, on August 9, 2018, the Ministry of Foreign Affairs and Human Mobility issued Ministerial Resolution No. 000152 declaring a state of emergency in the human mobility sector (Ministerio de Relaciones Exteriores y Movilidad Humana, 2018a).

If one observes the resolution above and each of the eighteen ministerial agreements (Ministerio de Relaciones Exteriores y Movilidad Humana, 2018c–h, 2019a–m, 2020a–b) through which the emergency was prolonged, all of them start with a preamble that strongly emphasizes the pro-migration principles contained in the constitution: migration as a human right. However, they gradually make a subtle shift towards the language of risk management and the unusualness of the migratory movements that the country is facing. Similarly, the official discourse of government authorities draws heavily on the language of solidarity and brotherhood for migrants (Ramirez, 2022) who are victims of the policies of a corrupt government (El Comercio, 2018b; El Universo, 2018b; El Universo, 2018c).

Within this framework, I argue that problematizing Venezuelan migration as a crisis allowed the implementation, without further analysis, of repressive and securitization measures that seek to expel Venezuelan citizens and prevent their further entry. Thus, the Ecuadorian government adopted humanitarian discourses, practices, and policies through which migrants are constructed as victims and at the same time as a security-related issue (Pereira, 2019). In this sense, the logic of crisis management is deployed together with discursive practices that seek to "save" and "protect" the Venezuelan "victim" who left their country in search of a better life. In this sense, this country carried out a strategic deployment of measures that can be understood as tactical humanitarianism.

Through this concept I want to capture the tactical way in which Ecuador used the vague concept of humanitarianism (Chimni, 2001) to filter out Venezuelan migrants already in its territory and prevent new entries. Thus, the responses deployed in this framework did not emerge as measures that seek to protect international human rights obligations. They were strategically constituted as humanitarian and temporary. Thus, without shedding its image of the benchmark for the protection of free human mobility (El Universo, 2018d; El Universo, 2018e; Ministerio de Relaciones Exteriores y Movilidad Humana, 2017, n.d.; SENPLADES, 2014; SENPLADES, 2017), Ecuador dissociated itself from the obligation to establish a long-term migration policy.

I identify the deployment of tactical humanitarianism observing the broader implications of the declaration of emergency. In Ecuador, a response of this nature implies the action of the Secretariat of Risk Management. As its name indicates, this secretariat is the institution in charge of planning and coordinating the necessary activities to face natural or human-made risks. Hence, this institution coordinates the necessary humanitarian aid to offer support during and after disasters or emerging situations (Rebotier, 2016, p. 145). In other words, its actions are focused on alleviating situations of vulnerability, but at the same time on facing threats that put at risk the security and integrity of the Ecuadorian territory.

Therefore, the Secretariat of Risk Management is at the same time conceived as a rescue and a risk containment institution. It seeks to implement measures that save and alleviate as well as measures that will safeguard the security of the Ecuadorian population. It is responsible for guiding and coordinating all state institutions called upon in case of a crisis (e.g., Ministry of Health, police). Therefore, this secretariat acted like a "relieving" institution that helped Venezuelan "victims" by coordinating actions that alleviated their basic needs. At the same time, it also acted as an institution that facilitated the exit of these unwanted victims from the Ecuadorian territory through the coordination of a humanitarian corridor.

In this context, and within this dialectic that represents Venezuelan migrants as a risk and as victims, Ecuador deployed four types of control measures that are embedded in these complex, ambiguous, and interrelated logics. Their aim was to accelerate the exit of these "migrant victims" by either facilitating their movement or pressuring it.

The Humanitarian Corridor: After the declaration of emergency, one of the first actions taken by the Ecuadorian government was to announce the opening of a humanitarian corridor (El Comercio, 2018b; El Universo, 2018f). Thus, the Secretariat of Risk Management, together with other institutions such as the Ministry of Transport, Ministry of Health and Police, etc., coordinated the transportation of thousands of Venezuelans on 36 buses, which departed from various Ecuadorian cities and transported more than 1,300 people (Secretaría Gestión de Riesgos, n.d). The objective was to take Venezuelan citizens to the southern border before Peru implemented a passport requirement (El Comercio, 2018c), which would have prevented many Venezuelans from entering this territory, leaving them stuck in Ecuador. Therefore, considering that most Venezuelan migrants travel on foot (OIM, 2020), the Ecuadorian government was incentivized to take quick action promoting an easy and fast transit through the country.

In this context, Ecuador presented Venezuelan migration as a vulnerable population that needed to be protected and supported in their transit through the country to Peru. Through this route, the government installed humanitarian assistance points where basic hygiene kits were handed out. In addition, primary medical care was provided (El Comercio, 2018d; Cancillería del Ecuador, 2018). In this way, Ecuador ensured that these "victim bodies" could leave its territory safe and sound. Consequently, Ecuador assumed the position of protecting victims while ensuring that the protection provided would be quick and temporary. To prevent these migrant bodies from being stuck in its territory, it decided to act as a facilitator of their transit. Although these corridors helped this population to move safely, the assistance granted by the Ecuadorian government was sufficient to maintain "bare life" (Agamben, 2005) needs; thus, reaffirming (Hameršak & Iva Plešela, 2018) the constitution of Venezuelan immigrants as victims who must be rescued so they could immediately be led out of the country.

With the establishment of the humanitarian corridor, Ecuador presented the growing arrival of Venezuelans as a transitory problem. In this way, it constructed its identity as a transit country in which this population does not want to remain. Although many of these migrants use Ecuador as a place of transit, as of 2017 a considerable increase in the migratory balance of this population can be seen (Herrera & Cabezas Galvez, 2019). Therefore, representing Ecuador as a place of transit does not match the reality, but it does allow Ecuador to disengage from the development of an effective policy of regularization and insertion of this population in the country.

Similar to what is explained by Bužinkić (2018) in the case of the humanitarian corridor established in Croatia, the Ecuadorian humanitarian corridor established that Venezuelan migrants were "welcome through" the country but not welcome to stay. In this context, Ecuador established a discourse in which it presented itself as a charitable country that faced the crisis in an extremely generous manner despite its limited resources (El Comercio, 2018f; El Comercio, 2018g;

Presidencia del Ecuador, n.d). This discourse has been maintained over time and through it the government of Ecuador has managed to obtain significant sums of money through the financial support of several countries and international institutions (El Universo, 2018f). However, Ecuador's identity as a transit territory is subsequently questioned through the measures developed by Ecuador itself when it decided to implement a migratory amnesty process, which will be subsequently analyzed.

Passports: Only a week after the emergency declaration, the Ecuadorian government determined that Venezuelan citizens wishing to enter Ecuador must present a valid passport (Ministerio de Relaciones Exteriores y Movilidad Humana, 2018b), a measure that violates treaties and the Ecuadorian constitution.[8] Thus, in a tactical manner, the image of the Venezuelan immigrant is used as a potential victim of smuggling human trafficking, determining that the only way to protect them is through greater entry restrictions (Secretaría Nacional de Comunicación del Ecuador, 2018).

The Ecuadorian government constantly expressed its commitment to fight human smuggling and human trafficking linked to Venezuelan migration. Hence, all measures framed within there declaration or emergency were also justified under this premise. Van Liempt and Sersli (2013) determine that the way in which the political discourse represents migrant smuggling has not only changed the way in which this phenomenon is understood, but also the type of responses that are developed to confront it. In this sense, this activity is seen as a threat to the state and not as an effect of the restrictive measures used to control migration (Kyle & Dale, 2001). In the case of Ecuador, the representation of human trafficking and smuggling as a crime linked to the violence of organized crime[9] supported the deployment of more severe migratory restrictions. Thus, the construction of the Venezuelan migrant as a victim that must be protected from these criminal activities legitimized the need to enhance border security in this country.

The passport requirement was suspended for 45 days by the Ecuadorian justice system (El Comercio, 2018e); however, the same restrictive logic remained in place. Ecuador decided that Venezuelan citizens were allowed to enter the territory only with their national identity document. Nevertheless, they had to present a certification validating its authenticity (Ministerio de Relaciones Exteriores, 2018i). The Ministry of the Interior of Ecuador affirmed that after having identified that several Venezuelans are trying to enter the country with false documentation, the government was obliged to take measures to verify authenticity (El Comercio, 2018f). By doing so, Venezuelans are no longer possible victims of trafficking, but are now conceived as potential document forgers who wish to enter the country in an irregular manner. Through the implementation of this mechanism of control, the migrant victim is again strategically represented as a risk to the country's security that must be contained.

Criminal Records: While the declaration of emergency was still in force, in January 2019, a Venezuelan citizen committed a femicide in Ibarra, a small town in Ecuador (El Comercio, 2019b). This tragic event led the president and vice president of Ecuador to make statements where immigrants were represented as victims who can easily become victimizers.[10] Thus, on January 25, 2019, the Ecuadorian authorities enacted Ministerial Agreement No. 0000001. It established that all Venezuelan citizens seeking to enter Ecuador must present their criminal records (Ministerio de Relaciones Exteriores y Movilidad Humana, 2019n), a measure that once again violated the constitutional framework. Dal Lago (2009) posits that identifying migrants with danger justifies the use of any type of measure to protect the "insiders" from the threats of the "outsiders" and therefore exclusion is the privileged measure. Following this logic, the Ecuadorian government used this tragic event to deploy a highly politicized, emotional response framed in the logic of exclusion (Aliverti, 2012). The requirement of criminal records was presented as an unwanted answer that this "charitable government" was forced to take in the face of the criminal acts of a foreign population. Consequently, through this measure, Ecuador played once again with the security and humanitarian dialectic. Hence, this requirement constituted the Venezuelan migrant as a suspect and a potential criminal who takes advantage of the solidarity of a country that welcomed him.

Visas: In July 2019, the Ecuadorian presidency enacted decree 826. This instrument establishes a mandatory amnesty process (Presidencia del Ecuador, 2019). The amnesty was presented as a mechanism to regularize the situation of thousands of Venezuelans in Ecuador (El Comercio, 2020a). For this purpose, the government decided to issue the so-called humanitarian visa, better known as the VERHU visa. This process came to an end in August 2020 (Presidencia del Ecuador, 2020). The establishment of this visa process was framed by the Ecuadorian government as an amnesty since it was not only intended for those migrants who wanted to enter the country but also for people who were already in the territory and did not possess a regular status.

The procedure established to obtain the VERHU visa was presented by the government of Ecuador as simple and free since the applicant "only" had to pay 50 US dollars, which was supposed to cover the cost of the application (Cancillería del Ecuador, 2019). However, the application process for this visa did not only have a cost, but the requirements necessary to access it were difficult to fulfill. All applicants had to present their passport (with at least five years of expiration for those already living in Ecuador), criminal records (legalized and apostilled in Venezuela), and birth certificates for children and adolescents (legalized and apostilled in Venezuela) (Cancillería del Ecuador, 2019). Given the economic and social situation that Venezuela is experiencing, obtaining these documents in most cases was an extremely difficult task (El Comercio, 2020b). In addition, many Venezuelan citizens in Ecuador were in a situation of extreme economic vulnerability, making the payment involved in this administrative process a difficult limitation to overcome. Most Venezuelans entered the country with the Andean card and obtaining a passport implied a high cost (US$280) that was very difficult to afford (Suárez Molina, Castillo Aguirre, Mera Zambrano, 2020). Likewise, the process of obtaining all the necessary documentation was a titanic task, not only because there were a series of failures in the electronic system implemented by the government (La Hora, 2019) but also because the Venezuelan government was unable to provide the required documents (passports and apostilled criminal records) (Herrera & Gálvez, 2019, p. 141).

All these inconveniences and requirements meant that many Venezuelan citizens already in Ecuadorian territory could not access these visas and remained in a state of irregularity. In addition, it must be considered that this regularization process was only intended for those Venezuelan citizens who entered the country in a regular manner but who stayed beyond the allowed time (180 days) and, therefore, found themselves in an irregular situation (Presidencia del Ecuador, 2019). This limitation implied that all those who entered the country through irregular crossings could not apply. These kinds of limitations, which increase the difficulty of regular entry, multiply the use of clandestine methods in the aim of gaining access to the destination country, and once inside, to remain in the territory (Armenta, 2017; Khosravi, 2010; De Genova, 2004; Inda, 2008). In this context, according to International Organization for Migration data, 31 percent of Venezuelans who entered Ecuadorian territory did so through "trochas" (i.e., irregular passages) (OIM 2021), which implies many Venezuelan citizens are in a legal limbo that perpetuates their irregular situation and therefore their state of vulnerability.

Exclusion can be created through legislation, and in general through policy responses. It is achieved by framing non-citizens in the borders of "illegality", which many scholars argue is an artificial category configured and shaped by the restrictions of different types (De Genova, 2004). In this context, conditions imposed by the Ecuadorian government define the non-citizens who are incapable of fulfilling them outside the scope of the law, turning them into irregular immigrants. However, this regularization process, which was presented by the Ecuadorian government as an "amnesty", was clearly exclusive for many Venezuelan citizens. Nevertheless, it was presented as proof of Ecuador's willingness to make humanitarian efforts and reaffirm its position as a reference in the defense of migrants' rights.

Similarly, it should be noted that before the introduction of this visa, Venezuela was still on the list of countries that could freely enter Ecuador, so the introduction of this visa sought to limit the number of entries of Venezuelans and their potential stay in the territory, an objective that was attained according to the numbers registered by the Ministry of Government (El Comercio, 2019d; Ministerio de Gobierno, n.d.). This limitation is a clear sign of the securitization logic underpinning this measure, which was presented as a humanitarian solution.

Conclusion

The Ecuadorian case explored in this chapter illustrated how the construction of a so-called crisis to regulate immigration legitimized the deployment of measures that restrict the movement of migrant populations, enabling their framing as potential dangers, and worsening their vulnerability. This chapter thus sought to expose how the form in which an issue is conceptualized in public policy delimits how policymakers think about solutions to address it. In the context of migration policy, the solutions that are thought to face a "crisis" are framed by an idea of urgency, danger, and temporality. In this sense, framing migration policy in terms of crisis fails to centre on policy development and the need for long-term measures. Therefore, policy responses seeking to contain immigration are prioritized to the detriment of those aiming to improve the quality of life of migrants as a permanent project.

The way in which migration is problematized to be governed has a significant impact on the lives of people who move across borders. Consequently, migration policy can be a tool that guarantees the rights of migrants or that perpetuates the dynamics of exclusion and stigmatization of these populations. By questioning the taken-for-granted designations that are deployed to govern issues such as migration, we are invited to think about issues in alternative forms, which could open a path for the development of more humane alternatives that challenge hegemonic frameworks of regulation.

Notes

1.   Bacchi uses the expression "representation of the problem" to simplify what is meant by "problematization"; she is not interested in doing a sociology of representations. "Representation of the problem" is the same as "problematization of an issue", "framing of an issue" (Bacchi, 2009; Bacchi, 2015; Bacchi & Goodwin, 2016) or to use Foucault's words, "how things are constituted as problems" (Foucault et al., 2003).

2.   Fiel Web is a database whose objective is the dissemination of Ecuadorian legal regulations published in the official state newspaper.

3.   In October 2018, the Presidential Decree No. 534 changed it to its name "Servicio Nacional de Gestion de Riesgos y Emergencias" (Presidencia del Ecuador, 2018).

4.   According to some research (e.g., Bonilla, 2008; Nasimba Loachamín, 2013; Valle Franco, 2017; Freier and Holloway, 2019) the visa withdrawal was announced by the Ministry of Foreign Affairs in Press Bulletin No. 398 of May 11, 2008. However, the electronic address (http://www.mmrree.gov.ec/mre/documentos/novedades/pol_exterior/junio/bol398.htm) presented in these texts no longer exists.

5.   Until the first half of the 2000s, these numbers did not exceed a few hundred people, but after the removal of visas they rose to several thousand.

6.   Ecuador withdrew from UNASUR in 2019.

7.   For the statute's full content visit: https://bit.ly/3oUUe5r.

8.   At the time, art. 133 of the Human Mobility Law established that South American citizens could enter Ecuador with a valid identification document, not specifying it should be a passport. Hence, this measure put in place just for Venezuelan citizens was discriminatory, violating the right to non-discrimination. It also violates the right to free movement and the right to equality.

9.   Several studies have shown that migrant smuggling is linked to small-scale economic activities that are far from the representations of violent criminality with which it is associated (Neske, 2006; Soudijn, 2006; Staring et al., 2005; Zhang & Chin, 2002). Nevertheless, migrant smuggling is presented as an activity intrinsically linked to organized crime and thus legitimizes the actions taken to combat it (Collyer, 2007; Mountz, 2010).

10.   In a public statement the president of Ecuador stated: "Ecuador is and will be a country of peace. I will not allow any antisocial to take it away from us. The integrity of our mothers, daughters and companions is my priority. I have ordered

the immediate formation of brigades to control the legal situation of Venezuelan immigrants in the streets, in workplaces and at the border. We have opened our doors to them, but we will not sacrifice anyone's safety. It is the duty of the Police to act harshly against delinquency and crime, and they have my support. We will apply the full weight of the law to those who did nothing in the face of violence, injustice and the criminal exercise of power" (El Comercio, 2019c).

References

Agamben, G. (2005). *State of exception*. University of Chicago Press.

Agier, M., & Fernbach, D. (2011). *Managing the undesirables: Refugee camps and humanitarian Government*. English ed. Polity Press.

Aliverti, A. (2012). "Making people criminal: The role of the criminal caw in immigration enforcement." *Theoretical Criminology, 16*(4), 417–434. https://doi.org/10.1177/1362480612449779

Armenta, A. (2017). *Protect, serve, and deport: The rise of policing as immigration enforcement*. University of California Press.

Bacchi, C. L. (2009). *Analysing policy: What's the problem represented to be?* Pearson.

Bacchi, C. L. (2015). The turn to problematization: Political implications of contrasting interpretive and poststructural adaptations. *Open Journal of Political Science, 5*(1), 1–12. https://doi.org/10.4236/ojps.2015.51001

Bacchi, C. L, & Goodwin, S. (2016). *Poststructural policy analysis: A guide to practice*. Palgrave Pivot.

Barbieri, N.G, Ramrez Gallegos, J., Del Pilar Ospina Grajales, M., Pincowsca Cardoso Campos, B., & Polo Alvis, S. (2020). Respuestas de los países del pacifico suramericano ante la migración venezolana: Estudio comparado de políticas migratorias en Colombia, Ecuador y Perú. *Diálogo Andino* (63), 219–233. https://login.proxy.bib.uottawa.ca/login?url=https://www.proquest.com/scholarly-journals/respuestas-de-los-países-del-pacífico/docview/2573033924/se-2

Bonilla, A. (2008). Análisis de política Exterior en la región Andina. Análisis del retiro de requerimiento de visados de turismo en el Ecuador. Master's diss., Flasco-Ecuador. https://www.flacsoandes.edu.ec/sites/default/files/agora/files/1224174871.por_que_s_1_._2.pdf

Bouillaguet, Annick, and André D. Robert (2007 [1997]). *L'analyse de contenu*. Paris: Presses Universitaires de France.

Burbano Alarcón, M. (2015). "Las asociaciones de migrantes haitianos en el Ecuador: Entre debilidad y resistencia." *Revista Interdisciplinar Da Mobilidade Humana, 23*(44), 207–220. https://doi.org/10.1590/1980-85852503880004413

Bužinkić, E. (2018). "Welcome to vs. welcome through. Crisis mobilization and solidarity with refugees in Croatia as a transit country." In E. Bužinkić & M. Hameršak (Eds.), *Formation and disintegration of the Balkan refugee corridor. Camps, routes and borders in the Croatian context* (pp. 43–167). Zagreb: Institute of Ethnology and Folklore Research, Centre for Peace Studies, Faculty of Political Science University of Zagreb. https://www. bib.irb.hr/1045672/download/1045672.Formation_and_Disintegration_ or_theBalkan_Corridor.pdf#page=143

Carson, L. (2013). The politics of the problem: How to use Carol Bacchi's work. *The power to persuade* (blog). http://www.powertopersuade.org.au/blog/ the-politics-of-the-problem-using-carol/12/2/2018

Chimni, B. S. (2000). Globalization, humanitarianism and the erosion of refugee protection. *Journal of Refugee Studies, 13*(3), 243–263. https://doi. org/10.1093/jrs/13.3.243

Cancillería del Ecuador. (2018). *Respuesta en Salud Movilidad Humana.* Cancillería del Ecuador. https://www.cancilleria.gob.ec/wp-content/ uploads/2018/09/msp_acciones_en_salud_venezezolanos_a_nivel_ nacional.pdf

Cancillería del Ecuador. (2019). *Manual de proseco para el usuario de consulado virtualproceso de aplicación de visas de ecepción por razones humanitarias verhu.* Cancillería del Ecuador. https://www.cancilleria.gob.ec/wpcontent/ uploads/2019/11/MANUALDEUSUecu.pdf

Cancillería del Ecuador. (n.d.). *Plan integral para la atención y protección de la población venezolana en movilidad humana en ecuador.* https://www. cancilleria.gob.ec/wpcontent/uploads/2020/09/tenci%C3%93n_y_ protecci%C3%93n_de_la_poblaci%C3%93n_venezolana_2020_-_2021- 16sept20-final0812999001600384661.pdf

Dal Lago, A. (2009). *Non-persons: The exclusion of migrants in a global society.* Translated by Marie Orton. Vimodrone: IPOC.

De Genova, N. (2004). The legal production of Mexican/migrant "illegality." *Latino Studies, 2*(2), 160–185. https://doi.org/10.1057/palgrave.lst.8600085

El Comercio. (2018a). Emergencia en Carchi, Pichincha y El Oro por crisis humanitaria de ciudadanos venezolanos en Ecuador. *El Comercio.* https:// www.elcomercio.com/actualidad/ecuador/ecuador-emergencia- venezolanos-pichincha-eloro.html

El Comercio. (2018b). Ecuador crea un corredor humanitario para paso de ciudadanos venezolanos. *El Comercio.* https://www.elcomercio.com/ actualidad/ecuador/ecuador-corredorhumanitario-venezuela-migra- cion-frontera.html

El Comercio. (2018c). Perú exigirá pasaporte a ciudadanos venezolanos por creciente migración. *El Comercio.* https://www.elcomercio.com/actuali- dad/mundo/peru-exigira-pasaporte-venezolanos-migracion.html

El Comercio. (2018d). 14 buses esperan a venezolanos en la frontera con Colombia otros 22 salieron a Perú en un corredor humanitario. *El Comercio.* https://www.elcomercio.com/actualidad/ecuador/ecuador- corredorhumanitario-venezolanos-colombia-peru.html

El Comercio. (2018e). *Rueda de prensa sobre la situación de los ciudadanos venezolanos*. [Video]. YouTube. https://youtu.be/_2qV1zVIMwg

El Comercio. (2018f). Jueza amplia plazo para ingreso de ciudadanos venezolanos sin pasaporte. *El Comercio*. https://www.elcomercio.com/ actualidad/politica/medidas-cautelares-efecto-pasaporte-venezolanos. html

El Comercio. (2018g). Moreno compara el éxodo venezolano con el feriado bancario de Ecuador. *El Comercio*. https://www.elcomercio.com/actualidad/ politica/leninmorenocomparacion-exodo-venezuela-feriadobancario. html

El Comercio. (2019a). Lenin Moreno reitera que la exigencia de visa a ciudadanos de Venezuela es para velar por el bienestar de todos. *El Comercio*. https://www.elcomercio.com/actualidad/politica/moreno-exigencia-visa-venezolanos-bienestar.html

El Comercio. (2019b). Feminicidio conmueve a Ibarra: La Fiscalía indaga la acción policial. *El Comercio*. https://www.elcomercio.com/actualidad/ seguridad/ femicidio-conmueve-ibarra-fiscalia-indaga.html

El Comercio. (2019c). Lenín Moreno anuncia brigadas para controlar situación legal deciudadanos venezolanos en Ecuador. *El Comercio*. https:// www.elcomercio.com/actualidad/seguridad/moreno-brigadas-control-venezolanos-ecuador.html

El Comercio. (2019d). La visa humanitaria desacelero el ingreso de ciudadanos venezolanos. *El Comercio*. https://www.elcomercio.com/actualidad/ ecuador/visa-humanitaria-ingreso-venezolanos-ecuador.html

El Comercio. (2020a). Ecuador aspira entregar 75 000 visas a ciudadanos venezolanos hasta septiembre. *El Comercio*. https://www.eluniverso. com/noticias/2020/08/31/nota/7961671/ecuador-venezolanos-visas-humanitarias-registro/

El Comercio. (2020b). Asociación Civil de venezolanos insiste por amnistía migratoria en Ecuador y habla de fallas en entrega de visas. *El Comercio*. https://www.elcomercio.com/actualidad/asociacion-venezolanos-amnistia-migratoria-visas/

El Universo. (2008). Ecuador ya no pedirá visa a ningún turista a partir del 20. *El Universo*. https://www.eluniverso.com/2008/06/11/0001/8/297741B18 5604F0CB8A436D44A3BC 5FD.html/

El Universo. (2018a). Ecuador declara emergencia migratoria, por llegada de 4.200 venezolanos al día. El estado de emergencia rige para las provincias de Carchi, Pichincha, El Oro. *El Universo*. https:// www.eluniverso.com/noticias/2018/08/08/nota/6897749/ecuador-declaraemergencia-migratoria-llegada-4200-venezolanos-dia/

El Universo. (2018b). Ecuador expulsa a embajadora de Venezuela. *El Universo*. https://www.eluniverso.com/noticias/2018/10/18/nota/7005572/ ecuador-expulsa-embajadora-venezuela/

El Universo. (2018c). Lenin Moreno en la ONU pide una accion continental por Venezuela. *El Universo.* https://www.eluniverso.com/noticias/2018/09/25/nota/6970505/lenin-moreno-onu-pide-accion-continental-venezuela/

El Universo. (2018d). Ofrecen apoyo por la migración venezolana en Ecuador. *El Universo.* https://www.eluniverso.com/noticias/2018/12/01/nota/7076451/ofrecen-apoyo-migracion-venezolana/

El Universo. (2018e). Ecuador, el país de América Latina que acoge más refugiados. *El Universo.* https://www.eluniverso.com/noticias/2018/06/25/nota/6829766/ecuador-pais-america-latina-que-acoge-mas-refugiados/

El Universo. (2018f). Ecuador implementa 'corredor humanitario' para venezolanos. *El Universo.* https://www.eluniverso.com/noticias/2018/08/23/nota/6919508/ecuador-implementa-corredor-humanitario-venezolanos

Foucault, M. (1983). "Discourse and truth-the problematization of parrhesia." Lecture given at Berkeley, CA. http://www.cscd.osaka-u.ac.jp/user/rosaldo/On_Parrehesia_by_Foucault_1983.pdf

Foucault, M., & Hurley, R. (1990). *The History of sexuality, Vol. I: An introduction.* Vintage Books.

Foucault, M., & Rabinow, P. (1984). *The Foucault reader.* 1st ed. Pantheon Books.

Foucault, M., Rabinow, P., & Rose, N. (2003). *The essential Foucault: Selections from essential works of Foucault, 1954–1984.* New Press.

Freier, L. F., & Holloway, K. (2019). The impact of tourist visas on intercontinental south-south migration: Ecuador's policy of "open doors" as a quasi-experiment. *The International Migration Review, 53*(4), 1171–1208. https://doi.org/10.1177/0197918318801068

Glynos, J., & Howarth, D. R. (2007). *Logics of critical explanation in social and political theory.* Routledge. https://doi.org/10.4324/9780203934753

Hameršak, M., & Pleše, I. (2018). Confined in movement: The Croatian section of the Balkan refugee corridor." In E. Bužinkić & M. Hameršak (Eds.), *Formation and disintegration of the Balkan refugee corridor: Camps, routes and borders in the Croatian context. Zagreb/Munich* (pp. 9–41). Zagreb: Institute of Ethnology and Folklore Research, Centre for Peace Studies, Faculty of Political Science University of Zagreb. https://www.bib.irb.hr/1045672/download/1045672.Formation_and_Disintegration_or_the_Balkan_Corridor.pdf#page=143

Harrell-Bond, B. (1999). The experience of refugees as recipients of aid. In A. Ager (Ed.), *Refugees: Perspectives on the experience of forced migration* (pp. 136–168). Continuum.

Herrera, G. (2018). From immigration to transit migration: Race and gender entanglements in new migration to Ecuador. In *New Migration Patterns in the Americas,* 285–315. Cham: Springer International Publishing. https://doi.org/10.1007/978-3-319-89384-6_11

Herrera, G., & Cabezas Gálvez, G. (2019). Ecuador: de la recepción a la disuasión. Políticas frente a la población venezolana y experiencia migratoria: 2015-2018. In L. Gandini, A. Fernando, & V. Prieto (Eds.), *Crisis y migración de la población venezolana. Entre la desprotección y la seguridad jurídica en Latinoamérica*, 125–155. México: UNAM. https://www.academia.edu/download/62287921/lku.pdf#page=135

Herrera, G., & Torres, A. (2005). *La migración ecuatoriana: transnacionalismo, redes e identidades*. Quito: Flacso-Sede Ecuador.

Inda, J. X., & Xavier Inda, J. (2008). *Targeting immigrants: Government, technology, and ethics*. Wiley.

INEC. (2014). *Anuario de entradas y salidas internacionales 2014*. INEC. https://www.ecuadorencifras.gob.ec/documentos/web-inec/Poblacion_y_Demografia/Migracion/Publicaciones/Anuario_ESI_2014.pdf

Khosravi, S. (2011). *"Illegal" traveller: An auto-ethnography of borders*. Basingstoke, Palgrave Macmillan.

La Hora (2008). Eliminan visados para ingresar por turismo en Ecuador por 90 días. *La Hora*. https://lahora.com.ec/noticia/732837/eliminan-visados-para-ingresar-por-turismo-en-ecuador-por-90-dc3adas

La Hora (2019). Venezolanos denuncian fallas en el sistema para visas humanitarias. *La Hora*. https://lahora.com.ec/noticia/1102286436/venezolanos-denuncian-fallas-en-el-sistema-para-visas-humanitarias-

Lukic, V. (2016). Understanding transit asylum migration: Evidence from Serbia. *International Migration, 54*(4), 31–43. https://doi.org/10.1111/imig.12237

Malkki, L. H. (1995). Refugees and exile: From "Refugee Studies" to the national order of things. *Annual Review of Anthropology, 24* (1), 495–523. https://doi.org/10.1146/annurev.an. 24.100195.002431

Ministerio de Gobierno. (2019). *Plan de accion conta la trata de personas en el Ecuador*. Ministerio de Gobierno. https://www.ministeriodegobierno.gob.ec/wpcontent/uploads/downloads/2019/12/PLAN-DE-ACCIO%CC%81N-CONTRA-LA-TRATA-DE-PERSONAS-1.pdf

——. 2020. Twitter post. Available at: https://twitter.com/mingobiernoec/status/1219703839504445447

——. n.d. *Nacionalidad y puerto mes a mes para página web del MDI 2010–2020*. Ministerio de Gobierno. Available at: https://www.ministeriodegobierno.gob.ec/nacionalidad-y-puerto-mes-a-mes-para-pagina-web-del-mdi-2010-20203/

Ministerio de Relaciones Exteriores y Movilidad Humana. 2017. Discurso de intervención del Sr. viceministro de Movilidad Humana, en el Panel No. 3 SOBRE 'Consecución de un enfoque gubernamental integral en materia de migración: perspectivas nacionales y locales. Speech given at Taller del Dialogo Internacional sobre migraciones de la OIM, New York, NY, 18–19. https://docplayer.es/57274304-Nueva-york-18-y-19-de-septiembre-2017.html

——. 2018a. *Resolución No. 000152*. Registro Oficial del Ecuador.

———. 2018b. *Resolución No. 000242*. Registro Oficial del Ecuador.

———. 2018c. *Resolución No. 000248*. Registro Oficial del Ecuador.

———. 2018d. *Resolución No. 000270*. Registro Oficial del Ecuador.

———. 2018f. *Resolución No. 000280*. Registro Oficial del Ecuador.

———. 2018g. *Resolución No. 000302*. Registro Oficial del Ecuador.

———. 2018h. *Resolución No. 000312*. Registro Oficial del Ecuador.

———. 2019a. *Resolución No. 0000006*. Registro Oficial del Ecuador.

———. 2019b. *Resolución No. 000021*. Registro Oficial del Ecuador.

———. 2019c. *Resolución No. 0000036*. Registro Oficial del Ecuador.

———. 2019e. *Resolución No. 00000046*. Registro Oficial del Ecuador.

———. 2019f. *Resolución No. 00000059*. Registro Oficial del Ecuador.

———. 2019g. *Resolución No. 0000079*. Registro Oficial del Ecuador.

———. 2019h. *Resolución No. 0000105*. Registro Oficial del Ecuador.

———. 2019i. *Resolución No. 0000126*. Registro Oficial del Ecuador.

———. 2019j. *Resolución No. 0000158*. Registro Oficial del Ecuador.

———. 2019k. *Resolución No. 0000178*. Registro Oficial del Ecuador.

———. 2019l. *Resolución No. 0000189*. Registro Oficial del Ecuador.

———. 2019m. *Resolución No. 0000201*. Registro Oficial del Ecuador.

———. 2019n. *Resolución No. 0000001*. Registro Oficial del Ecuador.

———. 2020a. *Resolución No. 000016*. Registro Oficial del Ecuador.

———. 2020b. *Resolución No. 0000023*. Registro Oficial del Ecuador.

———. n.d. Política Migratoria. Ministerio de Relaciones Exteriores y Movilidad Humana. https://www.cancilleria.gob.ec/2020/06/25/politica-migratoria/

Minteguiaga A., & Gemma, U.G. (2015). Regímenes de bienestar y gobiernos 'progresistas' en América Latina: los casos de Venezuela, Ecuador y Bolivia. *Política y sociedad* (Madrid, Spain), *52*(3), 691–718. https://doi.org/10.5209/rev_POSO. 2015.v52.n3.45379

Moffette, D. (2018). *Governing irregular migration: Bordering culture, labour, and security in Spain*. UBC Press.

Nasimba Loachamín, Rocío (2013). *La política de inmigración en el gobierno de Rafael Correa: entre el deber ser y el ser*. Quito: Universidad Andina Simón Bolívar, Sede Ecuador; Corporación Editora Nacional, Serie Magíster, No. 137.

OIM (2020). *Análisis comparativo del Monitoreo de Flujo de la población venezolana en Ecuador 2018–2019*. OIM. https://data2.unhcr.org/en/documents/download/84046

OIM (2021). *OIM publica la novena Encuesta de Monitoreo de Flujo de población venezolana en Ecuador*. OIM. https://www.oim.org.ec/2016/iomtemplate2/news/oim-publica-la-novena-encuesta-de-monitoreo-de-flujo-de-poblaci%C3%B3n-venezolana-en-ecuador

Pereira, A. (2019). El Nexo Entre Migración, Seguridad y Derechos Humanos En La Política Migratoria de Argentina (1990-2015). *Desafíos (Bogotá,*

Colombia), 31(1), 273–309. Available at: https://doi.org/10.12804/revistas. urosario.edu.co/desafios/a.6031.

Presidencia del Ecuador (2018). *Decreto No. 534.* Registro Oficial del Ecuador.

——. 2019. Twitter post. Available at: https://twitter.com/ Comunicacion Ec/ status/1045135096565641218

Presidencia del Ecuador. n.d. Ecuador garantiza cumplimiento de los derechos humanos a migrantes. News release, n.d. Available at: https:// www.comunicacion.gob.ec/ecuador-garantiza-cumplimiento-de-los-derechos-humanos-a-migrantes-venezolanos/

Presidencia del Ecuador (2019). *Decreto No. 826.* Registro Oficial del Ecuador.

Presidencia del Ecuador (2020). *Decreto No. 1020.* Registro Oficial del Ecuador.

Quiloango Tipanluisa, S. (2020). *Políticas públicas migratorias en el Ecuador.* Quito: Fundación Friedrich Ebert, 2011. https://library.fes.de/pdf-files/ bueros/quito/07897.pdf

Ramírez, J. De la ciudadanía suramericana al humanitarismo: el giro en la política y diplomacia migratoria ecuatoriana. *Estudios fronterizos* 21.

Ramírez Jacques, Yoharlis, L., & Emilio, U. (2019). (Geo) políticas migratorias, inserción laboral y xenofobia: migrantes venezolanos en ecuador. In C. Blouin (Ed.), *Después de la Llegada. Realidades de la migración venezolana* (pp. 103–127). Lima: Themis-PUCP.

Rebotier, J. (2016). *El riesgo y su gestión en Ecuador.* Quito: Publicaciones Pontificia Universidad Católica del Ecuador, 2016.

Rose, N. (2000). Government and control. *British Journal of Criminology, 40*(2), 321–339. https://doi.org/10.1093/bjc/40.2.321

Šabić, S. Š. (2017). Humanitarianism and its limits: The refugee crisis response in Croatia. In M. Barlai, B. Fähnrich, C. Griessler, & M. Rhomberg (Eds.), *The migrant crisis: European perspectives and national discourses* (pp. 93–106). Zürich: Lit Verlag.

Secretaría Nacional de Comunicación del Ecuador (2018). Comunicado Oficial. News release. https://www.cancilleria.gob.ec/2018/08/16/comunicado-oficial-35/

Secretaria de Gestión de Riesgos. n.d. *Alrededor de 1300 ciudadanos venezolanos fueron movilizados hasta Huaquillas.* Secretaria de Gestión de Riesgos. https://www.gestionderiesgos.gob.ec/alrededor-de-1-300-ciudadanos-venezolanos-fueron-movilizados-hasta-huaquillas/

SENPLADES (2014). *Agenda nacional de igualdad para la movilidad humana.* https://www.planificacion.gob.ec/wpcontent/uploads/down-loads/2014/09/Agenda_Nacional_Movilidad_Humana.pdf

SENPLADES (2017). *Plan nacional para el buen vivir 2017–2021.* https://www. gobiernoelectronico.gob.ec/wp-content/uploads/downloads/2017/09/ Plan-Nacional-para-el-Buen-Vivir-2017-2021.pdf

Siso, C. B. (2021). La migración venezolana: inicios y consecuencias. In R. Guzmán Ordaz & A. Belén Nieto Librero (Eds.), *Políticas públicas en defensa de la inclusión, la diversidad y el género III: migraciones y derechos humanos,* 43–53. Salamanca: Ediciones Universidad de Salamanca.

Suárez Molina, V., Castillo Aguirre, D. & P. Mera Zambrano, P. (2020). *Análisis: Situación de derechos humanos de migrantes de Venezuela en el Ecuador.* CARE Ecuador. https://www.care.org.ec/wp-content/uploads/2020/12/Analisis-Situacion-de-DDHH-migrantes-Venezuela-en-el-Ecuador-Ago2020-1.pdf

Ticktin, M. (2021). Transnational humanitarianism. *Annual Review of Anthropology, 43*(1), (2014), 273–289. https://doi.org/10.1146/annurev-anthro-102313-030403

UNHCR. *Monitoreo de protección – Informe Nacional – marzo 2021.* Ecuador: UNHCR. Accessed January 7, 2021. Available at: https://www.acnur.org/op/op_prot/610d7b064/ecuador-monitoreo-de-proteccion-informe-nacional-marzo-2021.htmlç

Valle Franco, A.I. (2017). Breve análisis histórico de la inmigración al Ecuador. *Revista Facultad de Jurisprudencia,* (2),1–30. Redalyc. https://www.redalyc.org/articulo.oa?id=600263744015

Van Liempt, I., & Sersli, S. (2013). State responses and migrant experiences with human smuggling: A reality check. *Antipode, 45*(4), 1029–1046. https://doi.org/10.1111/j.1467-8330.2012.01027.x

Vargas Ribas, C. (2018). La migración en Venezuela como dimensión de la crisis. *Pensamiento Propio (cries), 47,* 91–128.

Verso Books. (2013). The endless crisis as an instrument of power: In conversation with Giorgio Agamben. https://www.versobooks.com/blogs/1318-the-endless-crisis-as-an-instrument-of-power-in-conversation-with-giorgio-agamben

Watson, S. (2011). The "human" as referent object? Humanitarianism as securitization. *Security Dialogue, 42*(01), 3–20. https://doi.org/10.1177/0967010610393549.

Župarić-Iljić, D., & Valenta, M. (2019). "Opportunistic humanitarianism and securitization discomfort along the Balkan Corridor: The Croatian experience." In M. Feischmidt, L. Pries, & C. Cantat (Eds.), *Refugee Protection and Civil Society in Europe,* 129–160, Cham: Springer International Publishing. https://doi.org/10.1007/978-3-319-92741-1.

CHAPTER 4

Top Manta: Barcelona's Unionized *Manteros* in their Struggle for Recognition and Redistribution

Marina Gomá and Tatiana Llaguno

The current volume invites us to think about the manufactured language of "crisis" in its political function to obscure and maintain crises' underlying structures of power. To do so, this chapter discusses the work of the Popular Union of Travelling Vendors of Barcelona, with a particular focus on the anti-racist praxis of their clothing co-operative, Top Manta, created in 2018. In what follows, we examine how the union has used their brand to engage with migratory phenomena from a deeper understanding—not from a perpetual crisis perspective—of migrants as active citizens who are embedded in structural relations of inequality, collectively resist state illegalization, redefine the boundaries of political belonging, and enact alternative social imaginaries.

During the COVID-19 global pandemic (but also before), unionized street vendors in the highly touristic and cosmopolitan city of Barcelona, in their majority Black Senegalese men, formed exemplary civic coalitions to counter racial and economic inequalities. They countered the idea of a European immigration crisis by making visible the systemic processes that construct them as racialized subjects in Spain. As a European Union (EU) member state since 1986, Spain constitutes a southern border of Europe along Italy and Greece. Spanish immigration laws, which heavily rely on the idea of containing illegal immigration well before migrants reach the Iberian Peninsula (in the autonomous cities of Ceuta and Melilla, as well as the Canary Islands),

have played a central role in the deaths of thousands of migrants travelling across the Atlantic Ocean and the Mediterranean Sea. Strong
xenophobic, reactionary, and nationalist movements have followed
the plethora of so-called migrant crises in Spain, with far-right parties
such as Vox claiming that illegalized immigrants pose a security crisis
for Spanish citizens — discourses that have only been amplified in the
wake of the COVID-19 pandemic.

Top Manta is part of a co-operative project that includes stitching and serigraphy workshops, as well as a physical store in the Raval
neighbourhood of Barcelona, as a means to "enact resistance against
the system that condemns [them] to vending in the streets" (Sindicato
Popular de Vendedores Ambulantes, 2018; our translation).[1] Top
Manta's co-creator Papalae Abdoulaye explains that the brand's logo
simultaneously represents the *cayuco* (boat) in which many migrants
dangerously travel and the blanket that they take to the streets
(Palomo, 2020). Top Manta is a legally registered trademark and cannot be subjected to allegations of intellectual property and piracy
crimes. Top Manta's products are especially popular within activist
and progressive circles in Barcelona. The *sindicato*'s project has also
achieved broader public support from well-known figures and artists,
gathering a significant amount of attention from national and international news outlets.[2] With its creation, *manteros* have challenged
the pejorative connotations surrounding "top manta," a term now re-
appropriated and re-signified into a sign of "solidarity, struggle, and
vindication" (Iborra, 2017; our translation).

With Top Manta, the Popular Union of Traveling Vendors of
Barcelona aims to empower vendors both materially by legally employ-
ing them[3] and symbolically by igniting an anti-racist consciousness in
Spain. As argued by Fernández-Bessa (2019), *manteros'* combination
of unionizing and sensitization campaigns has challenged social stigmatization by positioning themselves as valid political interlocutors.
We additionally suggest that by including recognition and redistribution demands, the *sindicato mantero* is promoting a two-dimensional
conception of justice (Fraser, 2003, p. 9). By historically situating
their condition within the context of racial capitalism, *manteros* have
become producers of a complex social diagnosis that transcends one-
sided approaches. Furthermore, we claim that instead of following a
humanitarian frame, which is profoundly reliant on the idea of crises and emergencies (Ticktin, 2016), *manteros* constantly situate their
social conditions within a larger time narrative that includes the past,

the present, and the future, establishing connections between historical phenomena, ascribing responsibilities, and practicing alternatives.

We take the passages in Top Manta's designs as entry points of
discussion and complement them with the *sindicato*'s epistemic activisms (Medina, 2013), adding our analysis and contextualization with
theoretical and methodological frameworks developed by critical
theorists (Fraser, 2003), decolonial (Grosfoguel, 2016; Lugones, 2006;
Quijano, 2007), and critical race and migration scholars (Lowe, 2015;
Mbembe, 2003; Dawson, 2013). After offering an introduction to the
sindicato and its contextualization within Spanish migration politics,
the chapter's structure follows the migration route that migrants take
from Senegal to Spain.

First, we introduce the notion of racial capitalism and its suitability for exploring how unionized *manteros* situate themselves
historically within transnational and globalized capitalist power relations by locating the causes of migration in a long-standing history
of expropriation. Second, we present the necropolitical power at play
in the crossing of borders and the modalities of resistance that *manteros* exercise in their repudiation of deadly border regimes. Third,
we scrutinize the types of political and economic injustices to which
migrants are exposed once they arrive to Spanish territory. Here, we
pay attention to the intersections between class, race, sex, and citizenship that participate in the criminalization of migrants, which in turn
reveal the logics of contemporary liberal capitalist societies. Finally,
we delve into the re-shaping of public space, political participation,
and conceptions of belonging, in which *manteros* engage. We underline the activation of epistemologies and processes of self-definition
present in the *sindicato*'s coalitional practices, and their broader political incidence in the delineation of alternative socialities.

Before we proceed, we would like to clarify that we are outsiders
to the community of *manteros*. Our research is based on the *sindicato*'s
own media and the interviews that they have provided elsewhere,
though we are also informed by our personal experiences as witnesses
and beneficiaries of white supremacist oppression in Spain. From our
position of academic Anglo/Eurocentric power, we strive to make
our work accountable to illegalized migrants and the epistemologies that they produce. As Spanish citizens, but also as migrants, we
are interpellated by their call to dismantle the hypocrisy of our current border regime. We are aware that the practice of speaking about
and for others can be informed by a desire for mastery and entail a

reinscription of hierarchies, but we also reject a general retreat (Alcoff, 1991). Instead, we acknowledge our aim of contributing to immigrants' emancipatory goals and remain accountable to the effects of our analysis. While we frame our analysis within the context of global capitalist relations, we do not sympathize with solutions that displace the issue to migrants' countries of origin. We believe in the necessity of global economic justice and reparations as much as we defend the inalienable right to migrate.

Context

In October of 2015, the Popular Union of Traveling Vendors formed with the support of the Barcelona networks *Espacio del Inmigrante* (the Immigrant Space) and *Tras la Manta* (Behind the Blanket). The decision to unionize followed the death of Mor Sylla, a Senegalese *mantero* who died on the eleventh of August 2015 in Salou while being raided in his own apartment by *Mossos d'Esquadra* (the autonomous police force of Catalonia) in an operation against the theft of intellectual property associated with the sales of counterfeit goods (Espinosa Zepeda, 2017). The union was thus born out of an urgent necessity to fight the specific forms of discrimination, racism, and police violence targeted at *manteros* in Barcelona.

Street or travelling vendors (*manteros*) are typically referred to as "top manta" for the blanket (*manta*) that they spread out on the sidewalks of the street to sell a variety of clothing, accessories, and luxury brand imitation goods.[4] Their blankets are laced at each corner with strings that form a knot in order to quickly disperse in case of police persecution. *Manteros* are highly surveilled and often expelled from public space by urban authorities (Moffette, 2020).[5] In general, there are various negative stereotypes associated with street vending, including that it damages local commerce, that it is sourced by mafias, or that it has a negative impact on tourists' perceptions of the city (Berrio, 2015).

The progressive mayor of Barcelona, Ada Colau (2015–2023) acknowledged that the top manta problem needed social solutions, not carceral ones. However, three months later (August 2015), a massive police deployment through a joint police operation between Guardia Urbana, Mossos d'Esquadra, and the Port Police against street vendors in the Port Vell of Barcelona took place (Espinosa Zepeda, 2017, p. 68). The Generalitat of Catalunya (the Catalonian government) also produced and distributed a pamphlet in tourist areas titled "Say No!" advising tourists to refrain from illegal vendors, among other things "because it is controlled by mafias and organized by crime networks" (Leach, 2016). Yet, geographers have demonstrated that informal economic practices such as street vending are fluidly interwoven and equally constitutive of market relations (Alford et al., 2019, p. 1087). Most importantly, *manteros* have repeatedly shown, along with a variety of civil society actors, that there are no mafias or trafficking behind top manta; a reality corroborated in a Council of Barcelona report (Ajuntament de Barcelona, 2015).

While street vending is indeed an unauthorized activity in Spain (Moffette, 2020), the social abjection experienced by *manteros* is also related to the fact that many of the vendors are Black African migrants in a mostly white context who have been racialized, illegalized, and criminalized by the Spanish state. *Manteros* reclaim street vending as a rather non-harmful process of self-organization (Cosculluela, 2016; Sierra, 2015) that allows a precarious collective to survive at the margins of national citizenship and waged labour.

While *manteros* in Barcelona unionized formally in 2015, their organization is preceded by longer trajectories of migrant and anti-racist community "weaving" across the Spanish state. The Federation of Immigrant Collectives in Catalonia, a referent in migrant organizing, formed in the nineties to offer a heterogeneous associative space between collectives and individual migrants with the objective of reclaiming citizenship rights for all (Diagne Lo, 2019). The absolute electoral majority of the Conservative Party in 2000, which coincided with the violent racist riots of El Ejido, led to counter-reforms that practically reversed Spain's immigration policy to a "fortress Europe"-oriented 1985 Organic Immigration Act.[6] This shift in policy reinforced a hardline dichotomy of legal/illegal immigration that heavily curtailed the rights of non-citizens by externalizing and militarizing the borders, increasing police surveillance of immigrants, and denying migrants access to essential services (Moffette, 2018).

A *sin papeles* (without papers) nation-wide movement emerged to protest these changes and demand migrants' social and political recognition in the early 2000s. In Barcelona, the group Papeles para todos (Papers for everyone) took centre stage in organizing direct actions such as the sit-in of 1,700 illegalized migrants between the Cathedral of Barcelona and Church Santa María del Pi in 2004 (Toasijé, 2018; Fernández-Bessa, 2019).

A plethora of "scandals" regarding illegalized migrant workers' life (and death) conditions have surfaced in the wake of the COVID-19 pandemic: Temporary agricultural laborers who migrate to Spain on precarious contracts from Morocco and sub-Saharan Africa, like the anti-racist activist Serigne Mamadou (Gabón, 2020), have denounced exploitation, inhumane working conditions, sexual abuse, and a lack of access to health services and housing. A feminized care and domestic labour force, mostly from South American countries, is acutely underpaid, overworked, and subjected to racist and gendered violence, leading spokesperson Judith Espinola of the Active Domestic Service Association to assert that "we [migrant caregivers and domestic workers] sustain life yet remain exploited" (Rius, 2020, our translation). Over the years, it has become evident that the Spanish economy depends on socially unrecognized and state illegalized migrants' essential labor.

In this context, Barcelona's unionized *manteros* have joined other 1,217 organizations to demand *regularización ya* (papers for all) in a nation-wide movement that has advocated for the permanent and unconditional regularization of all migrants, who cannot and should not be seen as simply the victims (or, according to far-right discourses, the victimizers) of a crisis but as resistant subjects within a racist and imperialist immigration paradigm that criminalizes migrants and other working class sectors, pushing them further into precarity (Castán, 2021).

My Dream Was Not to Become a *Mantero*: Denouncing Capitalism's Expropriative Logics

In December 2020, Top Manta released a T-shirt with a message explaining the geopolitical processes that influence the migration of Senegalese origin to Europe. This T-shirt's passage explains how important aspects of Senegalese economy and culture have been disastrously affected by capitalist globalization. The front reads "my dream was not to become a *mantero*" and the back displays the following text:

> Fishing occupies a very important place in Senegal's economy.
> Many sectors made their living from fishing. Among them: young
> fishermen, transporters, and women in the markets. The typical
> Senegalese dish that everyone wants to eat at noon is *thiebou diene*
> or rice with fish. Unfortunately, our corrupt government sold all
> the sea to multinational ships that use blast fishing and harmful

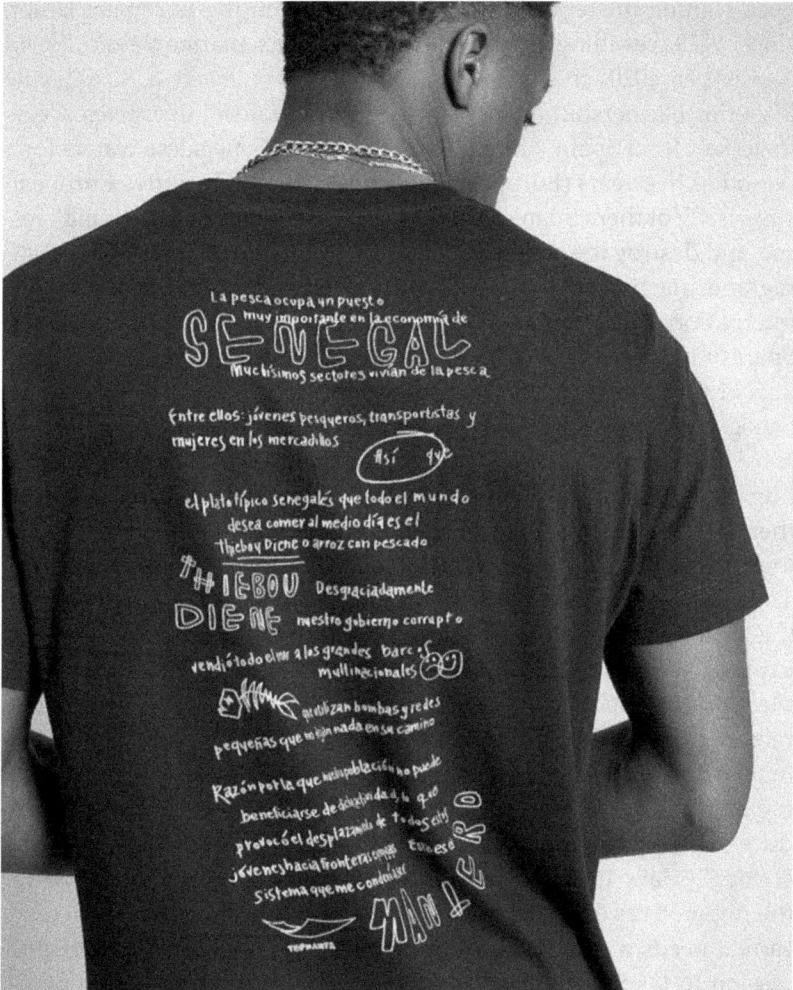

Figure 4.1. "I am a fisherman" T-shirt.

nets that leave nothing behind. The fact that our population can no longer benefit from fishing has provoked the displacement of all these young people towards European frontiers. This is the system that condemned me to be a *mantero*. (Top Manta, 2020; our translation)

To comply with the International Monetary Fund's (IMF) structural adjustment plans to liberalize the Senegalese economy and promote private sector activities (IMF, 1999), the Senegalese government has been signing bilateral fishing agreements with the European Union since 1979, resulting in the plundering of its marine resources. In November 2020, the European Parliament renewed a Sustainable Fisheries Partnership Agreements (SFPAs) protocol that gives access to vessels from Spain, France, and Portugal to Senegalese waters for a period of five years (European Parliament, 2020). Forty-five European vessels, 29 of them Spanish, both overpower Senegalese artisanal vessels and destroy the area's seabed. Apart from the decades of overfishing and inaction by the Senegalese government, there is a growing international fish oils and derivatives industry (which includes the Spanish company Barna) to feed fish farms, pigs, or poultry in markets of the Global North (Joaniquet & Ndiaye, *Mi sueño no es*, 2021). Senegalese locals have not received any compensation.

By denouncing the global economic injustices that push them to migrate, as well as the institutionalized forms of exclusion that keep them at the economic margins of society, *manteros* are identifying the logic behind racial capitalism (Robinson, 1983; Bhattacharyya, 2018). They are indeed showing that both the causes of unemployment and the reasons for migration begin with a process of land and resource expropriation in their country of origin. In *Capital*, Marx uncovered the "hidden abode of production," explaining how, under capitalist relations, rather than through voluntary contracting parts that engage in an equal exchange, the generation of surplus value is secured with the exploitation of wage labour by forcing the working class to produce "more work than the narrow round of its own life wants prescribes" (Marx 1996; p. 314). However, Marx also explained how for the imperatives of accumulation and profit-maximization to succeed, capital needs a prior process of primitive accumulation and dispossession to take place, usually associated with the destruction of the commons, enslavement, colonialism, and imperialism and with the direct use of deception, coercion, and force (Marx, 1996; Lenin, 1999; Federici, 2004; Luxemburg, 2004; Blackburn, 2010). As it has been remarked, it would nonetheless be a mistake to see these phenomena as remnants from the past; instead, we should see the logics of expropriation and dispossession as structurally imbricated within capitalist relations (Harvey, 2004; Dawson, 2016; Singh, 2016; Ince, 2018).

Capitalism hides its systematic dependence on a set of "background conditions"[7] and disavows the fact that "the official 'ex' of exploitation rests on the hidden 'ex' of expropriation" (Fraser & Jaeggi, 2018, p. 47). Behind the notion of expanded, colonial, and/

or racial capitalism, what we have then is a view of capitalism as a productive regime based upon expanding fields of appropriation and dispossession, fed by heterogeneous forms of labour, including wage-labour exploitation, as well as "the settler colonial dispossession of land and removal of Indigenous peoples, the colonial slavery that extracted labor from people to whom it denied human being, and the racialized exploitation of immigrants from around the world" (Lowe, 2015, p. 150).

A consequence of neoliberal changes in transnational employment markets is the production of gender-specific patterns of migration (Collins, 2000; p. 243). In their online blog, the *sindicato* has framed their understanding of migratory patterns within a patriarchal organization of society: "Families in Africa are large and it's the father who is responsible for all the expenses. When you turn eighteen you must take on the role that your father carried for years. It is thus easy to understand why sub-Saharan people risk their life to enter Europe" (Sindicato Popular de Vendedores Ambulantes *Nosotros*, 2016; our translation). The majority of street vendors in Spain are thus "unaccompanied" men (80 percent of them originating from Senegal) who began to arrive from the seventies onward to the Iberian Peninsula in large entries of *cayucos* via the Canary Islands coast (Diagne Lo, 2019; p. 172).

El Cayuco: Challenging Necropolitical Deathscapes

Top Manta's design "*El cayuco*" (the canoe) pays tribute to those who lost their lives at sea, those who made it but were deported upon arrival, and those who survived the border but now face institutional racism, classism, and xenophobia in Spain (Sindicato Popular de Vendedores Ambulantes, 2020). A *cayuco* is a boat made from wood typically used by Senegalese fishermen to work. However, due to the transnational and racial capitalist forces of dispossession mentioned above, *cayucos* have been re-purposed as migration vessels. The words *cayuco* and *patera* generally circulate in Spanish mass media to refer to the various types of boat crafts (often overloaded, small, or too fragile for long open-sea journeys) used by non-EU citizens to reach Europe. *El cayuco* is therefore symbolic of both a lost fisherman profession and the dangerous journey that migrants are forced to take.

To contextualize, in the space of two weeks in early November of 2020, 480 people died during their migratory route from Senegal. The organization Walking Borders reported a total of 2,170 victims

Figure 4.2. *El Cayuco* sweater.

who died in the access routes to the Spanish state in 2020 (Caminando Fronteras, 2020). While COVID-19 exacerbated the forced expulsion of many migrants from their territories, the 2006 "crisis of the *cayucos*" had already seen the entry of more than 31,678 people through the deadly Canary Islands route (ONU Migración, 2020). The crossing through the latter, which can take up to ten or 12 days (Joaniquet & Ndiaye, *El expolio extranjero,* 2021), is directly caused by the increasing militarization and surveillance of safer routes. According to activist Helena Maleno (cited in Sainz, 2020), the deterrence policies imple-mented by European states, which are designed to enrich the arms industries invested in migration control, are responsible for higher mortality rates since people will continue to migrate in search of a better life regardless of border controls.

Part of our interest in the framework of racial capitalism is that it allows not only to underline the centrality of unwaged or dependent forms of labour but also the question of management of populations which are simultaneously "trapped within the capital relation" and made "redundant in relation to capital" (Chen, 2013, n.p.). The lens of racial capitalism is therefore essential to understand how capital-ist institutionalized coercion does not only materialize in the compul-sion of market relations (including labor market relations) but also in the deathly militarization and disciplining of borders and cities. In fact, Gržinić (2017, p. 4-5) links the increasing number of deaths in the Mediterranean—and how they are overlooked by the media— to a much broader shift in the reconceptualization of life and death, "from biopolitical populations to necropolitical deathscapes."[8] If bio-power is the systematic management and optimization of life through the disciplinary regulation of bodies (Foucault, 1988), necropower is the sovereign administration of death (Mbembe, 2003). Importantly, the shift from biopolitics to necropolitics is established along a racial/ colonial classification of the world (Mignolo, 2006; Quijano, 2000). As the *sindicato* has put it, "these are not accidental deaths but the result of a violent model of life that expels us from our lands and, in turn, prohibits us from migrating legally and safely" (Sindicato Popular de Vendedores Ambulantes, *Jugándose la vida,* 2021, n.p.; our translation).

The militarization of borders that administer death at the edges of Europe is legitimized on the grounds of not holding a European passport, visa, or residency permit. The status of being a citizen, and not race per se, is what we currently see instrumentalized in anti-migratory discourse to draw the abyssal line between the zone of being and the zone of non-being, where people are dehumanized and managed by means of perpetual violence systemically, not just in a state of crisis or exception (Grosfoguel, 2016, p. 13). As Chen (2013) has shown, a considerable number of today's "ascriptive racialisa-tion processes" do not unfold straightforwardly as issues of race due to their re-coding as "race-neutral" questions, through expressions such as "illegal immigration" and "urban crime." While the racialized dimension of wage labour (Du Bois, 1999; Roediger, 2007) and the con-stitution of whiteness as property (Harris, 1993) have been extensively studied, the concealment of race when it comes to citizenship, that is, "the transfer of whiteness to the threshold of nationality" (Singh, 2016, p. 4)—has been less thoroughly scrutinized. Nonetheless, if as Alcoff maintains, "whiteness is not an illusion but a historically evolving identity-formation that is produced in diverse locations, while constantly undergoing reinterpretation and contestation" (2015, p. 22), we need to remain alert to the ways in which it might be deployed in the legal dispositif (Foucault, 1980) of citizenship. Following Dawson, we note that the "colonial logic of superior/inferior human includes not only ongoing expropriation and exploitation, but also disposability, and an attenuated extension of citizenship or subject 'rights,' if they are extended at all" (2016, p. 151). At this point, we can begin to grasp the materiality that informs the two-dimensional conception of justice (Fraser, 2003) that we see *manteros* promoting. As a matter of fact, the coming together of questions of recognition and redistribution that *manteros* exhibit in their discourse is based on lived experiences characterized by the profound imbrication of the two.

Arrival: Resisting the Borders Within

Fernández-Bessa (2019, p. 159) has argued that migrant "illegality" in Spain is paradoxically produced "by the demanding requirements set by immigration law (Organic Law 4/ 2020) to obtain and renew residence and labour permits." To opt for a temporary authorization of residence, immigration laws require migrants to hold a criminal record certificate and demonstrate continued permanence in Spain for a minimum of three years.[9] *Manteros* have denounced the law's inconsistency and contradictoriness in obliging migrants to live clandestinely for at least three years without relying on informal labour activities to subsist (Diagne Lo, 2019, p. 179).

Following migrant rights collectives' mobilizations to de-penalize street vending in 2010, the punishment for *manteros* de-escalated from years of prison to lesser sanctioning mechanisms, such as fines and community work. However, with the 2015 approval of the Penal Code Article 274.3 and the Citizen Security Law (also known as "gag law"), street vending has been newly criminalized, further pushing *manteros* into precarity given the need for a criminal record certificate to acquire administrative regularization (Moffette, 2020). Unionized *manteros* have thus concluded that the assemblage of the Immigration Law, the Penal Code, and the Citizen Security Law entraps racialized migrants into a labyrinth of impoverishment, illegality, and criminalization that is practically impossible to break (Sindicato Popular de Vendedores Ambulantes de Barcelona, *Manifiesto por la despenalización*, 2016).[10]

It is worth noting that the persecution and criminalization of migrants in Spain worsened after the imposition of austerity measures following the global economic crash in 2008 (Alford et al., 2019, p. 1087), which created a fertile ground for the appearance of the immigrant figure as a scapegoat. Tellingly, *Mossos d'Esquadra* invested 28,000 hours of work in persecuting *manteros* between 2011 and 2015 (Espinosa Zepeda, 2017). Regarding the death of Mor Sylla, Minister of the Interior of the *Generalitat* Jordi Jané publicly asserted that the persecution of *manteros* was indispensable because "top manta" puts the welfare of Catalonia at risk (Espinosa Zepeda, 2017, p. 68). The designation of *manteros* as criminals seen in this kind of "security" discourse problematically reinforces a boundary between "us" (law-abiding Catalonians) and "them" (migrant outlaws) to justify the latter's (dis)placement under surveillance, punishment, and containment (Mopas & Moore, 2012). Such criminalizing discourses present the so-called illegal immigrant as a self-inflicted outcome of lawbreaking rather than as the product of the law itself (Cacho, 2012).

The labyrinth of impoverishment, illegality, and criminalization denounced by *manteros* requires a continuous emphasis on what scholars working at the intersections between race and capitalism have theorized as the "ontological distinction between superior and inferior humans—codified as race" necessary to justify "slavery, colonialism, the theft of lands in the Americas, and genocide" (Dawson, 2016, p. 147).[11] Critical race and decolonial scholars have shown that the division between racialized superior and inferior human beings, human/subhuman, civilized/uncivilized, first-world/third-world subjects and/or full-citizens/second-class citizens mediates economic relations more broadly: Those deemed superior are allowed to "sell their labor power and compete within markets," while those seen as inferior become "disposable, discriminated against, and ultimately either eliminated or superexploited" (Dawson, 2016, p. 148).

The entanglement between racial classification and capital accumulation calls us to include but also move beyond the wage relationship in the analysis of capitalist societies. In its more comprehensive iteration, Marx's idea that "capital ceases to be capital without wage labor" is then re-articulated into "capital ceases to be capital without the ongoing differentiation of free labor and slavery, waged labor and unpaid labor" (Singh, 2016, p. 35). The differentiation between waged and unwaged labor, which is usually (though not always) racialized, ideologically reinforces capitalism and provides the possibility of consistently securing, through economic and extra-economic processes, unpaid labour that is then propelled into the circuit of capital.[12] The "confiscation plus conscription into accumulation" sequence is thus essential to understand that expropriated racialized labour does not remain outside the cycle of capital valorization, but gets integrated into it (Fraser & Jaeggi, 2018, p. 46). Ultimately, these economic/status social divisions materialize in the co-constitution of the "free exploitable citizen-worker" and the "dependent expropriable subject," a distinction that "correlates roughly but unmistakably with the color line" (Fraser & Jaeggi, 2018, p. 43).

By connecting migrants' economic precarity to their illegalization, we are hoping to expose their profound intertwinement, which has specific implications for *manteros*. *Manteros'* trade unionism is responding to the realities of a "two-dimensionally subordinated group," suffering "both maldistribution and misrecognition in forms where neither of these injustices is an indirect effect of the other, but where both are primary and co-original" (Fraser, 2003, p. 19). Fraser refers to racialized immigrants as an example of this two-dimensional social division: on one side, they undergo racially specific forms of maldistribution produced by capitalism, such as higher rates of unemployment and poverty or an over-representation in low-paying menial jobs; on the other, they are deemed inferior due to institutionalized cultural patterns that privilege whiteness (Fraser, 2003, p. 23).

Consequently, what we have is not economic versus cultural problems, but *both* a distributive injustice and a status subordination. Ultimately, what matters in terms of justice is that if social arrangements institutionalize economic disparities and systematically subject individuals to material deprivations, while impeding them to achieve equal social status, then they frustrate the possibility for those subjects to partake in political deliberations in equal terms. Trade unionism in this context emerges as a means to seek emancipation not only from labour precarity and exploitation, but also from "the relations of gender and interethnic domination in the public and private spheres" (Mélis, 2010, p. 20; our translation). We further elaborate how unionized *manteros* tackle both realms in the next section of this chapter.

In short, the *sindicato mantero* is adding nuance to discourses on migration by historically situating their entrapment within a cycle of impoverishment caused by global capitalism *and* criminalization operationalized by Spain's legal apparatus. While the establishment of Top Manta allows *manteros* to contribute "legally" to production networks, on an epistemic level, unionized vendors are doing much more. By helping those that hold Spanish citizenship understand that surviving as a migrant pushed into precarity by the state should not be criminalized, the *sindicato* is substantially correcting epistemic distortions (Medina, 2013) that circulate in the Spanish imaginary about street vending.[13]

Re-shaping the City: Weaving Networks of Solidarity and Reframing Political Belonging

Due to their lived experiences as illegalized African migrants, *manteros* have developed an intricate understanding of the workings of a racial/colonial matrix (Mignolo, 2006) operating at the heart of border regimes.[14] Union members remember the colonial structures sustaining "necropolitical deathscapes" (Gržinić, 2017) and challenge the complacent (Spanish or Eurocentric) cognitive-affective processes that legitimize such violence. For instance, in their response to the 2017 Catalan independence referendum, the *sindicato* voiced their support for the independence movement from a highly vigilant and critical standpoint. Performing what hooks (2014, p. 116) calls "the oppositional gaze," wherein Black people interrogate the colonizing gaze but also look back in an act of resistance, they stated:

> We are attentive to everything that is happening and, even though no one has invited us to be part of this historic moment, we migrants have invited ourselves. We are used to perceptions of us as unknowing non-citizens, who do not vote and do not know about politics, but they are wrong. We have been fighting and resisting for years against this colonial and racist Spanish government. (Sindicato de Vendedores Ambulantes de Barcelona, 2017; our translation)

In the face of an erasure or "forgetting" of the global colonial processes that make migrants "illegal" and define citizenship as the new abyssal line that can sovereignly "make die" (Gržinić, 2017), *manteros* remember and gaze back. Informed by their lived understanding of migratory phenomena, they point at the hypocrisies of a white supremacist border regime. They defy cycles of impoverishment and criminalization by making visible systemic processes of illegalization. In demanding a profound transformation of both objective and intersubjective relations, *manteros* deploy a richly informed notion of social justice, which has the enablement and fostering of new forms of political participation as one of its most notable purposes (Fraser, 2003, p. 30). Nonetheless, *manteros* do not merely demand for such injustices to be addressed by others. They actively engage in the social and political reconfiguration of the society in which they live. In line with this, we would like to advance a final reflection on the *sindicato*'s reshaping of both the city's and the country's political boundaries.

Apart from the establishment of their label Top Manta, which employs *manteros* legally, the union promotes "community-based" forms of agency (Alford et al., 2019, p. 1095) that amplify *manteros*' voices in Spanish society via the organization of workshops for migrants that offer legal advice and provide tools of survival, as well as interviews and open discussions where the *sindicato* makes visible migrant concerns and promotes anti-racism.[15] They also actively use their platforms to denounce police violence, organize anti-racist direct-actions, and debunk false stereotypes and criminal accusations by communication media. For example, in March 2021, the national public TV series *Servir y Proteger* (Serve and Protect) portrayed a police interrogation with a *mantero* "confessing" that street vending is used to finance jihad, to which the union responded that such representations disapprovingly a) reinforce anti-Black, Islamophobic, violent, and fanatical stereotypes of people who take up *mantero* activity as a means of survival, and b) fail to represent "truthful information about its citizens" and foster conviviality.[16]

Rather than expecting institutional solutions from above, *manteros*' strength comes from below, where they develop networks of solidarity with other civil society collectives such as SOS Racism (an anti-racist action group), Putas Indignadas (a collective defending sex worker rights), and Yayoflautas (an organized group of senior citizens that defend retirement pensions and the welfare state) (Iborra, 2017). In addition, while some scholars have noted a certain division between racialized and illegalized migrants on one hand and the black diaspora and Afro-Spanish people on the other (Toasijé, 2018; Diagne Lo, 2019), the *sindicato* has carefully bridged anti-racist struggles as well as feminist activisms with migrant-right issues, without relegating the former to the latter. Coalitional work is fundamental for enacting decolonial resistance and forming "alternative socialities" (Lugones, 2010, p. 748).[17] And, as Taylor maintains, it is indeed "within those struggles for the basic rights of existence that people learn how to struggle, how to strategize, and build movements and organizations" (2016, p. 216). The formation of these solidarity networks has thus reshaped *manteros'* relationship to the city and vice versa.

During the first wave of COVID-19, the *sindicato* turned their Top Manta store into a stitching workshop to make gowns and surgical masks for Catalonian hospitals (Press, 2020). With the collaboration of neighbors and local associations, the union also created a food bank and distributed necessities to more than 300 migrants (Efe, 2020). As it has been mentioned, the Popular Union of Traveling Vendors of Barcelona has also played a leading role in the *Regularización Ya* (Papers for All) movement that has unfolded in the wake of the COVID-19 pandemic and its consequent migratory "scandals." The platform is comprised of a remarkable coalition of 1,218 organizations, ranging from feminist assemblies to multicultural, Muslim, ecologist, animal rights, queer rights, and anti-capitalist organizations, as well as a plethora of migrant and anti-racist collectives. *Regularización Ya* has demonstrated that the only thing preventing the Spanish government from granting migrants legal residence permits is political will, not European agreements. But, while their non-legislative motion for universal regularization was denied by a (nonetheless divided) Spanish government, the Status for All movement asserts that it will continue to "embark on a recomposition of society that centers the preservation of life, the defense of common good, social justice and solidarity as principles for a national political agreement" (Regularización Ya, 2021, n.p.; our translation).[18]

We would like to suggest that the *sindicato mantero* is reframing the conversation around political belonging through their participation in the *Regularizacion Ya* campaign and their construction of a collective space of identification and action. According to McNevin, the idea of political belonging weaves together notions of political community, political identity, and political practice, ultimately framing "how one is positioned with respect to others and the agency one enjoys in that context" (2006, p. 135). The importance of such belonging for the (possibility of) protection of one's basic human rights has been extensively studied, with Hannah Arendt (1976) as one of the first and fiercest critics of those who appealed to an abstract humanity for rights' safeguard. Speaking from the perspective of the refugee,

Arendt's poignant discovery was that one loses human rights at very moment one becomes "a human being in general" (1976, p. 302), the world apparently finding "nothing sacred in the abstract nakedness of being human" (1976, p. 299). Practices of belonging are thus fundamental to the extent that losing one's place results not only in the destruction of one's home but, even more importantly, in the elimination of the social texture in which one's opinions are significant and one's actions are effective (1976, p. 296). For that reason, according to Arendt, the most elementary of rights is the right to have rights, a basic condition to establish for ourselves "a distinct place in the world" (1976, p. 293).

In that sense, it is worth noting that *manteros* do not usually deploy the language of a shared human condition in their demands. Rather, they make themselves apparent in the public sphere through references to their "walking together" (Ande Dem, 2021), their cultural heritage, their networks of solidarity, and to the fact that they live and work in Spain, thus forming part of and shaping Spanish society. Indeed, the *sindicato* offers material improvements in *manteros'* lives as much as it sustains the formation of affective webs. In his activist involvement with the *sindicato*, Espinosa Zepeda (2017) found that *manteros'* common belonging to a Wolof ethnic group and Sufi spirituality greatly informed the "weaving" of solidarity networks that extend both to their family members in Senegal and to each other in Barcelona, where "godfathers" (*diatungui*) take direct responsibility to support newly arrived migrants (*dajar*). In such a way, "the fight for survival and adaptation in a new context is added to the experience of remaining connected in active ways to the site of origin" (Espinosa Zepeda, 2017, p. 72; our translation). Therefore, through their practices, the *sindicato mantero* manages to work within the limits imposed by the Westphalian state system and beyond them, effectively challenging the idea of belonging as a "fixed relationship between state, citizen and territory" (McNevin, 2006, p. 136). Although their political belonging lacks the sanction of the Spanish state, *manteros* nonetheless succeed in reconfiguring the traditional and naturalized borders of citizenship. Furthermore, their discourse does not invoke a humanitarian sensibility and its characteristic "narrow emotional constellation" is dependent on claims of innocence and purity (Ticktin, 2016, p. 256). If, for Arendt, innocence was the mark of the rightless but also "the seal of their loss of political status" (1976, p. 295), in their refusal of such language, *manteros* can be seen as repudiating the hierarchies of humanity implicit in humanitarian approaches (Fassin, 2007). However, while avoiding the perils of an abstract universality and advocating respect for difference, *manteros* also seem to forgo a cultural relativism that would "preclude asking how we, living in this privileged and powerful part of the world, might examine our own responsibilities for the situations in which others in distant places have found themselves" (Abu-Lughod, 2002, p. 189).

Conclusion

In this chapter, we have argued that the *sindicato mantero* provides an active proof that recognition and redistribution must be thought of and practiced together for subjects to belong to their communities in fair terms. *Manteros'* anti-racist praxis consequently combines a profound questioning of the structural inequalities produced by global and racial capitalism with a far-reaching rejection of the racist institutions and practices that condemn them to social, economic, and political exclusion, and, as we have seen in the process of border crossing, to death. In their most recent *Ande Dem* (Walking Together) campaign, in which they claim that "it's not about just doing it" but about "doing it right," the normative relevance of their social analysis becomes explicit as they delineate five central tenets guiding their interventions: collectivity, non-exploitation, diversity, antiracism, and social justice (Ande Dem, 2021).

Manteros therefore expose the ways in which racial differentiation is an integral part of capitalism's ongoing expansion and, by self-organizing in economic terms, they also attempt to challenge the market's "predatory inclusion," that is, one that integrates subjects "but on more expensive and comparatively unequal terms" (Taylor, 2019, p. 5). In the process, *manteros* have importantly resignified pejorative connotations behind "top manta," showing that "all labor has dignity," as Martin Luther King Jr. (2012) eloquently put it.

In addition, the *sindicato* challenges colonial imaginaries embedded in Spanish society, pointing to their role in sustaining a deathly border regime, and actively superseding the language of legal integration in ways that reshape the boundaries of political belonging. Certainly, status and citizenship remain unwaivable demands and existential aspirations, and they must be granted by the Spanish state. It is also essential to challenge the ways in which borders, but also

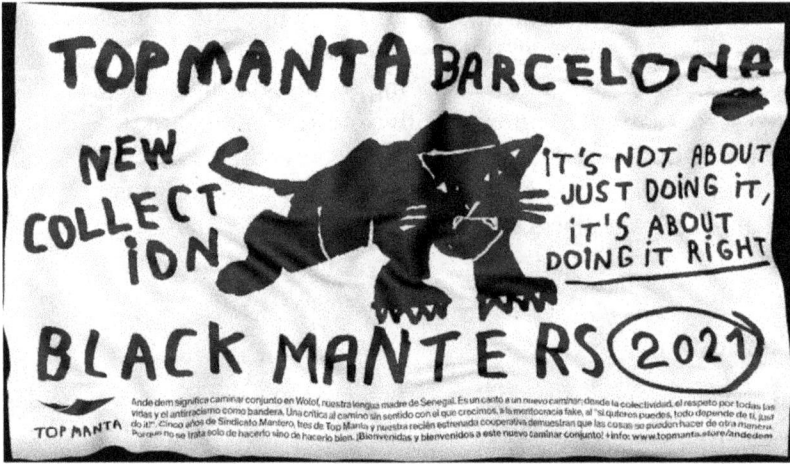

Figure 4.3. "It's not about just doing it, it's about doing it right."

access to citizenship, reproduce race and class exclusions (Ypi, 2018). Yet, *manteros'* subversion resides precisely in that they go much further than that: Their political practice shows that they remain vigilant about the intrinsic limits of legal equality, which, while necessary, does not guarantee complete liberation from oppression. As the evidence shows, racialized subjects continue to "find themselves subject to more intensive exploitation and restrictive controls," in spite of attaining formal equality (Glenn, 2002, p. 92). As it happens, even though political emancipation is "a big step forward" in our existing societies, it is certainly not the "last form of general human emancipation" (Marx, 1992, p. 221). By avoiding this reduction, the *sindicato mantero* participates in the construction of a "multidimensional conception of political belonging" (McNevin, 2006, p. 136) while simultaneously reinvigorating citizenship "in as much as it is not an institution or a statute but a collective practice" (Balibar, 2000, p. 42 cited in McNevin, 2006, p. 147). If the "calamity of the rightless" is that "they no longer belong to any community whatsoever" (Arendt, 1976, p. 295), then the *sindicato mantero* emerges precisely as a producer of rights, to the extent that it produces the conditions of possibility of a thriving community.

What is more, when *manteros* claim that they did not come "only in search of a dignified life for [them] and for [theirs]," but "to change the rules of the game and to make them fairer for all" (Sindicato Mantero de Barcelona, 2021, 1:12) they actively inscribe themselves within the community, a community that is not responding to the citizen/non-citizen binary. As a result, *manteros* prefigure "alternative horizons that may be emerging organically within struggles that refuse the citizen/migrant divide as a basis for imagining collective political futures" (McNevin, 2020). By engaging in a vigorous reshaping of the city's economic, social, and political life, they exhibit that "becoming citizens does not mark the endpoint of struggle or the point at which the contested nature of political belonging is settled" (McNevin, 2020). In sum, *manteros* can be seen as practicing what Tomba—in a reference to the historical struggles of women, mulattos, Blacks, and the poor—has named "insurgent universality," an act "structured around the gap between juridical citizenship and the practice of citizenship," by which individuals acting in common "put into question the hierarchical organization of the social fabric" (2019, p. 41). In particular, the notion of insurgent universality refuses to position the oppressed "in a status of victimhood that requires protection from above" and transforms passive victims into "active agents of a politics that demands freedom for everyone" (Haider, 2018, p. 109). Finally, in the importance that they ascribe to coalition building, *manteros* acknowledge that "while it is true that when Black people get free, everyone gets free, Black people [...] cannot 'get free' alone," reminding us that to the extent that "Black liberation is bound up with the project of human liberation and social transformation" (Taylor, 2016, p. 194), we *all* hold responsibility towards collective emancipation.

Acknowledgements

The Top Manta images in this chapter are reproduced with permission from the Popular Union of Traveling Vendors of Barcelona.

Notes

1. Top Manta is registered as a non-for-profit association under the name Associació Popular de Venedors Ambulants de Barcelona (Popular Association of Street Vendors of Barcelona). As of the second of June of 2021, it is also a co-operative that stands for "a horizontal space based on a social economy of solidarity" (Ande Dem, 2021, n.p.).
2. See for example "De Bad Gyal a Terribas: Así es como un grupo de famosos catalanes apoya a los manteros," *El Nacional* (2019); "Pedro Almodóvar elige en Venecia una mascarilla de Top Manta," *El País* (2020); "Top Manta: Spain's street sellers taking on the fashion world," *Al Jazeera* (2020); and "Barcelona street sellers take on Nike with own-brand trainers," *The Guardian* (2021).

3. In her theoretical typology of border activism, Fernández-Bessa (2019) situates unionized *manteros'* work within "de facto citizen struggles," whereby repertoires of contention against Spain's border regime are based on their positionality as workers, rather than on their migrant subjectivity.

4. We prefer referring to vendors as *manteros*, since the latter term more accurately signifies the practice of relying on the blanket to work.

5. David Moffette (2020) has analyzed the multilayered, complex ways in which immigrant street vendors are governed at the juncture of various levels: At a chiefly municipal law level enforced by the Guàrdia Urbana to repress bylaw violations for sales without proper licensing; at a criminal law level by the Catalan Mossos d'Esquadra to prosecute sales of counterfeit goods, as well as the National Police in order to prevent the import of counterfeit merchandise; and third, at an immigration law level to apply the Alien Act by the National Police. While these jurisdictional powers operate under different regimes, Moffette (2020, p. 266) has shown how they intersect to create a "municipal form of spatial borderwork," given that municipal bylaws not only target specific collectives of non-citizens, but also collaborate with the National Police for the purpose of immigration enforcement.

6. In early February of 2000, following the murder of two Spanish farmers by a Moroccan employee and a Spanish woman by a Moroccan individual, an extremely violent outbreak of racist riots directed towards Moroccan and Algerian migrant and agricultural workers unfolded in the Andalusian municipality of El Ejido, a town reliant on agricultural economy and migrant labor. The riots lasted for two days and two nights and have been described as one of the worst episodes of racism in recent Spanish history.

7. Fraser identifies social reproduction, expropriated racialized labor, nature and political power as capitalism's background conditions (see Fraser, 2014, 2016, 2018).

8. As a result of the increasing number of people taking the Canary Islands migration route, the Atlantic Ocean is also becoming a site of death.

9. In Spain, "illegal" migrants who have registered in the municipal register (Padrón Municipal) can apply for regularization via *arraigo* (entrenchment) after three years given that they provide a criminal record certificate, an employment contract, and a social integration report by the town council of residence. Migrants across the Spanish state have also denounced the administrative violence involved in the process to obtain regularization, such as the lack of appointments available to provide documentation.

10. Filigrana (2020) has poignantly argued that irregular migrants, similarly to the ways in which Romani people were criminalized in sixteenth-century legislation in Spain, are punished for *being* out of place in the national white body politic (racialized, illegalized, impoverished, unemployed, or employed beyond the parameters of formal labour) rather than for committing a crime. Espinoza Zepeda (2017) has drawn parallels between *manteros* and the white Spanish working-class "ragmen" in the Republican Barcelona of 1930, who were expelled from public space on similar grounds of preserving the image of a middle-upper-class body politic. However, the punishment for being a racialized illegal migrant trying to survive (Internment Centers for Immigrants, prison, deportation, police violence, and surveillance) is exceptional and differentiated from the one inflicted on the non-racialized national population (Filigrana, 2020, p. 41), in the sense that violence is considered an exception (not the norm) for citizens in democratic states (Grosfoguel, 2016).

11. For an analysis of how the relation between race and capital has varied, constituting differentiated "regimes of racialized accumulation," see Fraser (2018).
12. Appropriation is embodied, according to Singh, "in the figures of the slave, the migrant worker, the household worker, the chronically unemployed, and the like" (2016, p. 40), which are many times racialized but not always.
13. José Medina argues that when racialized images of the oppressed circulate in the social body, an epistemic distortion is produced and the so-called racial others are no longer perceived in their own identity, but as the effect of a white "boomerang perception." White people perceive the racialized other only through the image they created, projected onto the other and perceived back (2013, p. 192).
14. The union stated: "We have never, ever achieved independence in most African governments. From the era of slavery until now, the continent has been subjugated under Western rule. History repeats itself, but in different ways—that's what our experiences have taught us as we inhabit sites of slavery, territorial occupation, and economic capitalist colonization" (Sindicato Popular de Vendedores Ambulantes, 2017; our translation).
15. Unionized *manteros* have held public conversations tackling the struggles that illegalized migrants face with various Spanish intellectuals, artists, and activists. These conversations were widely followed in social media platforms such as Instagram. For example, in her interview with Top Manta spokesperson Aziz Faye, urban singer Bad Gyal compelled her followers (793,000 on Instagram at the time) to be informed about the highly precarious and unjust process that racialized working-class migrants go through in Spain (interview available in Casa Nostra, Casa Vostra, 2020).
16. In a social media post, the union stated: "This absolutely false statement contributes to creating a violent and fanatical image of people who are forced to uptake street vending as a means of survival because of the Immigration Law of the Spanish state that prohibits us from working legally. Not only do we have nothing to do with jihad, but we are tired of explaining that there is no one exercising power above us. We *manteros* organize ourselves, we help each other, we buy the products we sell in legal stores in Barcelona's industrial areas and with what we earn we survive until our papers arrive, so we can have access to decent employment with basic rights" (Sindicato Popular de Vendedores Ambulantes Queremos denunciar la serie Servir y Proteger, 2021, n.p.; our translation).
17. It has already been noted that Barcelona's unionized *manteros* have accounted for patriarchal social structures in their analysis of Senegalese migration to Spain. We wish to add that the union has consistently displayed the usage of gender inclusive language in their communications, signalling an alignment with feminist struggles within Spain's linguistic, cultural, and political context.
18, At the time of writing, the Spanish government is composed by the Spanish Socialist Workers' Party, which does not support the regularization of all migrants, in coalition with Unidas Podemos, which does.

References

Abu-Lughod, L. (2002). Do Muslim women really need saving? Anthropological reflections on cultural relativism and its others. *American Anthropologist, 104*(3), 783–790.

Ajuntament de Barcelona (2015). Estratègia d'inclusió per a persones que exerceixen la venda irregular al carrer a Barcelona. *City Council of Barcelona.*

https://bcnroc.ajuntament.barcelona.cat/jspui/bitstream/11703/86531/3/
estrategiavendairregular.pdf

Alcoff, L. M. (1991). The problem of speaking for others. *Cultural Critique*, (20), 5–32.

Alcoff, L. M. (2015). *The Future of whiteness*. Polity Press.

Alford, M., Kothari, U., & Pottinger, L. (2019). Re-articulating labour in global production networks: The case of street traders in Barcelona. *Environment and Planning D: Society and Space*, 37(6), 1081–1099.

Ande Dem (2021). Sobre Top Manta. June 3, 2021. https://topmanta.store/andedem/about/

Arendt, H. (1976). *The Origins of totalitarianism*. Harcourt.

Azarmandi, M. (2018). Los límites racistas del antirracismo moral español. *El Salto Diario*. April 12, 2018. https://www.elsaltodiario.com/1492/los-limites-racistas-del-antirracismo-moral-espanol

Berrio, A. G. (2015). Top Manta: De la estigmatización a las soluciones. *El Diario*. September 5, 2015. https://www.eldiario.es/catalunya/opinions/top-manta-estigmatizacion-soluciones_132_2493498.html

Bhattacharyya, G. (2018). *Rethinking racial capitalism: Questions of reproduction and survival*. Rowman & Littlefield International.

Blackburn, R. (1997). *The making of new world slavery: From the baroque to the modern 1492 – 1800*. Verso.

Bosniak, L. (2006). *The citizen and the alien: Dilemmas of contemporary membership*. Princeton University Press.

Burgen, S. (2021, June 9). Barcelona street sellers take on Nike with own-brand trainers. *The Guardian*. https://www.theguardian.com/global-development/2021/jun/09/barcelona-street-sellers-take-on-nike-with-top-manta-own-brand-trainers

Cacho, L. M. (2012). *Social death: Racialized rightlessness and the criminalization of the unprotected*. NYU Press.

Caminando Frontera (2020). Monitoreo del Derecho a la Vida año 2020. https://caminandofronteras.org/monitoreo/monitereo-del-derecho-a-la-vida-ano-2020/

Casa Nostra, Casa Vostra (2020, May 28). Bad Gyal + Aziz Faye (Top Manta) [Video]. YouTube. https://www.youtube.com/watch?v=LwoihaEP_Og&ab_channel=CasaNostra%2CCasaVostra

Castán, J. (2021, April 13). Un año de lucha por la regularización de las migrantes, un año sin respuestas del Gobierno "progresista." *La Izquierda Diario*. http://www.izquierdadiario.es/Un-ano-de-lucha-por-la-regularizacion-de-las-migrantes-un-ano-sin-respuestas-del-Gobierno

Chris, C. (2013). The limit point of capitalist equality: Notes toward an abolitionist antiracism." *Endnotes* 3.

Collins, P. H. (2000). *Black feminist thought: Knowledge, consciousness, and the politics of empowerment* (2nd ed.). Routledge.

Cosculluela, F. (2016, June 5). La Mina del "Top Manta." *El Periódico*. https://www.elperiodico.com/es/sociedad/20160605/badalona-sud-poligono-abastece-manteros-articulos-top-manta-5179330

Dawson, M. C. (2016). Hidden in plain sight: A note on legitimation crises and the racial order." *Critical Historical Studies, 3*(1), 143–161.

Diagne Lo, M. (2019). Más de tres décadas de la ley de extranjería: Los Manteros como principales víctimas. In *Migraciones y Población Africana en España: Historias, relatos y prácticas de resistencia.* Editorial Universidad de Granada.

Du Bois, W. E. B. (1999). *Black reconstruction in America 1860–1880.* Simon & Schuster.

Efe (2020, March 25). Un banco de alimentos creado para manteros ha ayudado a 300 personas. *El Periódico.* https://www.elperiodico.com/es/sociedad/20200325/banco-alimentos-manteros-coronavirus-7905267

El Nacional (2019, December 16). De Bad Gyal a Terribas: así es como un grupo de famosos catalanes apoya a los manteros. https://www.elnacional.cat/enblau/es/television/loteria-mantera-famosos-catalanes_452106_102.html

El País (2020, September 4). Pedro Almodóvar elige en Venecia una mascarilla de Top Manta, la marca de Barcelona que lucha por el futuro de los manteros. https://smoda.elpais.com/celebrities/vips/pedro-almodovar-mascarilla-top-manta-venecia/

Espinosa Zepeda, H. (2017). El Mercadillo Rebelde de Barcelona. Prácticas Antidisciplinarias en la Ciudad Mercancía. *Quaderns de l'Institut Catala d'Antropologi, 22*(1), 67–87.

European Parliament (2020). Parliament backs the renewed fisheries partnership with Senegal. https://www.europarl.europa.eu/news/en/pressroom/20201111IPR91303/parliament-backs-the-renewed-fisheries-partnership-with-senegal

Fassin, D. (2007). Humanitarianism as a politics of life. *Public Culture, 19*(3), 499–520.

Federici, S. (2004). *Caliban and the witch: Women, the body and primitive accumulation.* Autonomedia.

Fernández-Bessa, C. (2019). A theoretical typology of border activism: From the streets to the council. *Theoretical Criminology, 23*(2), 156–174.

Filigrana, P. (2020). *El Pueblo gitano contra el sistema-mundo: Reflexiones desde una militancia feminista y anticapitalista.* Akal.

Foucault, M. (1977). *Power/knowledge: Selected interviews and other writings.* Pantheon Books.

Foucault, M. (1988). *The History of sexuality.* Vintage Books.

Fraser, N. (2014). Behind Marx's hidden abode. For an expanded conception of capitalism. *New Left Review, 86,* 55–72.

Fraser, N. (2016). Is capitalism necessarily racist? *Proceedings & Addresses of the American Philosophical Association, 92*, 21–42.

Fraser, N., & Honneth, A. (2003). *Redistribution or recognition: A political-philosophical exchange.* Verso.

Fraser, N., & Jaeggi, R. (2018). *Capitalism. A conversation in critical theory.* Polity Press.

Gabón, A. (2020, May 8). Serigne Mamadou: "Trabajamos doce horas por 25 euros." *El Salto Diario.* https://www.elsaltodiario.com/temporeros/serigne-mamadou-trabajamos-doce-horas-por-25-euros.

Glenn, E. N. (2002). *Unequal freedom: How race and gender shaped American citizenship and labor.* Harvard University Press.

Grosfoguel, R. (2016). What is racism? *Journal of World-Systems Research, 22*(1), 9–15.

Gržinić, M. (2017). Political agency: The subject and the citizen in the time of neoliberal global capitalism. *AM Journal of Art and Media Studies,* (14), 1–11.

Haider, A. (2018). *Mistaken identity: Race and class in the age of Trump.* Verso.

Harvey, D. (2004). The "New" imperialism: Accumulation by dispossession. *Socialist Register, 40*, 63–87.

hooks, b. (2014). *Black looks: Race and representation.* Routledge.

Iborra, Y. S. (2017, July 5). Camisetas y zapatillas 'Top manta:' Los vendedores ambulantes de Barcelona crean su propia marca. *El Diario.* https://www.eldiario.es/catalunya/barcelona/top-vendedores-ambulantes-barcelona-comercial_1_3296598.html

International Monetary Fund (IMF) (1999). Senegal: Enhanced structural adjustment facility economic and financial policy framework paper (1999–2001). *Policy Framework Papers.* https://www.imf.org/external/np/pfp/1999/senegal/

Ince, O. U. (2018). Between equal rights: Primitive accumulation and capital's violence. *Political Theory, 46*(6), 885–914.

Joaniquet, M., & Ndiaye, I. (2021, February 22). Mi sueño no es ser mantero: Soy pescador. *Público.* https://blogs.publico.es/conmde/2021/02/22/mantero-pesca-senegal/

Joaniquet, M., & Ndaye, I. (2021, April 2). El expolio extranjero en Senegal nos fuerza a migrar: Por eso estamos aquí. *Catalunya Plural.* https://catalunyaplural.cat/es/el-expolio-extranjero-en-senegal-nos-fuerza-a-migrar-por-eso-estamos-aqui/

Keeley, G. (2020, June 1). Top Manta: Spain's street sellers taking on the fashion world. *Al Jazeera.* https://www.aljazeera.com/economy/2020/1/2/top-manta-spains-street-sellers-taking-on-the-fashion-world

King, M. L. (2012). *All labor has dignity* (M. K. Honey, Ed.). Penguin Books.

Leach, S. L. (2016, November 13). *Barcelona's illegal street vendors form union to defend their rights.* Medium. https://medium.com/cities-the-future/

barcelonas-illegal-street-vendors-form-union-to-defend-their-rights-4b4d83aafee8

Lenin, V. (1999). *Imperialism: The highest stage of capitalism.* Resistance Books.

Lowe, L. (2015). *The Intimacies of four continents.* Duke University Press.

Lugones, M. (2006). Heterosexualism and the colonial/Modern gender system. *Hypatia, 22*(1), 186–209.

Lugones, M. (2010). Toward a decolonial feminism. *Hypatia, 25*(4), 742–759.

Luxemburg, R. (2004). *The Rosa Luxemburg reader.* Monthly Review Press.

Marx, K. (1992). *Early writings.* Penguin Books.

Marx, K. (1996). *Capital.* Volume 1. Penguin Books.

Mbembe, A. (2003). Necropolitics. *Public Culture,* 30.

McNevin, A. (2006). Political belonging in a neoliberal era: The struggle of the sans-papiers. *Citizenship Studies, 10*(2), 135–151.

McNevin, A. (2020). Time and the figure of the citizen. *International Journal of Politics, Culture, and Society,* 33, 545–559.

Medina, J. (2013). *The epistemology of resistance: Gender and racial oppression, epistemic injustice, and resistant imaginations.* Oxford University Press.

Mélis, C. (2010). "Des syndicalistes comme les autres ?" L'expérience syndicale de migrantes et de filles d'immigrés d'Afrique du Nord et subsaharienne. *L'Homme la Société,* 176–177(2), 131–149.

Mignolo, W. (2006). The (Re) configuration of the racial imperial/colonial matrix. *Human Architecture: Journal of the Sociology of Self- Knowledge,* 5(1), 17.

Moffette, D. (2018). *Governing irregular migration: Bordering culture, labour, and security in Spain.* UBC Press.

Moffette, D. (2020). The jurisdictional games of immigration policing: Barcelona's fight against unauthorized street vending. *Theoretical Criminology, 24*(2), 258–75.

Mopas, M., & Moore, D. (2012). Talking heads and bleeding hearts: Newsmaking, emotion and public criminology in the wake of a sexual assault." *Critical Criminology, 20*(2), 183–196.

ONU Migración (2020, February 15). Tras un fatal naufragio, la OIM responde con protección y asistencia para migrantes en la zona norte de Mauritania. https://www.iom.int/es/news/tras-un-fatal-naufragio-la-oim-responde-con-proteccion-y-asistencia-para-migrantes-en-la-zona

Palomo, R. (2020, March 6). We are illegal people with legal clothing. *El País.* https://english.elpais.com/society/2020-03-06/we-are-illegal-people-with-legal-clothing.html

Press, E. (2020, March 27). Los manteros de Barcelona convierten su tienda en un taller de batas y mascarillas. *La Vanguardia.* https://www.lavanguardia.com/local/barcelona/20200327/48115935358/manteros-barcelona-tienda-taller-batas-mascarillas.html

Quijano, A. (2000). Coloniality of power and Eurocentrism in Latin America. *International Sociology, 15*(2), 215–232.

Quijano, A. (2007). Coloniality and modernity/rationality. *Cultural Studies, 21*(2–3), 168–178.

Regularización Ya. (2021, March 15). Inicio. https://regularizacionya.com/

Rius, N. (2020, February 1). Empleadas domésticas se reúnen con el Relator de Pobreza de la ONU: "Sostenemos la vida de los demás pero seguimos explotadas." *El Diario.* https://www.eldiario.es/desalambre/empleadas-relator-pobreza-onu-sostenemos_1_1052709.html

Robinson, C. J. (1983). *Black Marxism: The making of the black radical tradition.* The University of North Carolina Press.

Roediger, D. R. (2007). *The Wages of whiteness: Race and the making of the American working class.* Verso.

Rowe, A. C. (2008). Be longing: Towards a feminist politics of relation. In *Power lines: On the subject of feminist alliances.* Duke University Press.

Sainz, P. P. (2020, December 29). En 2020 murieron 2.187 personas en su intento de llegar a España por vía marítima. *El Salto Diario.* https://www.elsaltodiario.com/fronteras/en-2020-murieron-2.187-personas-en-su-intento-de-llegar-a-espana-por-via-maritima

Sierra, L. (2015, September 17). Un estudio desvincula el "top manta" de las mafias. *La Vanguardia.* https://www.lavanguardia.com/local/barcelona/20150918/54435335507/estudio-desvincula-top-manta-mafias.html

Sindicato Mantero de Barcelona (2021, June 1). *Ande dem, walking together // TOP MANTA // Barcelona's Union of Street Vendors* [Video]. YouTube. https://www.youtube.com/watch?v=k0CVmSkUBso&ab_channel=SindicatoManterodeBarcelona

Sindicato Popular de Vendedores Ambulantes de Barcelona (2016, March 15). Nosotros. https://manteros.org/nosotros/

Sindicato Popular de Vendedores Ambulantes de Barcelona (2016, March 15). Manifiesto por la despenalización del Top Manta. https://manteros.org/comunicados/#1488655372018-0124eea1-2b0a

Sindicato Popular de Vendedores Ambulantes de Barcelona (2018, July 8). "Top Manta. Nace Una Nueva Marca." https://manteros.org/top-manta-nace-una-una-nueva-marca-colectiva/

Sindicato Popular de Vendedores Ambulantes de Barcelona (2020, December 25). *No queríamos acabar el año sin presentar este nuevo diseño: ¡CAYUCO!* Facebook. https://www.facebook.com/watch/?v=388105092260925

Sindicato Popular de Vendedores Ambulantes de Barcelona (2021, January 25). *Jugándose la vida en un cayuco.* Facebook. https://www.facebook.com/watch/?v=3941176685915384

Sindicato Popular de Vendedores Ambulantes de Barcelona (2021, March 15). Sobre el Referéndum de Catalunya: 1 Octubre. https://manteros.org/comunicados/#1506965653699-78e69f4b-3b24

Sindicato Popular de Vendedores Ambulantes de Barcelona (2021, March 30). *Queremos denunciar la serie Servir y Proteger de RTVE por haber vinculado con muy mala intención al colectivo mantero con el yihadismo*. Facebook. https://www.facebook.com/watch/?v=489550725400624

Singh, N. P. (2016). On race, violence, and so-called primitive accumulation." *Social Text, 34*(3), 27–50.

Taylor, K. Y. (2016). *From #blacklivesmatter to Black liberation*. Haymarket Books.

Taylor, K. Y. (2019). *Race for profit: How banks and the real estate industry undermined black homeownership*. University of North Carolina Press.

Ticktin, M. (2016). Thinking beyond humanitarian borders. *Social Research, 83*(2), 255–271.

Toasijé, A. (2018). Activismo africano y afrodescendiente en España. *NGRXSMGZ*. https://www.negrxs.com/numero-2/2018/2/18/activismo-africano-y-afrodescendiente-en-espaa

Tomba, M. (2019). *Insurgent universality: An alternative legacy of modernity*. Oxford University Press.

Top Manta (2020). Pescador T-shirt. *Top Manta Store*. https://www.topmanta.store/pescador-t-shirt-verde-1.html

Top Manta (2020). Sudadera Cayuco. *Top Manta Store*. https://www.topmanta.store/sudadera-cayuco-blanco.html

Tuck, E. (2009). Suspending damage: A letter to communities. *Harvard Educational Review, 79*(3), 409–427. https://doi.org/10.17763/haer.79.3.n0016675661t3n15

Ypi, L. (2018). Borders of class: Migration and citizenship in the capitalist state. *Ethics & International Affairs, 32*(2), 141–152.

CHAPTER 5

COVID-19 in Montreal: Systemic Impact on Precarious Im/migrant Workers and their Organizing Responses[1]

Manuel Salamanca Cardona

A t the beginning of the pandemic crisis, early scholarship pointed in two directions. On one side, optimistic interpretations of the pandemic highlighted the possible "beginning of the end" to capitalist order, with the raising of class awareness and the creation of new social bonds based on re-emergent collective interests and solidarity (Žižek, 2020). Furthermore, limited responses from the neoliberal state and previous health and public services privatization led to sharpening critiques of capitalism (Berardi, 2020; Butler, 2020). Additionally, governments' interventions to maintain consumption levels increased the sense of the importance of states representing collective interests of the working class (Harvey, 2020). Equity came back as the only way out of this critical situation.

On the other side of the interpretative spectrum, negative views warned about increased fear, vigilance, and control (Berardi, 2020) intrinsic to an exceptional situation of crisis (Agamben, 2020). Governments and corporations would then increase the use of technology to monitor peoples' behaviours (Han, 2020) and control the labour force, and social distancing would gravely limit options for workers' responses (Han, 2020). Therefore, the crisis would increase precarization and fragmentation of exploited and marginalized groups (Galindo, 2020).

Nevertheless, as time passed, these analytical poles started to look simplistic. In just a few months, layers of complexity emerged regarding labour and the pandemic. The knowledge about the virus; the pandemic's evolution according to nations, territories, social groups, and actors; and the empirical data coming from research and state intervention added density and nuances to these initial interpretations. In addition, social learning and activism happening inside community and autonomous labour organizations started to reveal the experiences of vulnerable groups, especially precarious racialized im/migrants.[2] In Montreal, this role[3] was developed in part by the Immigrant Workers Centre (IWC) and their allies.[4]

Currently, some two years after the official end of the pandemic in Montreal, more in-depth reflections may arise from the analysis of specific local experiences attached to the reflection around the notion of *crisis*. First, we know that crisis is inherent to capitalism, but also that it may bring up all sort of political opportunities (Dobry, 2009), including political education and organizing. Crisis may become a political battlefield, a political arena (as it is interpreted by the authors of the book) whose battles include the disputes for installing a dominant narrative or installing disruptive narratives. These clashes between narratives may make visible what was naturalized before the beginning of the crisis (Roitman, 2013); i.e., the impacts of migration and immigration policies to contribute for the racialization and social vulnerability of several communities or the distrust and suspicion of these communities with the Canadian and Quebec polities. In line with one of the core arguments of this book, this chapter highlights the racial variable as determinant of the exclusion and marginalizing experience of migrant and immigrant workers during the pandemic in Montreal, especially concerning their role in keeping the economy alive despite the risks and dangers of contagion and death, as well as their ability to respond through organizing. These workers also show and teach us their capacity to dispute the meaning of crisis that juxtaposes their social stance (vulnerable, racialized, disposable and exploited) with their essential work in Canadian society (Henaway, 2023). Many of these capacities converged within the Immigrant Workers Centre (IWC).

Founded in 2000, the IWC is an example of labour organizing outside of trade union structures. It is part of a North American movement of workers' centres which emerged in the mid-1980s. The IWC has a broad base of precarious immigrant workers as well as methods different from unions (Fine, 2006; Fine, 2007). Popular education, casework, leadership formation, and direct action are pillars of its political responses. Therefore, research, learning, and education get intertwined in a process which usually sees individual or collective cases ending in stronger structural analysis (Salamanca, 2018). For the IWC, the pandemic brought a state of urgency and limitations but also opportunities to advance an agenda of social change.

Relying on the learning from the IWC and its allies, this paper explores three questions: How did precarious status im/migrants experience the crisis in terms of work, social protections, and according to their diverse migratory statuses? Which systemic realities of the crisis impacted their work situation and their private lives, and how did these emerge in popular education and organizing processes? What are their underlying critiques to the state's interventions and its discourse categorizing immigrants as *anges gardiens* ("guardian angels") and "essential workers"?[5]

This depiction uses some information from the research project *S'installer : Comprendre les enjeux du parcours et de l'intégration des demandeurs d'asile au Québec*.[6] In 2019, this project carried out a survey of 324 refugee claimants (in process, accepted or rejected) in Montreal who arrived between January 1, 2017 and December 31, 2018. It collected information regarding their labour conditions. Also, a set of 31 semi-structured interviews was done with refugee claimants who participated in the survey about their general experiences of installation in Quebec. Twenty-four of these interviews were conducted from April to December 2020, during the pandemic. These gave the opportunity to raise questions about their working conditions in the COVID period as well as how were they experiencing this critical period time. The information extracted from the survey about labour and employment (type of work, work with agency or not, salaries, occupation and work sectors, health and safety conditions) and from the interviews concerning the same subject allowed us to have a general view of the precarious working conditions before the pandemic and their experience of the COVID related to their vulnerability (isolation, financial concerns, immigration uncertainty, fear of contagion, employers' measures, mental health).

The identified main sectors within which precarious status im/migrant workers are in Montreal and its surroundings according to source are displayed in Table 5.1.

Table 5.1. Sources of identified precarious im/migrant workers' sectors.

Refugee claimants survey and interviews of the research project S'installer : Comprendre les enjeux du parcours et de l'intégration des demandeurs d'asile au Québec	IWC and its allies[7]
Work sectors	**Work sectors**
• Material Handlers • Nurses' aides, health care aides and orderlies • Live-in caregivers/home support workers • Kitchen staff, cooking and kitchen helpers, waitresses and related support staff • Maintenance and cleaning staff—light work • Specialized cleaners • Security guards and similar staff • Cab drivers	• Temporary agency workers in several sectors (warehouses—mainly Dollarama—cleaning, food and food processing factories) • Temporary agricultural workers and chicken catchers (farms attached to big industries of food processing and small farms) • Workers of food processing sector • Domestic cleaning workers • Hotel cleaning workers • Construction cleaning workers (new buildings cleaning) • CHSLD workers (cleaning and health care aids) • Slaughterhouse workers • Wood products production workers • Production of masks and covers workers

The analysis includes the author's personal reflections within the working group on precarious immigrant workers of the SHERPA Institute from September 2020 to April 2021, and the author's critical ethnography based on activism as member of the IWC; this last approach includes the review of archives, rapports, and press publications. I used reflexivity as a methodological strategy to link my own lived experiences as a member of the IWC supporting the provision of services and organizing of immigrants during the pandemic with structural determinants of the vulnerable conditions of im/migrants. For example, lack of control and regulations for temp agency workers, immigration policies and their effects on undocumented women of the ATTAP, or inaccessibility of migrant workers to financial support from the Canadian state. This reflexivity was immersed in a participant observatory process as a member of the IWC and the ATTAP. This process was accompanied with notes taken from field conversations in meetings, assemblies, outreach, and workshops with activists and im/migrant workers, including some workers I personally supported on their labour complaints processes and applications to federal financial assistance.

As way to ensure this document does not harm in any way im/migrant workers and activities of IWC and its allies, other members of the IWC read this document for veracity and accuracy. The research process and collection of data of the project *S'installer : Comprendre les enjeux du parcours et de l'intégration des demandeurs d'asile au Québec* had already passed by an ethics review process and approval at the SHERPA Institute and leading researchers approved the use of the data. Finally, the persons quoted in the report have read the complete document to approve the use of the quotes and their adequacy to the text they support.

Setting the Framework for the Crisis in Montreal

In Montreal, the pandemic hit hard by March 2020. Community and immigrant organizations were already expecting that racialized groups were going to disproportionately suffer its negative impacts (Cleveland et al., 2020). The first US reports were showing that racialized populations were more likely to catch the virus and faced severe conditions and deaths in greatest numbers (Kim & Bostwik, 2020). Interpretations pointed to a direct relationship between precarious labour and historic racial exclusion and vulnerability. Within Canada and Quebec, studies also showed that racialized communities and visible minorities were more likely to be contracting COVID and dying in greater numbers (Lourenco, 2020). In Montreal, the study carried out by Cleveland et al. (2020) concluded that some cultural communities were more vulnerable by way of the intersection of multiple economic and social factors, such as precarious financial situation; employment at high risk of exposure to COVID; precarious migration status or lack of status; lack of medical insurance; being allophone; low literacy; and being a racialized person. The monitoring of the Montreal Regional Public Health Direction (MRPHD) was showing high concentrations of COVID cases within neighbourhoods with large immigrant populations such as Montréal Nord. An analysis reported by CBC News on June 11, 2020 using statistical data from the MRPHD and the 2016 data censusfound strong correlations between the number of COVID cases in neighbourhoods according to the percentage of the population who self-identified as Black visible minority, who worked in manufacturing/utilities occupations, or who worked in health/social services as industry workers. The study also correlated COVID cases with unsuitable housing, low-income and legal status as refuees (Roch et al., 2020). Voices coming from the IWC and allies were also alerting as early as April 2020 that outbreaks would come from precarious labour workplaces to communities. In October, 30 percent of new coronavirus cases were linked to workplaces (Marotta, 2020). Dr. Horacio Arruda, the Quebec National Director of Public Health (2012-2022), also mentioned on October 22, 2020, that "46 per cent of all outbreaks involve a workplace" (Gordon, 2020). Although with time people would start taking social distancing more seriously and using masks in public places, the feeling was that workplaces were going to be key to the future of virus spread. Also, the IWC and allies' workshops and meetings between March and April led to better understandings of how COVID-19's negative impacts were being unequally distributed. Poverty, precarious work, migration status, racialization, and geographic location were setting a systemic shape for the pandemic. On its side, the federal government focused on providing financial relief to compensate for the first lockdowns in March 2020.[8] While these measures were necessary palliative, they did not target change to the inequalities existing before the virus. They were not attacking structural problems such as poverty related to work precarity or precarious migratory status (Noiseux & Hamel-Roy, 2020; Noiseux, 2020).

The federal and provincial governments were unable to evade their moral responsibility to asylum seekers working and struggling on the front lines as health care providers. Mobilizations coming from these groups pushed the federal government to announce in August 2020 the opening of the regularizing program for the so-called *anges gardiens*, a group mostly composed of racialized immigrants. The implementation of this program started in December 2020[9] with the participation of the Quebec provincial government. In May 2021 the federal government opened temporary residency up to a pathway to permanent residency, targeting 90,000 essential workers and international graduates who were already in Canada and contributing to Canada's economy.[10] However, the Quebec government did not participate in this program.

Other reactions within the province of Quebec were several municipal and provincial sanitary measures to prevent virus spread, such as lockdowns (starting on March 13), social distancing regulations, and measures for private and public spheres (implemented in general in workplaces, daycares, and schools). While these actions were consistently touted by the provincial government in media and press conferences as a concerted effort against an abstract enemy, they were subject to sharp criticisms coming from the activist milieu and community sector. In this context, the IWC and their allies paved a critical narrative exposing the continued gaps between the state government (both federal and provincial) and its institutions, ignoring the realities of discrimination and systemic racism experienced by im/migrant workers and their communities leading up to and during the pandemic.

Experiencing the Crisis in Terms of Work, Barriers to Social Protection, and Migratory Status

Before the pandemic, the IWC and its allies were addressing three campaigns: monitoring the new regulations for temp agencies, organizing the warehouse sector based on previous work done with Dollarama workers, and the campaign against sexual harassment of racialized immigrant women (Immigrant Workers Centre, 2020). The outbreak forced them to put these campaigns on hold. Resources were directed to plan actions to respond to the new labour situations im/migrant workers were reporting related to COVID-19.

The first element of this frame was the racist attitudes relating the pandemic to ethnic origin, nationality, and/or the social condition of workers. According to workers, employers had a racist rationale to explain contagion in workplaces and communities—i.e., blaming Asian workers for spreading the virus, or explaining neighbourhood outbreaks by the poor hygiene conditions of Filipino workers in their homes. In contrast, workers from Parc-Extension, Montréal-Nord, and Côte-des-Neiges–Notre-Dame-de-Grâce (CDN-NDG) were depicting the movement of the virus as from workplaces to communities happening in poor and racialized neighbourhoods with multigenerational housing.

Another element was the initial lack of knowledge of immigrant workers' situation by the CNESST (Commision des normes de l'équite, la santé et sécurité au travail) and its weak responses. In a press conference on April 4, many Dollarama workers reported that their complaints for the employers' non-compliance of the official recommended health measures were being systematically rejected by the CNESST. They also remarked that the number of CNESST officers was not enough to deal with effective controls, and that some officers were checking up on these conditions by telephone. This was subsequently echoed by the press, highlighting the high volume of labour complaints and complaint rejections within the CNESST (Crête, 2020). Public pressure and campaigning appeared necessary to push for improved government interventions.

As the lockdowns also increased layoffs, many workers were resorting to temp agencies to find a new job. Traditionally, refugee claimants are specific targets for agencies—the SHERPA Institute survey found in 2019 that 16 percent of refugee claimants were working through a temp agency (Cleveland et al., 2021). With refugee claimants being laid off from permanent jobs, this percentage likely increased. Also, the need for labour in the health sector and caregiving (CHSLDs and elderly residents) brought an increase in the demand for temp agency labour (Teisceira-Lessard & Touzin, 2020). It was clear that the demand for and offer of precarious labour was going to expand with immigrants as its main source. In addition, the temp agencies incapability and/or lack of willingness to apply the CNESST—and MRPHD—recommended measures was going to create difficult conditions for workers. It seemed unrealistic to ask small and medium-size temp agencies to take on the implementation and responsibility for sophisticated measures of health protection, given they had already failed in taking accountability for workers' health and safety under normal conditions (Choudry & Henaway, 2012; Salamanca Cardona, 2018).

Other labour situations workers mentioned were high density of workers, making it impossible for social distancing; employers' reluctance to adjust working methods; lack of gloves and masks; lack of cleaning and disinfection; threats of being fired if they complained (some Dollarama workers denounced being laid off by their agencies); the need for more bathroom stalls and separated sinks; lack of air ventilation; lockers without social distancing; crowded lunch rooms and food freezers, etc. The non-binding nature of the CNESST and the MRPHD recommendations was a great concern because in the milieu of non-unionized workers for im/migrants, it was difficult to challenge employers.

An important element was the high human cost undocumented workers were suffering. Although COVID-19 testing was never officially closed to undocumented residents, it took months until the provincial government implemented mechanisms to facilitate their access. Likewise, for the undocumented falling sick represented the risk of being identified, of paying high medical fees in the case of complications not related directly with the virus, and not being able to work. The main barrier was the fear of being identified, and the worst result was not having any financial income due to no access to federal benefits. Therefore, many workers needed to work even when they suspected they had symptoms. Regarding this issue, one community organizer of the IWC mentioned:

> Work, the loss of work. Non-economic livelihood. And at the same time, those who are still working, well, obviously the concern is that, to be careful not to get infected, at this moment, right? Because they are in a very vulnerable situation in terms of status and who could not, like, confront an infection, because it is not only in terms of health that they could, in a given case, have access to treatment, but also everything that is involved afterwards, paying the rent, how you eat, so it has to do with the economic aspect as well. (V. M., IWC community organizer)[11]

The imposition of the provincial curfew on January 6, 2021 also had strong impacts on the undocumented. They are called "invisible" because many must work night shifts doing cleaning and other jobs rejected by most Canadians. So, with the curfew many had to leave their homes earlier to start their shifts at 10 p.m. or afterwards. Some others decided to stay and sleep in their workplaces before coming back to their homes. The reason was the fear of being detained. The written permit delivered by their employers did not ensure them avoiding being stopped by the police and reported to the Canada Border Service Agency. On January 26, 2021, the IWC and their allies presented a press release asking for an immediate end to harassment, detention, ticketing, and the arbitrary bullying of essential workers without status in the curfew.[12] This press release was made after an urgent outreach in the borough of CDN-NDG about the problems the curfew was creating. These problems included more precarity within their personal life; i.e., not having enough time for sleeping, resting, cooking, and/or shopping, groceries, and doing other reproductive labour activities. In the end, this measure was not helping these workers but rather complicating their lives. Also, a flyer for precarious immigration status workers was produced regarding their rights during the curfew and it was disseminated in the neighbourhoods of Parc Extension, CDN-NDG, and Montréal Nord.[13]

In the case of temporary migrant workers, their shared stories were attached to their temporary status, their closed work permit, and their dependency on employers. Housing provided by employers made social distancing difficult to practice. Other workers described abuse and non-compliance with the mandatory two weeks' quarantine for recently arrived workers. Poor food, lack of food, and isolation were often mentioned (Immigrant Workers Centre and Migrant Workers Association of Quebec, 2020). In some cases, protective equipment was not provided by farmers, and recommendations to reduce productivity levels were not being followed.

The pandemic opened up complex situations, which made it difficult to identify employers' responsibilities for work stoppages or dismissals of workers. In a live-in domestic worker's case, the worker contracted the virus from the husband of her employer; when she showed symptoms, she was forced by her employer to leave the house. Her employer called the police without taking any responsibility for this situation, and the worker was left to deal with finding a place to live by herself while dealing with the illness (Coalition contre le travail précaire, 2021).

Truck drivers, fishing industry workers, and butchery employees were having problems related to barriers and lack of access to health services, social assistance, and to any form of support to understand their migratory situation in the case of work stoppages due to COVID. Language was a barrier because social services in general are provided only in French and English. In addition, the federal support measures proved complicated to understand. Workers outside of Montreal had further problems due to scarcity of community organizations for providing support, and access to English services was worse.

Transportation was a major issue for agency workers and migrant agricultural workers. Outreach by IWC and its allies in CDN-NDG and Parc-Extension boroughs identified places where agency workers were picked up by temp agency busses. Many of these workers were south Asian who came as students and became refugee claimants. Thanks to one Indian ex-Dollarama worker collaborating as a leader/organizer with the IWC, it was possible to learn from these workers about their specific migratory situations. Scam travel agencies in India and Pakistan promised them an easy avenue to permanent residency. However, once in Canada they were advised to apply as refugee claimants (Schué & Boily, 2021). This put them in an awful situation, with high amounts of debt, and working through agencies under the table in precarious jobs. Some were not able to speak in English or French. They described how social distancing was not being followed on agency buses. And their movements between various workplaces increased their chances to contract the virus.

In another transportation story, one ex-agricultural Mexican worker described how the employer used to load him in the car trunk to take him to the nearest town to buy his groceries. COVID regulations impeded transporting more than two passengers in a car, but the employer did not want to use more gas on several trips because he used to drive with two other seasonal workers in the back seat of the car. Other agricultural workers talked about the contradiction of being in crowded vehicles provided by employers while, just ten minutes before, wearing masks and practicing social distancing at work.[14]

The complexity of situations (in workplaces, homes, transportation) revealed two things. First, most white, Quebecois, middle class and high skilled employees working from home, and unionized workers in general were buffered from the full extent of the pandemic. These groups had more possibilities to limit the impacts of the virus in their lives. But in the case of precarious im/migrant workers, they were extremely limited in avoiding the damages of COVID in their lives, and those effects depended very much on employers' willingness and actions. Second, though the many government responses were directed toward supporting vulnerable communities, at the end of the day they also created and reproduced differences between privileged labour groups and unprotected and precarious groups. As the government responses were based on the pre-pandemic social and institutional structure of exclusion, its efforts to reach these marginalized sectors were insufficient and, in many cases, amplifying of differences and harms done.

Highlighting Systemic Effects of the Pandemic, Auto-organizing, and Questioning the State Exclusion

The described situations illustrate some of the specific effects the pandemic had on racialized and precarious immigrant and migrant workers. That specificity is part of those life trajectories which are hugely different from non-racialized groups with permanent residency or citizenship (Salamanca Cardona, 2019). When telling their stories, many workers did not differentiate between the impact COVID had on their work sphere or private sphere (family, extended family, neighbourhood, community, labour reproduction time). On the contrary, their stories deeply related and connected to these two worlds. This is interesting because before the pandemic, organizers, worker leaders, and facilitators needed to invest more educational work to create links between precarious work and precarity in other life dimensions. However, with the pandemic this relationship arose more spontaneously in workers' narratives, adding a systemic dimension to the educational processes carried out by organizers with workers. That was also the reason why suddenly IWC staff, volunteers, and worker leaders started to become overwhelmed with work. Now, in addition to submitting labour complaints or to providing immigration guidance, they had to learn how to guide, support, and follow up on applications to federal benefits; serve as translators and mediators with government officers; find sources of economic support for the undocumented; organize the provision of food baskets to those in need; accompany workers to do COVID tests; be mediators with health staff in clinics, etc. In this way all these new tasks were examples of the systemic effects of the pandemic, now visible and immediately tangible for organizers and worker leaders. Therefore, the lack of access and barriers to health services, the fear of going out in the public sphere for doing tests or interacting with health staff and social workers, desperate financial situations, the virus spreading within multi-generational families and dense living conditions, barriers to accessing community services, increased uncertainty due to delayed immigration responses in light of COVID, and more, were all vivid situations now present within the organizing discussions. Though this greatly increased the workload of organizers, it had the advantage of providing a bigger picture of the structures of inequality deeply related to im/migrant status. The IWC along with workers were able to position this whole set of circumstances within public discussion and to make them intelligible to other workers. This also fostered the interest of some of the media to report on this issue, and to focus on COVID effects beyond work.[15]

Workers' anger and indignation opened opportunities for radicalizing class awareness. While the mainstream media started spreading the state-sanctioned message of gratitude to "essential workers" and "guardian angels", many workers were upset with the lack of consideration and care by employers towards their health. This reaction was channelled into press conferences, workshops, rallies, and media coverage describing the pandemic experience from the "workers' point of view", contrasting with dominant points of view highlighted by government apparatuses and mainstream media. The contrast between the "gratitude" to "essential workers" and "guardian angels" then started to appear as hypocritical to those im/migrant workers participating in IWC and allies' meetings (Toutee, 2020).

The message from these responses was that while they were called "essential", they were also maintained as precarious, mistreated, excluded, getting sick, and without proper access to benefits and protections, putting themselves and their families at risk. Even in some sectors, such as in the case of agricultural work, being a foreign worker appeared to be more productive than local workers (Valiante, 2020, Asselin, 2020). In April 2020, one of the measures undertaken by the provincial government was to incite local Quebec workers to go to the agricultural field through a weekly prime of one hundred dollars through the program J'y vais sur-le-champ! However, employers had difficulties with the local labour force, preferring not to hire them and to await the delayed arrival of migrant workers from Mexico and Guatemala. Many employers said that productivity levels were much lower than foreign workers (Noiseux & Hamel-Roy, 2021). Despite more than 3,700 local workers responding to the call, until May 2020 the UPA (Union des producteurs agricoles) only counted a little bit more than one hundred workers hired in the agricultural sector (Noiseux et Hamel-Roy, 2021). So, it seemed more contradictory than ever that those maintaining the economy of Quebec during the crisis were those most left behind while being publicly "appreciated." This rupture with *useless gratitude*—which is not new, but now more tangible than ever—had some echoes in the press, which started questioning the lack of tangible recognition of im/migrant workers (Nicolas, 2020). Though many articles focused only on workers from temp agencies in the health sector, refugee claimants, and care workers, others were questioning this state attitude toward undocumented and other precarious immigration status workers. This led to the Canadian and provincial governments to expedite the proposal for regularizing the so-called "guardian angels" in Quebec (Schué, 2020). The provincial government, under the pressure of local and community organizations, announced in August a path for the regularization of these workers through a QSC (Quebec Selection Certificate). However, the measure was fiercely criticized later because it came with several restrictions, imposing as aforementioned requirements that could not be accomplished for many of those workers. Though

IWC and its allies applauded the work of many organizations that asked for a path to regularize "guardian angels", their position was that this measure was not enough. Essential workers were also hospital cleaners, hotel cleaners, domestic cleaners, caretakers, guards, security guards, domestic workers, agricultural workers, chicken catchers, butchers, truck drivers, warehouse workers, and not only refugee claimants who were working in the health sector with an identifiable role on the front lines. Another important critique by the IWC was that this program excluded those who could not work during the crisis, for many different reasons, particularly because of health issues and workplace injury. This point was emphasized when the IWC decided not to participate in the Coalition pour la régularisation des statuts, whose position at that moment was not clear about the regularization of non-status workers other to those called essential workers, a category which at the end was mostly defined by government discursivity.[16]

At this point, the IWC considered it important to reactivate the Coalition Against Precarious Work to set concrete demands for a unified position with all its allies. This coalition was already formed in 2012 but it was necessary to renew its demands as well as the member groups, given the new context of crisis. Thus, after several meetings and workshops, the coalition was re-launched in December 2020 by seven organizations and concretized a series of demands relating labour to immigration and minimum wage.[17] While those demands emerged from what the pandemic was teaching them, they were not only reactive, and they were based on an analytical framework coming from before and going beyond the urgency of the crisis. This frame took shape in the mobilization and discourse of racialized im/migrant workers and leaders. The coalition also made visible the institutionalization of exclusions from the state through the Bill Project 59. Those workers whom Quebec Premier François Legault called *anges gardiens* in daily press conferences were being excluded from the new law.[18]

Self-organizing, Critics, and Co-existence with the State and its Institutions in Times of Pandemic

The crisis also raised internal discussions in the IWC about its role during the pandemic. The emergency was forcing IWC to evaluate its possibilities to cooperate with some government actors given the problems many groups were facing; i.e., the bad humanitarian situation of undocumented women. Inside the IWC, the Women's Committee of the TAWA was highly active in reaching and supporting undocumented women and denouncing the need for government support.[19] These actions challenged the IWC to assess its acceptance to work along with the state and other actors close to the state for the provision of funded support services. However, taking this role created legitimate concerns about becoming a sort of "junior partner" in the provision of social relief and charitable services instead of questioning the state's exclusionary practices. This type of organizational trend has happened before in the community sector in Montreal with the advent of the neoliberal state (Shragge, 2003, DeFilippis et al., 2010) and has had the effect of depoliticizing issues associated with poverty, exploitation, immigration, and racialization, transforming them into a matter of technical and palliative intervention (Choudry & Kapoor, 2013). On the other hand, it raised the question about the relationship with precarious migration status workers: Will the IWC be a service and resource provider, or a space for self-organizing? How could its political role be limited or affected? However, despite these concerns, there was an overarching need to address the urgent and systemic effects of the pandemic in the most vulnerable groups. As such, this collaboration was understood as a political opportunity to reach more precarious workers and to include IWC's political view in technical and institutional contexts. In this sense, IWC began a process of collaboration with the Covivre Program from the SHERPA Institute[20] in September 2020, and the Support Program for Workers in situations of complex precarity in February 2021. It also was funded by Immigrant Quebec in February 2021, an NGO receiving federal funds to support precarious status workers, mostly migrant workers in Montreal and in some regions of Quebec where the IWC already has networks of workers and allies.[21]

The first two projects also came with their share of discussion spaces between IWC members and members of institutions linked to governments, such as the Public Health Direction of Montreal, the CNESST, and others from the community such as the TCRI (Table de concertation des organismes au service des personnes réfugiées et immigrantes) and Médecins du Monde.[22] IWC participation contributed to deploy an analysis of the specific vulnerabilities of workers with precarious status. It also allowed the production and refinement of official outreach and communication intervention tools. These instruments were focused on improving information about labour and health rights, about the provision of health assistance (COVID tests, medical baskets, etc.), about access to entitlements (coming from labour health and safety recommendations from the MRPHD and the CNESST for employers), access to federal assistance benefits programs, and to the creation of multilingual channels support. The second project was designed to provide financial assistance for undocumented workers in need of isolation due to COVID-19.

IWC's participation as a field actor raising the experiences of im/migrant workers had an impact in these official discussion spaces. It allowed for the blurring of artificial boundaries between the technical work and the political work regarding the situation of precarious status people. Many officials appeared then to have a much more open view regarding the possibility of a broad regularization program for people without status. It seemed to be a good structural solution. This is no small thing, considering the taboo this issue holds in government spheres. However, it was also noticed that this tendency was occurring at the local level and only in Montreal among mid-level officials. At the level of provincial senior officials and in regions, for example, no political approach and solution to this problem could be felt.[23] However, it is also important to mention that IWC and allies work were part of the echoes influencing for the city council of Montreal to adopt in February 2021 a unanimous motion calling the federal government for the regularization of people without status.[24]

In addition, this participation did not work like the usual "consultation" process driven by the federal and provincial governments, which disguises an intention to legitimize policies and state actions. In this case, IWC's participation was active and they directly questioned state limitations in their responses. And while this participation generated certain tensions within IWC around its political role, it also got recognition for alternative knowledge emerging from organizing and popular education as legitimate ways to learn about those who have been excluded by the neoliberal state.

I think that the involvement of the IWC was essential, honestly, because […] first of all, there were several reasons. One of the reasons is that the IWC is an organization that has an extreme knowledge […] I think, a knowledge of the field, but also a strategic knowledge, you know? In relation to the reality of immigrant workers. So, I think it's important for us, to work […] in fact, to carry out a new initiative, it was important to bring people who know the reality on the ground and that's what [...] we had an objective, not necessarily to work with an institution, we needed to work with people who know the reality on the ground, like the people from the IWC, it was important for us, for the Covivre project and also because I think that IWC has something interesting for us, it is a community-based organization that does advocacy, that does policy work, and for us that is important because for Covivre's approach, because as the pandemic exacerbated things that existed even before the pandemic, so it was important to understand what situations existed before, that were only exacerbated by the pandemic. (E. B. Covivre Program agent)[25]

Conclusion

The experiences of the IWC and its allies and the responses of racialized and precarious im/migrant workers suggest that the crisis presented itself as an opportunity to display and to use a repertoire of action and resources already built up over more than 20 years through activism and popular education. Now these resources were adapted to the new situations the pandemic brought within the labour sphere of racialized im/migrant workers. But these capacities for response were also extended to those situations taking place in the sphere of the reproduction of their labour force: family and community spheres.

In addition, the IWC and its allies successfully linked a pre-pandemic narrative with the pandemic impacts.[26] Two achievements of the workers' mobilization have been, first, to maintain the political relevance of its previous structural analysis, and second, to give political projection to the urgency of their responses.

The urgency for responses can illustrate another element. While the crisis produced by the financial meltdown of 2007–2008 had profound impacts on im/migrant workers, they were also gradual. Thus, the shock was managed in subsequent years through a state's neoliberal discursivity leveraging the continuation of hidden privatizations, austerity, labour deregulation, and the hardening of immigration policies. The result was the creation of vast sectors of cheap, fragmented, and racialized labour, ready to accept precarious jobs. In this way, the financial meltdown found in *the crisis* its own justifications and reasons to allow the reproduction of neoliberalism. However, the pandemic had immediate socio-economic and human impacts, requiring urgent responses from both the state and community organizations.

Faced with this urgency, the neoliberal state was not in a position to articulate a neoliberal discursivity, but rather a welfarist one.

However, this faint welfarism aimed at supporting vulnerable communities was based on the pre-pandemic structure of inequality defined by the neoliberal policies of the last 40 years. The exclusion and barriers of various types for precarious immigrant workers to access federal benefits have increased the impact of the crisis upon them, mainly upon im/migrant women with precarious status. Consequently, an unexpected effect was to reproduce and widen the inequalities for some groups instead of countering them.

The visibility of labour situations and abuses made much more vivid than ever the asymmetry of power between employers and racialized precarious immigrants. The impact of the pandemic was experienced by these not only in the workplaces, but in other dimensions of their private and community life. This contrasts with the majority group of white people, citizens, and permanent residents who were able to work from home and with more individual agency to minimize the negative impacts of the pandemic in their lives.

However, the urgency also opened — within a historical framework of oppositional relationship with the state — some spaces for cooperation of the IWC and its allies with certain private, provincial, and municipal state actors or other actors linked to the state. This cooperation occurred based on the tenuous acceptance that precarious immigrant workers are marginalized by the state and its policies. This collaboration created a limited degree of permeability inside these institutions with opportunity for further pressure to regularize and grant equal rights to all people living and working in Quebec.

Likewise, both the Canadian state and the Quebecois state reacted rhetorically by making use of signifiers such as "essential workers", "guardian angels," etc., that were challenged in their propagandistic and media framing by the factual structural narrative of exploitation and exclusion produced from the mobilizations generated from IWC and their allies (and other organizations not mentioned in this chapter). Here, this movement lays bare the hypocrisy of a state and a capitalist society that maintains colonial structures of racism and exploitation disguised as gratitude, as if expressing thanks was about multicultural coexistence. However, pressure from these groups has led to concessions and the implementation of some quite limited regularization programs that continue to exclude many immigrant groups. It is to be hoped that this dynamic push back on the state further prioritizes the need to recognize the place of immigrants in the Quebec and Canadian society. Hopefully, the result of this crisis will be a process of total regularization, of "Status for all", or at least the guide for the conception of a new paradigm of immigration, as it was mentioned by Cheolki Yoon and other community organizers in a letter sent to *Le Devoir* on 18 December 2020.[27] In 2022 the Canadian government announced the possibility of implementing a comprehensive program of regularization. This announcement triggered a pan-Canadian and pan-provincial campaign to push these governments to implement this program; however, the political path and struggles remain long and complex.

Finally, in terms of the notion of *crisis*, this experience leaves us with the feeling that other global crises will develop in the future. Possibly the main mark of the pandemic was its global character; however, the struggles of the IWC and other anti-capitalist organizations were still locally situated. Yet for organizations like the IWC it is necessary to develop more knowledge about the global implications of their local struggles in moments of global crisis. However, we also believe that for organizations such as the IWC, who support and organize vulnerable communities, there has been important learnings. It is desirable these learnings could be kept for future crises. Among these main learnings we can mention: the increased capacities to articulate fast responses, to build coalitions and alliances, the capacities to create immediate new educational endeavours to reach vulnerable communities, and the capacities to develop new frames of collective analysis for struggling against the dominant and exclusionary capitalist narratives that emerge in periods of global crisis.

Notes

1. I would like to thank immensely Cheolki Yoon, Koby Rogers Hall, and Émilie Noel for their readings and comments on this chapter.
2. In the Canadian academic literature and context, the term "migrant" is commonly used to refer to temporary foreign workers. These are workers who come in a temporary basis under the umbrella of temporary foreign worker programs with a valid immigration document such as a work permit (Faraday, 2012). On the other hand, the term "immigrant" usually refers to citizens and permanent residents with origins other than Canada (Goldring, Berinstein, and Bernhard, 2009). In this chapter I use the term "im/migrant" to group those categories of people but including others which have a temporary status such as international students and visitors. I also include refugee claimants, and accepted refugees waiting for the permanent residency, and sponsored persons who are waiting

for a response from Immigration Canada. I also include in the term rejected refugees, humanitarian applicants, and extemporary foreign workers who abandoned their programs or were laid off by their employer and who remain in the country. Usually, the last three categories do not have work permits and/or their visas have expired, so, they are commonly called "undocumented."

3.   This is not to say that the im/migrant movement revolves only around the IWC in Montreal. There are particularly important organizations such as SAB (Solidarity Across Borders), which had an incredible impact in this regard. Likewise, the *anges gardiens* movement itself, and the mobilizations led by Le Quebec c'est nous aussi had immense repercussions in questioning the neoliberal state and putting into discussion the exclusion of immigrants. However, the author does not have a direct involvement with these organizations, so he only focuses on the analysis of the experience of the IWC and its close allies.

4.   The IWC and its allies are composed of the Temporary Agency Workers Association (TAWA), the ATTMQ (Association de Travailleurs et travailleuses migrantes du Quebec), PINAY (Filipino Women's Organization of Quebec), Mexicans United for the Regularization, the Committee of Women with Precarious Status, Guineans United for the Regularization, and other immigrant groups organized around migrant justice. From here on, I refer to the IWC and its allies.

5.   The term *anges gardiens* was created to describe nurses, auxiliary nurses, and beneficiaries' attendants who were on the front line fighting the virus, whether this was in clinics, long-term care facilities, or hospitals. Many of them were refugee claimants, either in process or rejected.

6.   "Settling in: Understanding the challenges of the journey and integration of asylum seekers in Quebec," a research project funded by the FRQSC (Fonds de recherche du Québec – Culture et Société) and executed by the SHERPA Institute of Montreal. Research team: Janet Cleveland, Jill Hanley, Manuel Salamanca Cardona, Marianne Turcotte-Plamondon, Tamar Wolofsky, Xavier Leloup, Lisa Merry, Damaris Rose.

7.   Based on the final report *Review of the partnership* of the support project developed between COVIVRE and the IWC.

8.   The first financial aid implemented was the Canadian Emergency Response Benefit (CERB) from 15 March until 26 September 2020. It was provided by Employment Insurance Canada and the Revenue Agency of Canada. It replaced the traditional employment insurance program, extending it to more people. Its requirements were a valid work permit, a valid social insurance number, and a $5,000-earned income within the previous 12 months. In October 2020, this system reverted to Employment Insurance Canada with supposedly easier and flexible access. In parallel, the Canada Recovery Benefit Plan was implemented for independent workers and for people who get COVID and need to be in quarantine. Finally, the Canada Recovery Care Giving Benefit was implemented for people who had to stay at home to take care of children when their school or daycare closed due to COVID outbreaks.

9.   When it was announced in August 2020, the conditions were: 1) to have applied for asylum before March 13 and to have obtained a work permit; 2) to have worked in the health care sector and/or in health care institutions; 3) to have worked, according to the above criteria, at least 120 hours between March 13 and August 14, 2020; 4) possess six months of experience, according to the above criteria; 5) meet the eligibility criteria for permanent residence, including security and health requirements.

10. https://www.canada.ca/en/immigration-refugees-citizenship/news/2021/04/
new-pathway-to-permanent-residency-for-over-90000-essential-temporary-
workers-and-international-graduates.html.

11. The original interview was conducted in Spanish and translated by the author.

12. The press release may be read at this link: https://iwc-cti.ca/end-curfew-
repression-stop-police-harassment/.

13. Also, IWC and allies developed an information booklet for the rights of im/
migrant workers during the curfew. The link is here: https://iwc-cti.ca/wp-con-
tent/uploads/2021/01/The-Quebec-Curfew-Your-Rights-JAN-22.pdf.

14. From transcriptions of the workshop carried out on December 12, 2020, with
migrant agricultural workers from Mexico and Guatemala for the federal consultation process on housing conditions of migrant workers launched in October
2021.

15. Some examples of media reports are given in these links: "L'heure du test"
(https://www.ledevoir.com/opinion/chroniques/587441/l-heure-du-test),
"Vivre sans statut pendant la pandémie" (https://www.rad.ca/dossier/actua-
lite/409/immigration-travailleurs-sansstatut-montreal-immigrants-essentiels),
"Essentiels mais sans droits" (https://www.ledevoir.com/opinion/libre-opi-
nion/597217/essentiels-mais-sans-droits), "Limiter la vulnérabilité des sans
papier affectés par le couvre-feu" (https://www.ledevoir.com/societe/594024/
limiter-la-vulnerabilite-des-sans-papiers-affectes-par-le-couvre-feu).

16. Although the federal government program, which was launched in May 2021,
for the economic class was more comprehensive, it was also widely criticized by
immigrant organizations because of its limitations, mostly in Quebec. This was
because the province has greater power to define access to migratory status in
its territory, and in doing so closing chances for temporary migrant workers and
other precarious status workers to apply for this program (Rodriguez, 2021).

17. Which are: The Immigrant Workers Centre, the TAWA (Temporary Agency
Workers Association), the Association des travailleurs et travailleuses migrants
du Québec (ATTMQ), PINAY, MUR (Mexicans United for the Regularization),
India Civil Watch–Montréal, and the South-Asian Women's Community.

18. The position of the coalition is laid out in a document here: https://iwc-cti.ca/
category/projects/campaigns/.

19. The letter was published in the print version of the newspaper *Le Devoir* on May
10, 2020: https://iwc-cti.ca/fr/lettre-ouverte-a-francois-legault/.

20. The information about the program can be found in this link: https://sherpa-
recherche.com/en/sherpa/partner-projects/covivre-program/.

21. The information about this program is in this link: https://immigrantquebec.
com/fr/actualites/actualites/du-concret-pour-soutenir-les-travailleurs-etrangers-
temporaires.

22. One of these spaces was the working group on precarious immigrant workers,
which started its meetings on September 2020.

23. This reflection stems from observations made during participation in the meetings of the committee for precarious status immigrant workers happening inside
the SHERPA Institute as a research agent and as an IWC member between
September 2020 and April 2021. It also came from a personal conversation with
one of the Covivre agents and from conversations with one of the organizers
of the IWC, who also noticed a seemingly more open attitude towards regularizing the undocumented within official meetings with functionaries from the
Municipality of Montreal. There was a more visible tendency to agree with the
regularization of precarious migration status people as the main solution for the

problems they were having due to the pandemic. It seemed easier there to create links between the structural character of the problem with the questioning of the limits of the palliative character of the neoliberal state responses.

24.   https://www.solidarityacrossborders.org/en/city-of-montreal-calls-for-regularization-of-non-status-migrants.

25.   The original interview was conducted in French and translated by the author.

26.   This has been a noticeably big challenge for the IWC and its allies. I mean to keep alive and ignite its actions through communicational technology (various social media, online demands for casework support, etc.), but it is another element that deserves to be worked further in another article with more details and space to establish its advantages and disadvantages within this movement.

27.   IDIR, Mouloud, DEPATIE-PELLETIER, Eugénie, CAMARA, Thibault et YOON, Cheolki. (2020, 18 décembre). Migrants : un changement de paradigme s'impose. *Le Devoir*: https://www.ledevoir.com/opinion/idees/591982/migrants-un-changement-de-paradigme-s-impose

References

Agamben, G. (2020). Contagio in Sopa de Wuhan. *Pensamiento contemporáneo en tiempo de pandemias*, 31–34. ASPO.

Agamben, G. (2020). Crónica de la psicodeflación in Sopa de Wuhan. *Pensamiento contemporáneo en tiempos de coronavirus*, 35–54. ASPO.

Agamben, G. (2020). La invención de una epidemia in Sopa de Wuhan. *Pensamiento contemporáneo en tiempos de pandemias*, 17–20. ASPO.

Agamben, G. (2020). Reflexiones sobre la peste in Sopa de Wuhan. *Pensamiento contemporáneo en tiempos de pandemia*, 135–138. ASPO.

Asselin, C. (2020). De la main d'œuvre incompétente dans ses champs. *L'eveil*, 22 April, 2020.

Badiou, A. (2020). Sobre la situación epidémica in Sopa de Wuhan. *Pensamiento contemporáneo en tiempos de pandemia*, 67–78. ASPO.

Berardi, "Bifo" Franco (2020). Crónica de la psicodeflación in Sopa de Wuhan. *Pensamiento contemporáneto en tiempos de pandemia*, 35–54. ASPO.

Butler, J. (2020). El capitalismo tiene sus límites in Sopa de Wuhan. *Pensamiento contemporáneo en tiempos de pandemia*, 69–66. ASPO.

Choudry, A., & Kapoor, D. (2013). Introduction in *NGOization: Complicity, contradictions and prospects*, 1–23. Zed Books.

Choudry, A., & Henaway, M. (2012). Agents of misfortune: Contextualizing migrant and immigrant workers' struggles against temporary labour recruitment agencies. *Labor, Capital and Society*, 45(1), 36–65.

Cleveland, J., Hanley, J., A. James, A., & Wolofsky, T. (2020). Impacts du criss de la covid-19 sur les "communautés culturelles" montréalaises. Enquéte sur les facteurs socioculturels et structurels affectant les groupes vulnérables. Sherpa Institute.

Cleveland, J., Hanley, J., & Wolofsky, T. (2021). S'installer : Comprendre les enjeux du parcours et de l'intégration des demandeurs d'asile au Québec. Sherpa Institute.

Coalition contre le travail précaire. (2021). Pour mieux protéger la santé et la sécurité de tous les travailleuses et travailleurs. Mémoire déposé à la Commission de l'économie et du travail dans le cadre des consultations particulières sur le projet de loi n° 59. Document for the National Assembly of Quebec, Montreal.

Crête, M. (2020, July 3). La CNESST inondée de plaintes. *Le Devoir.*

DeFilippis, R., Fisher, R., & Shragge, E. (2010). *Contesting community: The limits and potential of local organizing.* Rutgers University Press.

Dobry, M. (2009). *Sociologie des crises politiques. La dynamique des mobilisations multisectorielles.* Presses de Sciences Po.

Fine, J. (2007). Marriage made in heaven? Mismatches and misunderstandings between worker centres and unions. *British Journal of Industrial Relations,* 335–360.

Fine, J. (2006). *Worker centres. Organizing communities at the edge of the dream.* ILR Press.

Hage, G. (2015). La critique de la crise et la crise de la critique. In A. Tremblay & M-C Haince (Eds.), Cris et mise en crise. Actes du colloque de l'ACSALF 2012. ACSALF. 143–152.

Galindo, M. (2020). Desobediencia, por tu culpa voy a sobrevivir in Sopa de Wuhan. *Pensamiento contemporáneo en tiempos de pandemia,* 119–128. ASPO.

Gordon, S. (2020, October 23). In Quebec, the battle against COVID-19 shifts to workplaces. *CBC.*

Han, B.C. (2020). La emergencia viral y el mundo del mañana in Sopa de Wuhan. *Pensamiento contemporáneo en tiempos de pandemia,* 97–112. ASPO.

Harvey, D. (2020). Política anticapitalista en tiempos de pandemia in Sopa de Wuhan. *Pensamiento contemporáneo en tiempos de pandemia,* 79–96. ASPO.

Henaway, M. & Walia, H. (2023). *Essential work, disposable workers.* Fernwood Publishing.

Immigrant Workers Centre (2020). Rapport d'activité du Centre des travailleurs et travailleuses immigrants (CTI) 2019–2020.

Immigrant Workers Centre (2021). Review of the partnership between the Covivre Project and the IWC. *Report of activities developed between 2020-2021,* Montreal.

Immigrant Workers Centre and Migrant Workers Association of Quebec (2020). Decent housing for migrant agricultural workers. Report submitted for the stakeholder consultations on mandatory requirements for employer-provided accommodations in the TFW program. Research report, Montreal.

Kim, S. J., & Bostwik, W. (2020). Social vulnerability and racial equality in COVID-19 deaths in Chicago. *Health Education & Behavior, 47*(4), 509–513.

López Petit, S. (2020). El coronavirus como declaración de guerra. In Sopa de Wuhan. *Pensamiento contemporáneo en tiempos de pandemia*, 55–58. ASPO.

Lourenco, D. (2020, December 29). ctvnews.ca. https://www.ctvnews.ca/health/coronavirus/how-covid-19-affects-different-communities-based-on-race-and-ethnicity-1.5247269

Markus, G. (2020). El virus, el sistema letal y algunas pistas… in Sopa de Wuhan. *Pensamiento contemporáneo en tiempos de pandemia*, 129–134. ASPO.

Marotta, S. (2020, October 8). Quebec workplaces linked to almost 30% of new coronavirus cases. *The Globe and Mail.*

Mouloud, I., Depatie-Pelletier, E., Camara, T., & Yoon, C. (2020, December 18). Migrants: un changement de paradigme s'impose. *Le Devoir.*

Nancy, J. L. (2020). Excepción viral. in Sopa de Wuhan. *Pensamiento contemporáneo en tiempo de pandemias*, 29–30. ASPO.

Nicolas, E. (2020, October 8). L'heire du test. *Le Devoir.*

Noiseux, Y. (2020, April 20). gireps.org. Available at: http://www.gireps.org/wp-content/uploads/2020/04/Autour-de-la-nature-de-la-b%C3%AAtenotesociopo-2.pdf

Noiseux, Y., & Hamel-Roy, L. (2021). Notre agriculture cultive-t-elle l'exploitation. *Relations 913*, Été, 20–21.

Noiseux, Y., & Hamel-Roy, L. (2020, April 4). Pour une protection des travailleurs et des travailleuses qui survivent à la crise. *Le Devoir.*

Rocha, R., Shingler, B., & Montpetit, J. (2020, June 11). Montreal's poorest and most racially diverse neighbourhoods hit hardest by COVID-19, data analysis shows. *CBC.*

Rodriguez, J. (2021, May 4). Thousands left out of plan to give workers permanent residency: Migrant Rights Network. *CTV News.*

Roitman, J. (2013). *Anti-crisis.* Duke University Press.

Salamanca Cardona, M. (2018). Les agences de placement à Montréal et le travail immigrant : une composante du racisme systémique au Québec? *Sociologie et societés, 50*(2), 49–76.

Salamanca Cardona, M. (2019). Activism, popular education and knowledge production against temporary employment agency exploitation of im/migrant workers in Montreal. McGill University - Faculty of Education.

Schué, R. (2020, August 13). Le statut des "anges gardiens" de la santé sera régularisé. *Radio-Canada.*

Schué, R., & Boily, D. (2021, February 11). *Radio Canada.* https://ici.radio-canada.ca/recit-numerique/1718/immigration-canada-inde-reseau-passeurs

Sharma, N. (2011). Canadian multiculturalism and its nationalisms. In M. Chazan, L. Helps, A. Stanley & S. Thakkar (Eds.), In *Home and native land: Unsettling multiculturalism* (pp. 85–207). Between the Lines.

Sharma, N. (2002). Immigrant and migrant workers in Canada: Labour movements, racism and the expansion of globalization. *Canadian Woman Studies / Les cahiers de la femme*, 21(4), 18–25.

Shragge, E. (2003). *Activism and Social change: Lessons for community and local organizing*. Broadview Press.

Teisceira-Lessard, P., & Touzin, C. (2020, May 3). Pandémie. Une manne pour des agences aux pratiques douteuses. *La Presse*.

Thobani, S. (2007). Exalted subjects. University of Toronto Press, 2007.

Toutee, L. (2020). "Anges gardiens" : derrière l'hypocrisie. *The McGill International Review*.

Valiante, G. (2020, April 4). Farmers say it takes more than two Quebecers to replace one migrant worker. *National Observer*.

Voss, K., & Sherman, R. (2000). Organize or die: Labor's new tactics and immigrant workers. In R. Milkman (Ed.), *Organizing immigrants: The challenge for Unions in Contemporary California*, (pp. 81–108). Cornell University Press.

Zibechi, R. (2020). A las puertas de un nuevo orden mundial. In Sopa de Wuhan. *Pensamiento contemporáneo en tiempos de pandemia*, 113–118. ASPO.

Žižek, S. (2020). El coronavirus es un golpe al capitalismo a lo Kill Bill. In *Sopa de Wuhan. Pensamiento contemporáneo en tiempo de pandemias*, 21–28. ASPO.

CHAPTER 6

International Students and the "Crisis" of Higher Education in Canada

Tahseen Chowdhury and Chiedza Pasipanodya

Immigration and migration law are the cornerstone of Canada's nation-building project. Over the past two decades, the role of international students in this project has continued to grow. From 2008 to 2018, the number of international students in Canada has more than tripled as higher education institutions have grown increasingly dependent on their tuition revenue to offset provincial government funding cuts (Statistics Canada, 2020). In 2021, international students are responsible for nearly 40 percent of tuition fees across Canada (Hune-Brown, 2021). The field of international education is increasingly steeped in the grammar of prosperous market economy, with international students positioned as the idealized conduits for trade and commerce.

This chapter investigates the commodification of international higher education, manufactured by neoliberal policies, and how this has been maintained and reproduced by the perceived crises of "scarcity" and "invasion" by the "other" in immigration discourse. This commodification leads to a continued reproduction of crises, an almost ripple effect of crises creating sub-crises. A critical analysis of this crisis-making also highlights how the rhetoric of "scarcity", and the grammar of "opportunity" is leveraged to justify the continued exploitation of international students and the shifting boundaries of their rights and protections. Scarcity denotes the perceived limited opportunities for Canadians when international students are drawn to

Canada by the promise of opportunities. By building on the patterns of global inequities produced by colonial practices, the post-secondary education (PSE) sector is able to ensure that wealth, knowledge, and power remain concentrated in places that already have them, renewing the colonial logics of Western supremacy and exceptionalism.

Methodology

This chapter employs critical race theory (CRT) to analyze and critique the constant state of crisis manufactured at the nexus of the immigration and PSE systems. CRT interrogates the role that race and racism play in society and the way it is embedded in its systems and institutions, particularly the immigration and economic systems.[1] The barriers faced by international students are also compounded by the way various systems of oppression (e.g., racism, sexism, classism) interact and intersect in their experiences.[2]

Migration control has historically been augmented to respond to the evolving concerns of colonial administration in Canada. From the 1885 Chinese Immigration Act that instituted a head tax on each person of Chinese origin immigrating to Canada, to the disproportionate cases and deaths of migrant farm workers due to poor work and health protections during the COVID-19 pandemic, the Canadian immigration system has its foundation in exclusion, racism, and white supremacy (McRae, n.d.; Gagnon, n.d.).[3] The Canadian Immigration Act of 1910 empowered cabinet to bar immigrants on grounds of "race deemed unsuitable to the climate and requirements of Canada" and the 1919 amendments extended the list of excluded persons to those with "peculiar customs, habits, modes of life and methods of holding property and because of their probable inability to become readily assimilated" (Jones & Baglay, 2007, p. 5; Matas, 1985, p. 8). In 1967, Canada adopted the *points* system to better meet Canada's economic needs as the face of immigrants was changing in a rapidly decolonizing world. However, after many more "progressive reforms," the system continues to produce racist outcomes such as African study permit applicants experiencing a 75 percent rejection rate, compared to a global 39 percent rejection rate (Kennedy, 2019). Through the lens of CRT, we will assess how in Canada, "racism is codified in law, embedded in structures, and woven into public policy," and continues to reproduce inequality, precarity, and the perpetuity of crises (George, 2021).

Neoliberalism has remained pervasive and continues to reinvent itself following crises, partially due to the challenges in defining it. In this chapter, neoliberalism is defined as a school of thought that prioritizes deregulation of the market, competition, and privatization of public services, which is believed to increase efficiency. Neoliberal policies shrink the state and have facilitated the rise of private pathway colleges, private language schools, huge tuition increases, and overreliance on international students. Neoliberal approaches argue that the state should minimize its involvement in social welfare as it has a comparative advantage in governing the rules allowing free and fair competition in the market.

This chapter relies on primary and secondary sources to identify the experiences and outcomes of international students. Primary sources include the Government of Canada's International Education Strategy (IES) (2019–2024), the internationalization strategies of five universities and one college, and Statistics Canada data.[4] Secondary sources include journal articles, books by various academics, and newspaper articles.

We conducted a content analysis of the IES and press coverage of its release to observe tone and classify language related to international students in public discourse. This research method involved coding text passages to create categorical variables that allow us to make inferences.[5] We analyzed the IES and three articles from major daily Canadian newspapers during a one-week news reporting period immediately after its public release on August 22, 2019, given that a news cycle typically lasts for a median of seven days (O'Neill, 2019). We intentionally excluded grammar or content pertaining to study abroad as the target audience for study abroad is domestic students. These portions of the IES are not focused on international students and their experience, making them irrelevant for this review. The articles were collected through the ProQuest News & Newspapers database using the search terms "International Education Strategy"; limiting results to "documents with full text", by publication dates between August 22, 2019 and August 29, 2019, the week following the release of the Government of Canada's IES; and by document type "article", "commentary", "front page/cover story", and "news." The database only contained English Canadian newspapers, thus limiting the scope of our content analysis to anglophone commentary. Of twenty-eight total search results, only seven results were directly related to the IES, four of which were republished stories. According to political scientist

Alexander George (cited in Pool, 1959), "qualitative analysis of a limited number of crucial communications may often yield better clues to the particular intentions [...] at [a] moment in time." While there was a relatively small sample size, the lack of media narrative and coverage itself suggests that international student education policy is not "newsworthy", framing the basis of our investigation of public discourse regarding international students and the visibility of their experiences in Canada (Friesen, 2019; Labine, 2019; La Grassa, 2019).

Context

Over the course of Canadian history, most of Canada's immigration policy has "explicitly favored white Protestants", with immigration occurring during labour shortages (Abu-Laban 1998, p. 71). Just as immigration has become more stringent, policy shifts in the education sector have worked in tandem to sustain the racism inherent within this system and Canada's colonial legacy. Under the 1867 Constitution Act, immigration is an area of concurrent jurisdiction between federal and provincial governments. The Canadian immigration landscape is complex, with immigration ministries at both the federal and provincial levels. Though most programs fall under federal jurisdiction, there are select programs (e.g., provincial nominee programs and Quebec's right to select its own immigrants under the Canada-Quebec Accord Relating to Immigration and Temporary Admission of Aliens) that fall under provincial jurisdiction (Government of Canada, 1991). Education is under provincial jurisdiction, which leaves most international students between two levels of government (Young, 1992).

Throughout the 1990s, large cuts to education were a pillar of the Ontario government's "common sense revolution" to ensure economic recovery and rationality. Ontario's conservative premier marketed the cuts to education and social services as home-grown common sense (Johnstone and Lee, 2014). Neoliberal economic policies were adopted across the country to address Canada's massive debt load. In Quebec, the government made massive cuts to education and health to move the province out of a series of deficits (CBC News, 2009); in Alberta, Premier Ralph Klein came to power in 1993 on the promise of balancing the budget, which led to deep cuts in health care, education, and municipal services (Hughes et al., 1996); similarly, Nova Scotia experienced a decade of cuts in the 1990s, with later research showing that cuts to expenditure slowed the economy and reduced tax revenue growth (Canadian Centre for Policy Alternatives – Nova Scotia, 2000). The Broadbent Institute argues that cuts to education are justified by conservative governments under the guise of "economic crisis" (Broadbent Institute, n.d.). Even federally, the Liberal government of the day had undertaken an aggressive austerity approach to cut federal debt and grow the economy, in line with global trends driven by the International Monetary Fund, the World Bank, and the US government in the 1980s. The spread of neoliberal economic policies promoting austerity and privatization as key to reducing state intervention in the economy for greater economic efficiency, recovery, and growth created a funding gap for PSE institutions across Canada. Prior to this, international students were viewed as part of Canada's charity commitments, regarded as future presidents and CEOs and an investment in Canada's global influence (Stein & de Andreotti, 2016).

This need for a new source of funding for PSE saw the approach to international students shift from "aid to trade" (Stein & de Andreotti, 2016). Between 1999 and 2009, university tuition fees for international students increased by 86 percent, despite low levels of inflation during that period of about 2 percent a year. In 2018, international students contributed over $4 billion in revenue to Canadian universities, $21.6 billion to the economy, and helped sustain 170,000 jobs as international students pay up to four times the tuition domestic students pay. Even during the COVID-19 pandemic, when students received limited to no services on campus, international student tuition continued to rise (Stacey, 2020). On the contrary, provincial funding has continued to fall as a total share of post-secondary funding, with a decrease from 38.6 percent in 2013–2014 to 35.4 percent in 2018–2019, while tuition grew as a source of total revenue from 24.7 percent in 2013–2014 to 29.4 percent in 2018–2019 (Statistics Canada, 2020). The continued defunding of public post-secondary education is in line with neoliberal policies and has manufactured a crisis of chronic underfunding.

Drastic cuts to public funding of education in the last 25 years have also contributed to a shift in educational values from centring knowledge, thinking, and responsible citizenship to a focus on occupational training and business (Johnstone & Lee, 2017). This has facilitated the rise of pathway colleges, which have increased corporatization of higher education as they privilege a "consumerist vision of education, and relies on contract and precarious academic labour" (McCartney & Metcalfe 2018, p. 206). As the cost of education continues to rise and provincial government funding continues to decrease, international students have become a lucrative source of untapped and uncapped revenue. The pricing of Canada's education, and in particular their international education product, has continued to balloon during its ongoing commodification.

As education, once regarded as a public good, has become increasingly commodified, policy and ideological decisions have led to the need for, and reliance on, international student tuition. In the past 10 years, international student enrollment has more than tripled while domestic enrollments grew by only 10.9 percent. International students accounted for 57.2 percent of total program enrollment growth between 2008–2009 and 2018–2019 (Statistics Canada, 2020). This has implications for domestic students and the overall accessibility of higher education; however, national discourse on this has been limited.

Over the decades, the profile of the international student has largely shifted to racialized individuals from the Global South.[6] A 2014 survey highlighted that dramatic increases in international tuition were attracting wealthier students that could afford the tuition and not necessarily the "best and the brightest" as the number of international students from families of "below average wealth" decreased from 12 percent in 1988 to 6 percent in 2009 (Humphries & Knight-Grofe 2014, p. 65). Today, any stereotyped caricatures of the "pampered young foreigner" are disconnected from the reality of the emerging international student profile (Hune-Brown, 2021). In 2019, 34 percent of international students in Canada were from India, ahead of 22 percent of students from China, a significant proportion of whom belong to low-and-modest income families seeking a Canadian education with the hope to improve their family's economic situation (Hune-Brown, 2021; Kahlon, 2021).

In 2011, the Government of Canada's Economic Action Plan established the pathway to the first IES, which aimed to increase Canada's share of the global international education sector by capitalizing on the already increasing growth rate of international students (an average of 8 percent per year). At the time, Canada attracted approximately 239,131 international students (Hune-Brown, 2021). In 2014, the federal government launched the second IES (Building on Success 2019–2024), setting a target of 450,000 international students by the year 2022 (Government of Canada, 2014). This target had already been exceeded by the outbreak of the COVID-19 pandemic in

2020. The second IES strategy aimed to diversify the education sector, boost Canada's innovation capacity, promote global ties, and foster a vibrant Canadian economy. As a result, the Canadian international student population has tripled in the last 10 years to 642,000 international students in 2019. This rapid increase has not been met with corresponding increases in investment to improve international student experience and transition.

Many international students come to Canada viewing it as a beacon for quality education and opportunities for the future given the constant and growing need for immigrants. However, their experiences involve denying any immigration ambitions and the dire financial challenges of integrating with limited support. Statistics Canada has highlighted that Canada is increasingly selecting its permanent residents from its Temporary Foreign Workers (TFWs) and international students, in a phenomenon known as two-step immigration, to improve labour market outcomes (Crossman et al., 2020). This is despite the lack of access to federally funded settlement support prior to transitioning to permanent residency.

Discussion

Colonial Grammar and the Myths of Western Supremacy

The expansion of the international education sector is typically represented as a supply in response to the natural demand for high quality education, without considering that educational policy directives are also designed to support the expansion of Western perspectives, power, and hegemony. The desire of Western higher education institutions to recruit international students is framed within a dominant global imagery that is rooted in Western supremacy and "in this imaginary, the West is understood to be at the top of a global hierarchy of humanity with the rest of the world trailing behind" (Stein & de Andreotti, 2015, p. 226). As it stands today, the characteristics pushing international student enrollment has little to do with the quality of education offered by the PSE sector, and "much more to do with the fact that Canada is an English-speaking country" with immigration pathways (Hune-Brown, 2021). With the West pervasively positioning itself as the reference point of best practice, most international students are left vulnerable, possessing limited knowledge of a foreign country's education system, and viewing all Western institutions as good quality.

The valorization of Western skill standards prevents the global majority from understanding the colonial forces behind the commodification of international higher education in Canada; namely, how this has maintained a system that lures many low- and middle-income families to have their children pursue "lucrative" higher education for the promise of economic success. The recent trend of "aggregator recruiters" makes this easier than ever by providing a platform for universities and colleges to interact with "agents" that recruit international students at scale (Hune-Brown, 2021). Aggregators like ApplyBoard are backed by venture-capital funding and have facilitated sub-networks of geographically situated "recruiters", or agents that universities and colleges partner with to "funnel in all the students they need" (Hune-Brown, 2021). The economic model has given birth to international recruitment industries around the world, many of whom operate with unlicensed agents, to lure youth wanting to obtain a study visa and settle in Canada. A Council of Ministries of Education of Canada survey found nearly 80 percent of Canadian education institutions rely on agents (Kahlon, 2021). The biggest impact of the agent-recruitment model is seen at smaller PSE institutions across Canada, where enrollment at community colleges like Langara College in Vancouver grew twelvefold from 2009 until 2019 (Hune-Brown, 2021).[7] Already susceptible to market exploitation, this for-profit model leaves international students more vulnerable than ever and enables agents and partner PSE institutions to operate without consequences. In Canada, Manitoba is the only province with specific legislation to regulate overseas recruiters (Hune-Brown, 2021).

Lee (2007) discusses the discrimination faced by students from Africa, the Middle East, the Latin Americas, and East and South Asia as "neo-racism," which is attributable to skin colour, national origin, and foreign policy relationships between countries. Despite many hardships, cases of discrimination are not reported on the basis of fear and inadequate reporting mechanisms, and international students endure difficulties in anticipation of a degree they believe will provide greater rewards and opportunities than obtaining a degree in their home country, thus accepting discrimination as a natural cost of their education (Lee, 2007).

The Manufactured Crisis of Scarcity, Competition, and Fraud

The inequitable paradigm created by Western imperialism continues to be sustained by discriminatory immigration law, which operates on manufactured crises of scarcity. In 1967, there was significant backlash to immigration policy reforms that attempted to make criteria for entry into Canada more objective and neutral, because it encouraged migration to Canada from countries of the Global South (Agnew, 2007). Instead of being dominantly Anglo-Saxon, a settlement hub like Toronto became "diluted by the immigrant surge [...] and was now not only multicultural, but multiracial", leading to outcry in the media about the burden that the new, racialized immigrants were imposing on social services and structures (Empire Club of Canada, 1978).[8] In the late 1970s, "Canadian" (read: "white") communities reported experiencing culture shock, not understanding "why they found so many people with different coloured skins on the bus, subway, in the public parks. [....] who were taking the jobs which rightly belonged to other Canadians" (Empire Club of Canada, 1978).

The narrative of immigrants taking away opportunities from Canadians is a fallacy that silences ongoing structural racism in administration processes and how they are designed to work against racialized migrants. This perceived scarcity of opportunities forms the basis of the crisis of scarcity. In a memorandum on the 1960 immigration policy reforms, Deputy Minister George Davidson acknowledged that "we know for a fact that the cards will be stacked against [the West Indian [...] compared to the Western European] to some extent in Canada, and that therefore he needs more skills or more resources if he is to have an even chance with the others" (cited in Triadafilopoulos, 2013, p. 26). And yet, when international students achieve success, they are perceived as threats who diminish Western entitlement and priority to resources and opportunities. A *MacLean's* article, from 2010, titled "Too Asian: some frosh don't want to study at an Asian university" featured complaints "that competing with Asian students requires an unreasonable expense of time and effort" (Findlay & Köhler, 2010). This maintains a form of racism wherein "the nation and the citizen are in a binary relation to the alien, foreigner, and immigrant, who are collectively described as 'the other,' [which then] poses a threat and [...are] often blamed for all the social and economic ills that befall the nation" (Agnew, 2007, p. 14), which forms the basis of the perceived crisis of invasion.

The grammar of access and opportunity in Western societies continues to be articulated against the "other" to perpetuate unequal rights and entitlements for migrants. In 2008, city councillor Rob Ford described how Toronto's Asian population served the economy: "Those Oriental people work like dogs. They work their hearts out. They are workers non-stop. They sleep beside their machines" (cited in Khan, 2021). In October 2021, the Premier of Ontario, Doug Ford, cautioned prospective immigrants with just "one criteria [sic]", stating that: "You come here like every other new Canadian has come here. You work your tail off. If you think you're coming to collect the dole and sit around, not going to happen. Go somewhere else" (cited in Khan, 2021). While the rhetoric of these comments is rooted in the language of scarcity and invasion, the reality is that newly arriving immigrants are ineligible for the province's social-assistance program until they have permanent residency status, a complicated and burdensome process that takes years (Stone & Gray, 2021).

Pitman (Empire Club of Canada, 1978) critiqued the irony of claiming that immigrants were "collecting welfare and consuming taxpayers' money at the same time as they were taking the jobs from other Canadians, scarcely a situation which was possible" within Canada's regulatory framework. Despite growing admission targets set out in government policy priorities, Canada's study visa program continues to be misrepresented as a back-door immigration ticket or in the grammar of a global "black market" (Todd, 2017). In 2019, Harpreet Kochhar, the assistant deputy minister for Immigration, Refugee and Citizenship Canada (IRCC), stated that about one in every ten study-permit applications are "clearly fraudulent" (Todd, 2019). This continues the narrative of invaders despite the watchful eyes of Canada's immigration authorities that turned down more than 100,000 study-visa applicants in 2019 alone (Todd, 2019).

Federal data illustrates that immigration officials reject two of five people applying to study in Canada, with African nationals having the most difficulty securing permission to visit Canada than travellers from any other continent (Mussa, 2019). Canadian immigration lawyers have suggested that legitimate applications are rejected because required study plans for international students, and the programs they apply for, "appear unreasonable to visa officers", and that visa officers increasingly do not believe that foreign nationals will return home after studying (Tomlinson, 2019). In 2019, CBC News conducted an analysis of IRCC data of temporary visa applicants and found that the approval rate for African applicants fell by 18.4 percent between 2014 and 2018, documenting "a pattern of continuing, discriminatory, and inconsistent treatment of visa applications made by academics from African countries" (Mussa, 2019). The same time period saw an increase for European applicants by 4.4 percent, compared to a 7.3 percent reduction in approvals of applicants from the Asia-Pacific region, and a 10.3 percent approval drop for applicants from the Middle East (Mussa, 2019).

Section 216(1) of Canada's Immigration and Refugee Protection Act lays out the provision for issuing study permits and includes establishing the foreign national's intention to depart. Although there is a provision in the Immigration, Refugees and Protection Act (IRPA) that legitimizes having a "dual intent" in applying to Canada as a temporary resident with the intention to become a permanent resident, the onus remains on applicants to satisfy visa officers that they are a "genuine'" temporary resident and not an immigrant (Desloges & Sawicki, 2018, p. 146). So, while the IRPA recognizes that the concepts of immediate temporary intention and future permanent intention are not mutually exclusive, international students still have to premise their application in grammar that proves they will eventually leave Canada or otherwise risk being denied admission. A former enrollment director of Bishop University in Sherbrooke, Quebec, argued this policy approach sends mixed signals to migrant students, where on one hand they are encouraged to "come to Canada to study but [get] rejected for your study permit if there is a belief you won't leave after your studies", and on the other hand, "after you complete your studies you can stay, work and possibly immigrate" (Chantler, 2020). This paradox largely positions international students as unwelcomed outsiders who are likely to overstay their conditional welcome, feeding into the perceived crisis of invasion.

The Business and Branding of International Education

Public narrative framing international students as "problematic intrusions into the state" can be traced back to a 1994 report from what is now Global Affairs Canada, where a recommendation to develop an international marketing strategy for higher education was met with hesitancy and concern "about adequate space for Canadians" (Robertson, 2011, p. 2193; Department of Foreign Affairs and International Trade, 1994). Today, post-secondary institutions aggressively market and

■ Media Coverage   ■ International Education Strategy

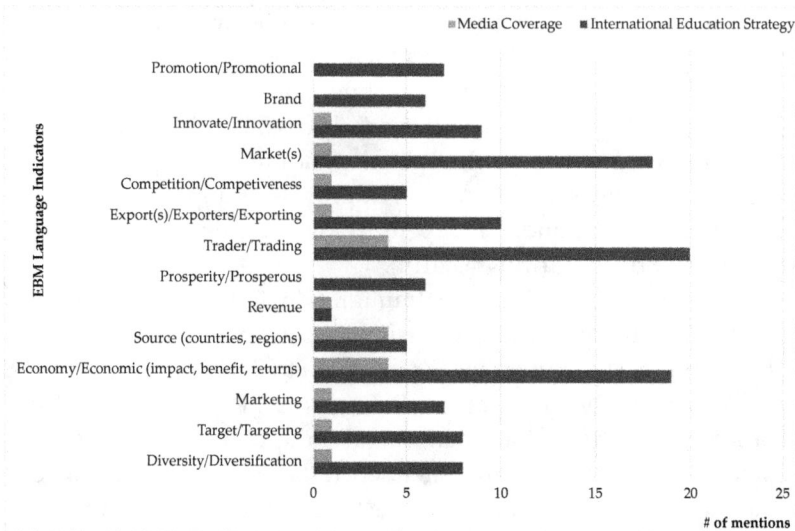

A content analysis of the International Education Strategy reveals 129 total mentions of language indicators categorized as EBM (economics, business, marketing). Subsequent media coverage by Canadian dailies *Globe and Mail, Edmonton Journal,* and the *Windsor Star* capture an additional 20 mentions.

Figure 6.1. Content analysis of "economic, business, marketing" vernacular in the international education strategy and subsequent media coverage.

recruit international students to sustain their revenue, and hosting international students is considered a hallmark of Canada's economic success. The opening statement of Canada's IES is from the then-minister of international trade diversification, who states that the IES is an integral part of Canada's Trade Diversification Strategy and that "international education is an essential pillar of Canada's long-term competitiveness", reinforcing the idea that the core motivation of the strategy is to increase Canada's economic power (Government of Canada 2014, p. 1).

In this commodification of education, it is clear "policy language [is now] increasingly infused with the strategies of business" (Johnstone & Lee, 2014, p. 209). To investigate this, we applied a content analysis of the IES and carefully examined message characteristics and naturally occurring language in subsequent news coverage (Neuendorf, 2017). Our findings in figures 6,1 and 6.2 illustrate the prevalence of economic, business, and marketing appeals in the IES,

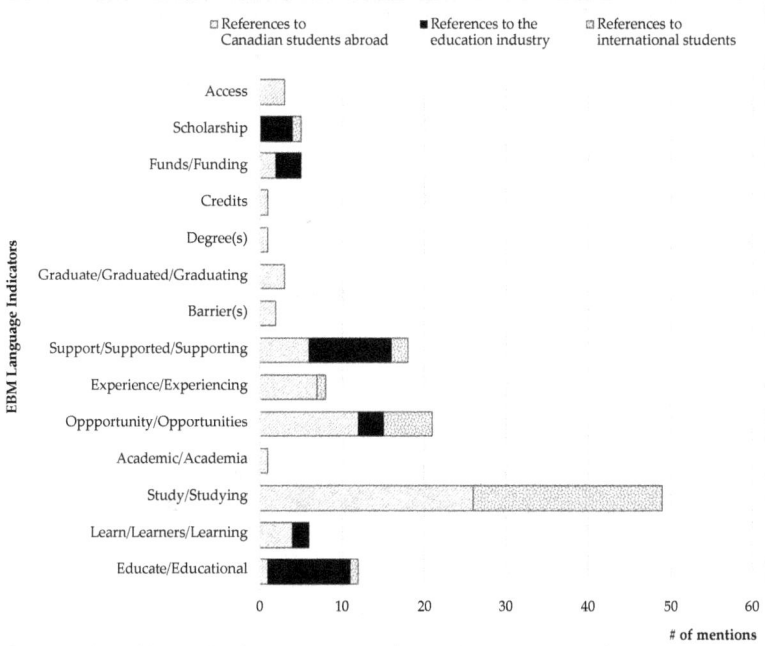

A content analysis of the International Education Strategy found that of 135 total mentions categorized as ELS (education, learning, studies), 51% of the text passages were in reference to Canadian students (69 mentions). International students were mentioned 25% of the time, with 24% of the mentions specific to the education industry as a business sector.

Figure 6.2. Content analysis of "education, learning, studies" vernacular in the international education strategy.

and that the strategy largely focuses on the interests and experiences of Canadian students. We also found that even in the vocabulary of education, learning and studies, the IES highlights business rhetoric.

The usage of the language of economics, business, and marketing reveals that the language used in reference to international students is "remarkably consistent in its commitment to maintaining Western onto-epistemological and economic supremacy" (Stein & Andreotti, 2016, p. 236). The 2019–2024 IES boasts that "international students have a greater impact on Canada's economy than exports of auto parts, lumber or aircraft" (Government of Canada, 2019, p. 2). The grammar of education as a trade export is consistent with the 2014–2019 IES, which noted that international student expenditure "is greater than our export of unwrought aluminum, and even greater than our export of helicopters, airplanes and spacecraft to all other countries" (Foreign Affairs and International Trade Canada, 2012).

The Grammar of Internationalization

Not only is internationalization ripe with the grammar of economic, business, and marketing exceptionalism, international students are positioned for the benefit of, and to support the identity development of, domestic students. The non-monetary contributions of international students are often understated while their economic contributions are centred. These contributions include the circulation of knowledge and improving cultural literacy and capital in university campuses and the broader host community, who benefit from an image of openness and progressiveness due to the perceived diversity of their student population (Deloitte Access Economics, 2016). A 2014 survey conducted by the Association of Universities and Colleges of Canada found that "95% of Canadian universities have included internationalization in their strategic plans, the majority of which also identified it as a top priority" (Stein & de Andreotti, 2016, p. 230). These internationalization strategy documents frame international students as diversity metrics to help improve their institutional reputations; for example, the University of Waterloo states that international students "contribute to the diversity of the student body" and Queen's University suggests that international student recruitment will cultivate an "inclusive, culturally diverse student body" (Buckner et al., 2021, p. 37). Similarly, Mount Allison University claims that international students "enhance the cultural diversity of campus and bring a different and important array of perspectives to the classroom" (Buckner et al., 2021, p. 37).

While these strategies demonstrate how international students are portrayed as agents or carriers of diversity, the stated commitments in federal policy documents like the IES are void of substantial commitments to further internationalization approaches and enhance international student experiences. James Gordon Carr, the minister of international trade diversification suggested that the IES "ensures that Canada will remain among the top destinations for learning" (Government of Canada, 2019). However, the IES does nothing to persuade readers how exactly the nation is prepared or will enhance their preparedness in hosting international students. Without genuine, adequate support from their host universities, international students face various ongoing stressors, including "culture shock, discrimination, adjustment to unfamiliar cultural norms, values and customs, [...] education system differences, financial hardships, lack of appropriate accommodation, [...] and loss of established support and social networks" (Khawaja & Stallman, 2011, p. 204). Our literature review consistently revealed a range of challenges that inhibit the interactions of international students with their domestic counterparts, which can exacerbate feelings of dissatisfaction and reduce opportunities for all students to gain global perspectives in higher education (Marangell et al., 2018, p. 1442). Though there is much literature discussing the experiences of isolation heightened by Canadian university environments, ultimately these experiences "are a symptom of greater societal issues" (Marangell et al., 2018, p. 1444).

Despite documented knowledge regarding the host of challenges migrant students face, Canada's IES does not acknowledge the structural, cultural, or financial barriers faced by international students and their need for support. Figure 3 illustrates the findings from our content analysis, highlighting the way the IES uses terms like *opportunities, experiences, supports, barriers, access,* or even *learning* largely in relation to domestic students.

The IES identified issues with outbound mobility as Canadian students reporting barriers related to "the cost of studying outside Canada and difficulties in transferring credits earned at educational institutions abroad" and how government financial supports are "often allocated based on merit, without considering the needs of certain under-represented students who face unique barriers" (Government of Canada, 2019, p. 5). In contrast, the discussion on inbound mobility (related to international students) centres on the presumed advantages of being young, Canadian-educated, and proficient in English/French, and how this "can help address this country's current and pending labour market needs" (Government of Canada, 2019, p. 5).

Even in the context of discussing barriers and challenges, international students are reduced to labour supply for Canada's knowledge and market economy. Though international students also lack financial support and have difficulties transferring work and education credentials obtained outside of Canada, the same lens of evaluating barriers of student education is not extended to their experiences. The IES also fails to distinguish the existence of under-represented groups and unique barriers within the international student population,

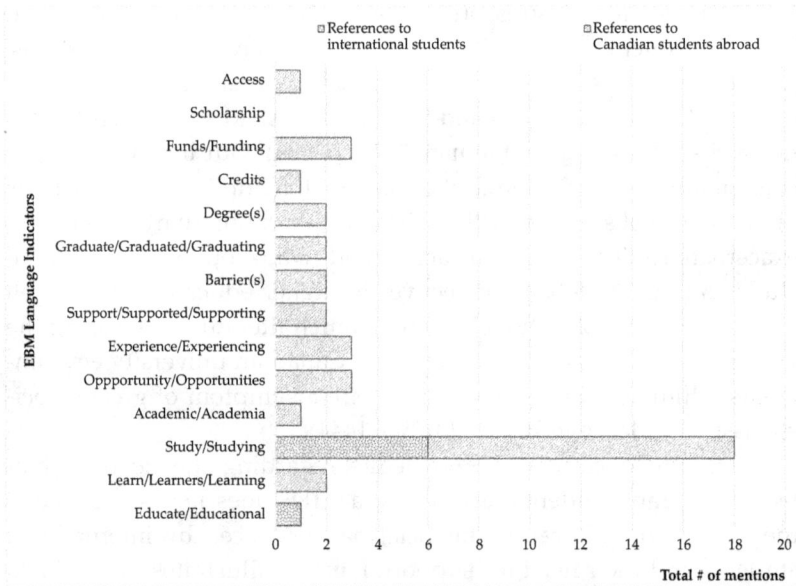

Media coverage after the release of the 2019 International Education Strategy overwhelmingly focused on the study abroad aspects of the strategy for Canadian students, who were referred to 83% of the time within the vocabulary of education, learning and studies (ELS). International students were mentioned 17% of the time within the ELS category across the three Canadian dailies (the *Globe and Mail*, *Edmonton Journal*, and the *Windsor Star*).

Figure 6.3. Content analysis of "education, learning, studies" vernacular in media coverage of the international education strategy.

which incorrectly implies that the international student experience is homogenous. This in turn maintains a duality to student life in higher education, furthering the divide of domestic and international experiences and reproducing the lack of belonging felt by international students on and off campus. Ultimately, the logic applied in the IES reveals internationalization as a marketing ploy ripe with subliminal vocabulary to position international students as "others" even within the borders of the imagined nation-state (Stein & de Andreotti, 2016, p. 236).

Language and vocabulary "create social meanings, [have] power relations embedded in it, and defines others", which explains why we explored the assumptions underlying the words used to describe international students in Canada (Agnew, 2007, p. 6). Even with a limited sample size, the consistent findings of coded language across each article strongly supports the assertion that Canada's IES frames higher education in a grammar of economic supremacy and international students as "sources of income, intellectual capital that support the continued prosperity of the Western university (i.e., as 'cash')" (Stein & de Andreotti, 2016, p. 226).

Student, Migrant, or Worker? Crisis by Design

While educational administrators spotlight the "internationalization" of PSE on paper, the challenge of truly integrating international students in the university and broader local community remains. Instead, the manufactured crises by neoliberal education policies marginalizes international students, deeming them "suitable as labourers but undesirable from the perspective of membership" (Triadafilopoulos, 2013, p. 17). Strategic planning at the university, community, and national level fails to include post-secondary career and international student services as part of the settlement and integration ecosystem.

The precarity faced by international students due to their status as temporary residents creates specific challenges and the lines between the identities of student, migrant, and worker have increasingly blurred (Robertson, 2011, p. 2193). While it is clear their priority is to study, the financial burden of attaining this education and the need to gain work experience necessitates their participation in the labour market. On paper, international students are simply students; however, in reality, they often wear multiple hats as workers and have limited access to the rights and protections that come with permanent status and a clearly defined identity. Hari and Liew (2018, p. 170) argue that Canada's "temporary migration policies facilitate the production and maintenance of multitude forms of temporariness," which means "limited rights, conditionality, and increased risk of abuse and exploitation". Applying a CRT lens, it is apparent that the precarity and vulnerability experienced by international students due to their temporary status is a sub-crisis manufactured by Canadian policy and regulations.

International students are regarded as consumers of Canada's education as a product, but from a nation-building perspective, they are also regarded as potential agents of national prosperity. Once they graduate, they are "enticed to stay as part of an industrious, yet temporary, workforce" while being vetted for their suitability as citizens (McCartney & Metcalfe, 2018, p. 215). The racialized other is regarded as inherently unsuitable for membership, but Canada's dire labour market needs have allowed for the acceptance of highly skilled racialized workers that can be co-opted into the existing structures and institutions. Temporary workers carrying out work the COVID-19 pandemic highlighted as being essential, such as agriculture and care work, and international students that are unable to thrive in the labour market while on their post-graduate work permit, are viewed to be undesirable as members. Nourpanah (2019, 1009) argues that TFWs and international students provide an "illustration of how class divisions and socioeconomic inequalities are reproduced minutely via closely engineered migration categories." The closed and open work permit system enables "the state [to award] privileges to those who are willing to spend a significant amount of money in the form of international tuition fees" (Nourpanah, 2019, p. 1009). TFWs experience heightened precarity and lack of options due to the design of the immigration system and its programs. This too facilitates the reproduction of power inequalities through the creation of hierarchies within the system which critical race theorists argue is key to the maintenance of white supremacy within the state.

In 2017, Jobandeep Singh Sandhu, an international student from India, was arrested for working more than the 20 hours allowed off-campus. He was arrested during an alleged "routine traffic stop" by the Ontario Provincial Police and handed to immigration officials, ten days before he was due to receive his diploma in mechanical engineering. A petition to stop his deportation received over 50,000 signatures and the Migrant Workers Alliance for Change was contacted by over 900 current international students alleging labour violations (Nasser, 2019). Despite many international students working, especially in essential jobs, they are not identified or protected as migrant workers. In surveys, international students consistently point to high tuition and lack of scholarships as the greatest challenges they face. International students also continue to point to the 20-hour limit for off campus work and longer times job hunting as barriers to their success and as key elements of their experiences (Humphries & Knight-Grofe, 2014).

According to Hutcheson and Lewington (2017, p. 27), the challenges faced by international students are "habitually oversimplified and ultimately left unaddressed," which leaves them vulnerable within unfamiliar legal systems. They are left exposed to the vulnerability often associated with temporary status and are unsure and uncertain of their rights and the protections they are entitled to. If they are working beyond the legally permitted 20 hours a week, as many are due to the high cost of tuition and the limited financial support, then they are in more precarious situations as reporting employer behaviour (labour violations or sexual harassment) is more challenging due to the fear of deportation. Female international students are particularly vulnerable to sexual violence as they are more likely to be unsure of where to seek help and could face challenges to reporting this violence partially due to different cultural norms and financial dependency (Kahlon, 2021). Post-secondary initiatives that aim to combat sexual violence on campus often do not target international students' cultural norms or needs, leaving them less empowered to advocate for themselves. These power dynamics created and maintained through these immigration policies make international students vulnerable and more susceptible to employer abuse, another sub-crisis in the making. These conditions were exacerbated by the COVID-19 pandemic as the families of international students struggled to support them.[9]

Research shows that international graduates earn less money compared to their Canadian graduates even six years after graduation. In the first year after graduation, international students earned 20 percent less than Canadian graduates, largely due to fewer years of pre-graduation work experience and lower levels of pre-graduation earnings than Canadian students (Choi et al., 2021). Policies and regulations limit the number of hours international students can work and discrimination in the labour market leads to the undervaluing of international work experience and credentials, and bias against racialized workers. The lower post-graduation earnings of international students is a crisis by design—a result of policy decisions that continue to erect barriers to international students' equitable participation in the labour market.

Conclusion

Canadian multiculturalism, a touted source of national pride, has been politically constructed to serve white settler hegemony from the very inception of its imagined community. The systemic reproduction of that in the post-secondary sector is articulated by the phenomenon of "brain drain", where Western countries contribute to their own nation-building and economic prosperity at the expense of developing nations, while positioning these decisions as "market-driven" (Stein & de Andreotti, 2015). Though the pursuit of different living conditions and work opportunities is certainly individually motivated, at a structural level, international education may have expanded the global equity gap, with governments leveraging international education and its "cultural, ideological, and political-economic significance to further migration projects at [...] regional, and national levels" (Nourpanah, 2019, p. 1009).

International students find themselves in the nexus of the *ad hoc* agreement with PSE and the immigration sector, which is increasingly commodified by national initiatives like Canada's IES. The international student experience is juxtaposed by the crisis of "scarcity" and the grammar of "opportunity", driven by policymaking at both the federal immigration level and provincial PSE. Seldom have policymakers centred the needs and experiences of international students, instead regarding them with suspicion while benefiting from their money and their labour. In 2021, the former Immigration, Refugees, and Citizenship Canada Minister, Marco Mendicino, highlighted that international students' "status may be temporary, but [their] contributions are lasting", thus acknowledging how invaluable their contributions are despite their continued exclusion.

Notes

1. Critical race theory (CRT) was popularized by law professors Derrick Bell and Kimberlé Crenshaw. According to Delgado and Stefancic (2012), CRT builds on the work of critical legal studies and radical feminism, thus informing its intersectional approach.
2. Intersectionality is an approach coined by Kimberlé Crenshaw (2017) to describe the way multiple forms of discrimination overlap in the experiences of marginalized individuals or groups.
3. According to Mickey Ellinger and Sharon Martinas (2010), "white supremacy is an historically-based, institutionally-perpetuated system of exploitation and oppression of continents, nations and peoples of colour by white peoples and nations of the European continent; for the purpose of establishing, maintaining and defending a system of wealth, power and privilege."
4. Reviewed were the internationalization strategies of the University of British Columbia, Durham College, Memorial University of Newfoundland, University of Ottawa, Queen's University, and University of Regina.
5. Created the alphanumeric codes of Economics, Business, and Marketing (EBM) and Education, Learning, and Studies (ELS) to capture content indicators.
6. According to Nour Dados and Raewyn Connell (2012), the phrase "Global South" refers broadly to the regions of Latin America, Asia, Africa, and Oceania.

It is one of a family of terms, including "Third World" and "Periphery," that denote regions outside Europe and North America, mostly (though not all) low-income and often politically or culturally marginalized.

7. According to Nicholas Hune-Brown (2021), Lambton College (Sarnia, Ontario) earned twice as much revenue from international students as it did from domestic students and government funding combined in 2019.

8. In 1977, Walter Pitman was appointed as a one-man task force (the Task Force on Human Relations) to probe the issue of racism in Metropolitan Toronto and addressed the Empire Club of Canada regarding the 1960s changes to immigration policy and how it affects the host community.

9. Canada's top sending countries were hard hit by the pandemic. In 2020, the top five sending countries for study permit holders were India, China, South Korea, Vietnam, and Brazil, in that order (CIC News 2020).

References

Abu-Laban, Y. (2014). Keeping 'em out: Gender, race, and class biases in Canadian immigration policy. *Painting the Maple: Essays on race, gender, and the construction of Canada.* UBC Press, 71–79.

Agnew, V. (2007). *Interrogating race and Racism.* University of Toronto Press.

Alvarez, M. (2007). Too visible: Race, gender and resistance in the construction of a Canadian identity in the poetry of Himani Bannerji." *Miscelánea: A Journal of English and American Studies, 36,* 11–23.

Buckner, E., Lumb, P., Jafarova, Z., Kang, P., Marroquin, A., & Zhang, Y. (2021). Diversity without race: How university internationalization strategies discuss international students. *Journal of International Students, 11*(1), 32–49.

Broadbent Institute. n.d. The short-sighted vision of conservative education policy. *Broadbent Institute.* https://www.broadbentinstitute.ca/the_short_sighted_vision_of_conservative_educational_policy

Canadian Centre for Policy Alternatives – Nova Scotia. (2000). A better way: Putting the Nova Scotia deficit in perspective. *A CCPA–NS Background Paper for an Alternative Approach to Nova Scotia's Provincial Budgets, April 2000.* https://www.policyalternatives.ca/sites/default/files/uploads/publications/Nova_Scotia_Pubs/NS_abetterway.pdf

Canadian Museum of History. n.d. The rail, from sea to sea. https://www.historymuseum.ca/history-hall/the-rail-from-sea-to-sea/

Cashmore, E. (1978). The social organization of Canadian immigration law. *Canadian Journal of Sociology, 3*(4), 409–429.

CBC News. (2009, March 19). "Quebec budget predicts 4 years of deficits." *CBC News.* https://www.cbc.ca/news/canada/montreal/quebec-budget-predicts-4-years-of-deficits-1.777318

Chantler, G. (2020, June 24). How Canada snatched away a foreign student's hopes. *The Tyee.* https://thetyee.ca/News/2020/06/24/Canada-Snatch-Away-Foreign-Student-Hopes/

Chatterjee, S. (2015). Skills to build the nation: The ideology of "Canadian Experience" and nationalism in global knowledge regime. *Ethnicities*, 15(4), 544–567.

Choi, Y., Feng, H., & Ping, C. (2021, February 24). Early earnings trajectories of international students after graduation from postsecondary programs. *Statistics Canada*. https://www150.statcan.gc.ca/n1/pub/36-28-0001/2021002/article/00004-eng.htm

Crenshaw, K. (2017). *On intersectionality: Essential writings*. The New Press.

Crossman, E., H. Feng, & P. Garnett (2020, July 22). Two-step immigration selection: A review of benefits and potential challenges. *Statistics Canada*. https://www150.statcan.gc.ca/n1/pub/11-626-x/11-626-x2020009-eng.htm.

Dados, N., & Raewyn, C. (2012). The Global South. *American Sociological Association*, 11(1), 12–13.

Delgado, R., & Stefancic, J. (2012). Introduction. *Critical race theory: An introduction, second edition*. NYU Press. 1–18.

Deloitte Access Economics (2016). The value of international education to Australia." *Australian Government*. https://internationaleducation.gov.au/research/research-papers/Documents/ValueInternationalEd.pdf

Department of Foreign Affairs and International Trade (1994). The international dimension of higher education in Canada: Collaborative policy framework."

Desloges, C., Fournier-Ruggles, L., & Sawicki, C. (2018). *Canadian immigration and refugee law: A practitioner's handbook*. Third edition. Emond.

El-Assal, K. (2020, February 20). "642,000 international students: Canada now Ranks 3rd globally in foreign student attraction." *CIC News*. https://www.cicnews.com/2020/02/642000-international-students-canada-now-ranks-3rd-globally-in-foreign-student-attraction-0213763.html

El-Assal, K. (2020, June 20). Where are Canada's international students arriving from? *CIC News*. https://www.cicnews.com/2020/06/where-are-canadas-international-students-arriving-from-0614717.html#gs.e1pxgd

Ellinger, M., & Sharon, M. (2010). Passing it on: Reflections of a white anti-racist solidarity organizer. *Accountability and white anti-racist organizing: Stories from our work*, 14–168.

Empire Club of Canada (1978). Now is not too late. *The empire club of Canada addresses*, 216–228. https://speeches.empireclub.org/details.asp?ID=61631

Findlay, S., & Köhler, N. (2010, November 10). Too Asian: Some frosh don't want to study at an Asian university. *Maclean's*. https://www.macleans.ca/news/canada/too-asian/

Foreign Affairs and International Trade Canada (2012). Archived – Economic impact of international education in Canada – An update. *Government of Canada*, December 20, 2017. https://www.international.gc.ca/education/report-rapport/economic-impact-economique/index.aspx?lang=eng

Friesan, J. (2019, August 25). Trudeau government outlines five-year, $148-million plan to attract more foreign students to Canadian universities. *The Globe and Mail.* https://www.theglobeandmail.com/politics/article-trudeau-government-outlines-five-year-148-million-plan-to-attract/

Gagnon, E. n.d. Continuous journey regulation, 1908. *Canadian Museum of Immigration at Pier 21.* https://pier21.ca/research/immigration-history/continuous-journey-regulation-1908

George, J. (2021, January 11). A lesson on critical race theory. *Human Rights Magazine.* https://www.americanbar.org/groups/crsj/publications/human_rights_magazine_home/civil-rights-reimagining-policing/a-lesson-on-critical-race-theory/

Government of Canada (2019). Canada's international education strategy (2019-2024). *Government of Canada.* https://www.international.gc.ca/education/strategy-2019-2024-strategie.aspx?lang=eng

Government of Canada (1991). Canada–Québec accord relating to immigration and temporary admission of aliens. *Government of Canada.* https://www.canada.ca/en/immigration-refugees-citizenship/corporate/mandate/policies-operational-instructions-agreements/agreements/federal-provincial-territorial/quebec/canada-quebec-accord-relating-immigration-temporary-admission-aliens.html

Grant, T., & Lan, B. (2021, May 5). Five migrant farm workers have died since mid-March, four while in COVID-19 quarantine, advocacy group says. *The Globe and Mail.* https://www.theglobeandmail.com/canada/article-five-migrant-farm-workers-have-died-since-mid-march-four-while-in/

Hari, A., & Chai Yun Liew, J. (2018). Introduction to special section on Precarity, illegality and temporariness: Implications and consequences of Canadian migration management. *International Migration, 56*(6), 169–175.

Hughes, K.D., Lowe G. S., & McKinnon, A. L. (1996). Public attitudes toward budget cuts in Alberta: Biting the bullet or feeling the pain? *Canadian Public Policy / Analyse de politiques, 22*(3), 268–284.

Humphries, J., & Knight-Grofe, J. (2014). Canada first: The 2009 survey of international students." *Canadian Bureau for International Education.* https://files.eric.ed.gov/fulltext/ED549797.pdf

Hune-Brown, N. (2021, October 18). The shadowy business of international education. *The Walrus.* https://thewalrus.ca/the-shadowy-business-of-international-education/

Hutcheson, S., & Lewington, S. (2017). Navigating the labyrinth: Policy barriers to international students' reporting of sexual assault in Canada and the United States. *Education Law Journal, 27*(1), 81–XI.

Immigration and Refugee Protection Act, SC 2001, c. 27, s 22(2), definition of "dual intent" [IRPA].

Immigration and Refugee Protection Regulations, SOR/2002-227, r 216, Issuance of study permits [IRPR].

Immigration, Refugees and Citizenship Canada (2021, January 8). Government of Canada announces new policy to help former international students live in, work in and continue contributing to Canada. *Government of Canada.* https://www.canada.ca/en/immigration-refugees-citizenship/news/2021/01/government-of-canada-announces-new-policy-to-help-former-international-students-live-in-work-in-and-continue-contributing-to-canada.html

Johnstone, Marjorie, & Eunjung, L. (2017). Canada and the global rush for international students: Reifying a neo-imperial order of western dominance in the knowledge economy era. *Critical Sociology, 43*(7–8), 1063–1078.

Jones, M., & Baglay, S. (2007). *Refugee law.* Irwin Law.

Kahlon, B. (2021). The realities of international students evidenced challenges. *One voice Canada.* https://onevoicecanada.org/report/

Kennedy, K. (2019, September 13). Canada immigration rejects three out of four African students. *Pie News.* https://thepienews.com/news/canada-immigration-african-students/

Khan, A. (2021, October 21). Doug Ford says the quiet part about Canada's view of immigrants out loud. *The Globe and Mail.* https://www.theglobeandmail.com/opinion/article-doug-ford-says-the-quiet-part-about-canadas-view-of-immigrants-out/

Khawaja, N.G, & Stallman, H. M. (2011). Understanding the coping strategies of international students: A qualitative approach. *Australian Journal of Guidance and Counselling, 21*(2), 203–224.

Labine, J. (2019, August 22). Learning abroad: Ottawa spending $148M on international student strategy. *Edmonton Journal.* https://edmontonjournal.com/news/local-news/learning-abroad-ottawa-spending-148m-on-international-student-strategy

La Grassa, J. (2019, August 22). Feds announce $95M for study abroad: "Just do it," St. Clair alum urges. *Windsor Star.* https://windsorstar.com/news/local-news/feds-announce-95m-for-study-abroad-just-do-it-st-clair-alum-urges

Lee, J. J. (2007). Bottom line-neo-racism toward international students. *About Campus, 11*(6), 28–30.

Marangell, S., Arkoudis, S., & Baik, C. (2018). Developing a host culture for international students: What does it take? *Journal of International Students, 8*(3), 1440–1458.

Matas, D. (1985). Racism in Canadian immigration policy. *Refuge* (Toronto. English edition), *5*(2), 8–9.

McCartney, D. M, & Scott Metcalfe, A. (2018). Corporatization of higher education through internationalization: The emergence of pathway colleges in Canada. *Tertiary Education and Management, 24*(3), 206–220.

McRae, M. n.d. The Chinese head tax and the Chinese exclusion act. *Canadian Museum for Human Rights.* https://humanrights.ca/story/the-chinese-head-tax-and-the-chinese-exclusion-act

Mussa, I. (2019, November 26). African visitors least likely to obtain Canadian visas. *CBC News.* https://www.cbc.ca/news/canada/ottawa/canada-s-temporary-visa-approval-rate-lowest-for-african-travellers-1.5369830#:~:text=Visa%20applicants%20from%20Africa%20have,whether%20the%20system%20is%20discriminatory

Nasser, S. (2019, May 24). Thousands join effort to stop international student from being deported for "working too hard." *CBC News.* https://www.cbc.ca/news/canada/toronto/international-student-deportation-work-permit-1.5149434

Neuendorf, K. A. (2017). The content analysis guidebook (Second edition). SAGE, 1–35.

Nourpanah, S. (2019). Drive-by education: The role of vocational courses in the migration projects of foreign nurses in Canada. *Journal of International Migration and Integration, 20*(4), 995–1011.

O'Neill, J. (2019, November 19). How long does a news story last? *Vuelio.* https://www.vuelio.com/uk/blog/how-long-does-a-news-story-last/

Pool, I. D. S (1959). *Trends in content analysis.* University of Illinois Press.

Robertson, S. (2011). Cash cows, backdoor migrants, or activist citizens? International students, citizenship, and rights in Australia. *Ethnic and Racial Studies, 34*(12), 2192–2211.

Stacey, V. (2020, August 18). International students question tuition fee hikes at Canadian HEIs. *Pie News.* https://thepienews.com/news/international-students-question-fee-hikes-at-canadas-heis/

Statistics Canada (2020, October 10). The Daily – Financial information of universities for the 2018/2019 school year and projected impact of COVID–19 for 2020/2021. *Government of Canada.* https://www150.statcan.gc.ca/n1/daily-quotidien/201008/dq201008b-eng.htm

Statistics Canada (2020, November 11). The Daily – International students accounted for all of the growth in postsecondary enrolments in 2018/2019. *Government of Canada.* https://www150.statcan.gc.ca/n1/daily-quotidien/201125/dq201125e-eng.htm

Stein, S., & Oliveira de Andreotti, V. (2016). Cash, competition, or charity: International students and the global imaginary. *Higher Education, 72*(2), 225–239.

Stone, L., & Gray, J. (2021, October 19). Ontario premier Doug Ford refuses to apologize for comments about immigrants and "the dole." *The Globe and Mail.* https://www.theglobeandmail.com/canada/article-ontario-premier-refuses-to-apologize-for-comments-about-immigrants-and/

Todd, D. (2017, July 3). International students in fake marriage schemes to Canada. *Vancouver Sun.* https://vancouversun.com/news/local-news/international-students-in-b-c-caught-in-fake-marriage-schemes

Todd, D. (2019, November 16). Canada rejecting more and more study-visa applicants. *Vancouver Sun.* https://vancouversun.com/opinion/columnists/douglas-todd-ottawa-rejecting-more-and-more-study-visa-applicants

Tomlinson, K. (2019, June 26). The foreign students who say they were lured to Canada by a lie. *The Globe and Mail.* https://www.theglobeandmail.com/canada/article-international-students-coming-to-private-colleges-say-they-were-duped/

Triadafilopoulos, T. (2013). *Wanted and welcome? Policies for highly skilled immigrants in comparative perspective.* Springer.

Young, M. (1992). Immigration: Constitutional issues. *Government of Canada law and government division,* October 1991. https://publications.gc.ca/Collection-R/LoPBdP/BP/bp273-e.htm

Studies in International Development and Globalization

Series editor: Christina Clark-Kazak

The *Studies in International Development and Globalization* series offers new perspectives on a range of topics in development and globalization studies—including Indigenous peoples, women, social movements, labour issues, agriculture, governance, and migration—revealing the tensions and conflicts of development and highlighting the quest for social justice in global contexts.

Previous titles in the *Studies in International Development and Globalization* collection

Younès Ahouga, *Gouverner les migrations pour perpétuer la mondialisation : gestion migratoire et Organisation internationale pour les migrations*, 2024.

Pierre Beaudet, Dominique Caouette, Paul Haslam and Abdelhamid Benhmade (eds.), *Enjeux et défis du développement international : acteurs et champs d'action. Édition nouvelle et actualisée*, 2019.

Hany Gamil Besada, M. Evren Tok, and Leah McMillan Polonenko (eds.), *Innovating South-South Cooperation: Policies, Challenges and Prospects*, 2019.

Charmain Levy and Andrea Martinez (eds.), *Genre, féminismes et développement : une trilogie en construction*, 2019.

Mahmoud Masaeli and Lauchlan T. Munro (eds.), *Canada and the Challenges of International Development and Globalization*, 2018.

Stephen Brown, Molly den Heyer and David R. Black, *Rethinking Canadian Aid: Second Edition*, 2016.

Henry Veltmeyer, *Des outils pour le changement : une approche critique en études du développement*, 2015.

Stephen Brown, Molly den Heyer and David R. Black, *Rethinking Canadian Aid: First Edition*, 2015.

Pierre Beaudet and Paul Haslam (eds.), *Enjeux et défis du développement international*, 2014.

Daniel C. Bach and Mamoudou Gazibo (eds.), *L'État néopatrimonial : genèse et trajectoires contemporaines*, 2011.

Andrea Martinez, Pierre Beaudet and Stephen Baranyi (eds.), *Haïti aujourd'hui, Haïti demain : regards croisés*, 2011.

Jacques Fisette and Marc Raffinot (eds.), *Gouvernance et appropriation locale du dévelop¬pement : au-delà des modèles importés*, 2010.

Isabelle Beaulieu, *L'État rentier : le cas de la Malaysia*, 2008.

Saturnino Borras, *Pro-Poor Land Reform: A Critique*, 2007.

For a complete list of our titles, please visit:
www.Press.uOttawa.ca